Self-evaluation in European Schools

This is a unique book. It tells the story of one school seen through the eyes of a pupil, a parent, a teacher, a headteacher and a critical friend. The story is a compelling journey through the process of school improvement; theories of school effectiveness and school improvement are progressively clarified.

The book is based on a well-known and well-documented research project involving individuals from eighteen European countries, which clearly sets it in a European policy context. It includes a wealth of practical tools for raising standards for teachers and school managers to refer to, and guidance on how to use them.

Self-evaluation in European Schools is a vital and useful source of good ideas, challenging insights and practical strategies for real schools.

John MacBeath is Director of the Quality in Education Centre, University of Strathclyde, and author of the acclaimed *Schools Must Speak for Themselves* for Routledge; **Lars Jakobsen** co-ordinated the project for the European Commission; **Denis Meuret** teaches at the University of Dijon and **Michael Schratz** teaches at the University of Innsbruck.

Self-evaluation in European Schools

A story of change

John MacBeath, Michael Schratz, Denis Meuret and Lars Jakobsen

London and New York

First published 2000
by RoutledgeFalmer
11 New Fetter Lane, London EC4P 4EE

Simultaneously published in the USA and Canada by RoutledgeFalmer
29 West 35th Street, New York, NY 10001

RoutledgeFalmer is an imprint of the Taylor & Francis Group

Typeset in Goudy by Bookcraft Ltd, Stroud, Gloucestershire
Printed and bound in Great Britain by St Edmundsbury Press,
Bury St Edmunds, Suffolk

British Library Cataloguing in Publication Data
A catalogue record for this book is available from the British Library

Library of Congress Cataloging in Publication Data
MacBeath, John E. C.
Self-evaluation in European schools : a story of change / John
MacBeath with Michael Schratz, Denis Meuret, and Lars Jakobsen.
p.   cm.
1. School improvement programs – Europe – Cross-cultural studies.
2. Educational evaluation – Europe – Cross-cultural studies.
I. Title.
LB2822.84.E85 M23 2000 0-031138E3
379.1'58'094–dc21

ISBN 0–415–23014–4

Contents

List of figures vii
Acknowledgements ix
Introduction xi

1 Serena 1

2 Mrs Kaur: Serena's mother 18

3 Tom Ericson: the history teacher 27

4 Mrs Barre: the headteacher 41

5 Ursula: the critical friend 53

6 Coffee with the professor 62

7 The professor revisited 73

8 A change of story 82

9 Self-evaluation: the power of three 94

10 The SEP: what it is and how to use it 103

11 Methods of self-evaluation 115

12 The work of the critical friend 158

13 The schools 165

14 What have we learned? 184

Notes 191
Bibliography 195
Index 199

Figures

1.1	The school self-evaluation profile	11
3.1	History questionnaire	31
3.2	The collated results	39
4.1	The completed profile	44
4.3	The self-evaluation form	51
5.1	The swamp	55
7.1	Variables associated with school effectiveness: British and North American schools	74
7.2	Variables related to effectiveness: French middle schools	75
7.3	Differences between very contrasting schools	79
8.1	Interrelationships within a legislative framework	90
8.2	The cube model of evaluation	93
9.1	The school self-evaluation profile	97
9.2	Stakeholder groups	98
9.3	How to choose the best method or instrument	100
9.4	A simple framework in the use of the SEP	101
10.1	Protocol for the session	110
10.2	Ground rules for discussion	111
10.3	Content of the areas	112
10.4	How one school represented the SEP in graphic form	114
11.1	The main activities in the process of self-evaluation	115
11.2	The structure of evaluation	116
11.3	Interview types	117
11.4	The interview triangle	117
11.5	Evaluation by sentence completion	119
11.6	A graphical interpretation of a multiple choice question	121
11.7	A graphical interpretation of a rating scale	121
11.8	Rating using simple questions	121
11.9	Rating between two opposite poles	122
11.10	An example of a questionnaire	123

11.11 Survey sheet   126
11.12 Time log   127
11.13 Force field   128
11.14 Protected area checklist   131
11.15 The Jarvis Court questions relating to pupil shadowing   133
11.16 Cards from school effectiveness studies   136
11.17 Worksheet for peer review   140
11.18 Measuring school performance   149
11.19 Starting picture for a Danish imaging exercise   152
11.20 Profiling diagram   156
11.21 Professional map   156
11.32 Drawing of relationships between system partners   157
 12.1 Checklist of key issues important for the work of the
       critical friend   159
 12.2 Forms of relationship between a critical friend and a school   160
 12.3 Partners of the critical friend in school   161
 12.4 Range of competencies of the critical friend   163
 12.5 Do's and don'ts for a critical friend   164
 12.6 How to be successful as a critical friend   164
 13.1 Finding a silent voice   177
 13.2 A major theme: reaching out for time   178
 13.3 Teachers' quality evaluation poster   178
 13.4 Pupils' photomontages   181
 13.5 Evaluation of a photo survey   182
 13.6 A photo evaluation exercise in a Swedish school   182
 13.7 Graphics from a Swedish school   183

Acknowledgements

We owe a debt of gratitude to a very large number of people who not only made this book possible but actually made this book. Anders Hingel, Head of DGXXII at the European Commission, was the first to mention the word 'book' during our writing up of the final report on the project. His support and encouragement throughout were major contributory factors in the success of the project and the brainstorming, writing and critical review phases of book production.

The ideas for the Serena story emerged out of one of our many brainstorming sessions, inspired by the lone school student, Chloe, who represented her school at the Luxembourg conference and was not intimidated by headteachers, teachers, policy makers and professors. Having pioneered the way and convinced us of the importance of student involvement, she was joined at the second conference in Vienna by another twenty students.

Many schools from around Europe took part and it would be invidious to name any of them individually but we enjoyed working with them tremendously and we made many new friends. We would have to say the same of the critical friends, too, numerous to mention by name, but who worked with the schools and gave us so many useful insights into school quality and self-evaluation.

National co-ordinators, too, made a significant contribution and we learned a lot through those national conferences and workshops which they facilitated and sometimes even paid for as well. Our thanks to them.

We had many long sessions in Brussels with the steering group representing each of the eighteen countries in the study. With each meeting they became more and more absorbed in the project as initial reservations turned to wholehearted enthusiasm and people began to report exciting advances in their schools and school systems. We learned much from these meetings and we would like to express our appreciation to those who contributed to our thinking and confidence in the value of both the project and of the book.

Thanks to Elaine Kirkland of the Quality in Education Centre in Glasgow who did a great job of proofreading and re-proofreading successive drafts and juggling the many graphics which either barely survived transmission internationally or became an incoherent scramble.

Our warm appreciation of Nina Stibbe, Jude Bowen and Judith Exley of

Routledge who have been extremely helpful and forbearing. We will work with them again any time.

Warren Dennis has written about 'great groups' and what makes them tick. We became a great group through the facilitation of our chair, Lars Bo, who took his three country 'experts' in hand and allowed challenges and sometimes sharp disagreements to flow into something constructive, creative and congenial.

John MacBeath
Lars Jakobsen
Denis Meuret
Michael Schratz

Introduction

This book is about how schools can improve using self-evaluation. It draws on a large body of research literature to make the case but leans most heavily on a unique European Socrates project called 'Evaluating Quality in School Education'. This involved 101 schools in eighteen countries, all of whom agreed to work with a common approach while at the same time developing thinking and practice within the context of their own cultures and histories. All of these schools learned important lessons about the process of improvement and change. All opened doors that had previously been closed or were only half ajar. All helped us to deepen our understanding of school education, where and how it works best and what exciting things can happen when we involve key stakeholders – students, parents and teachers.

The story is told in two ways, one conventional, the other unconventional. One narrative is at a broad, general level of all schools, the other is at the micro level of individual experience. One describes structures and sequences that are prerequisites of measured improvement. The other seeks to penetrate the culture of classroom, school and home, and how they interlink in a common journey of change. One narrative offers a step by step description of the process – introduction and climate setting, tools of evaluation, the important work of critical friends. The other explores how students, teachers and parents make meaning for themselves.

Because there are two stories there are two possible starting points for this book. The first section deals with the story of change seen through the eyes of an individual student, Serena, aged sixteen. Serena is in some senses fictitious but in a more important sense very real. Through her experience of her school we are led to some important truths and deep questions about what matters. Then we see her and her school through different lenses, from the perspectives of her mother, her teacher, her headteacher and the critical friend who works with the school. Finally she brings her questions to the 'experts' who were consultants to the European project in which she played her own small but significant part. We discover through the dialogue that there is a meeting point for the two, seemingly remote, worlds of European policy making and individual student learning.

Serena, her family and her teachers are not located in any identifiable school or country. Their school is, in some respects 'everyschool' and her home and community life 'anywhere'. In a very limited sense this is a work of fiction but as such it permits the reader access to ideas and insights not easily accessible through more conventional research. We were inspired, in part, by the landmark Presidential address of Elliot Eisner to the American Educational Research Association when he posed the question: 'Can a novel be good research?' His case for the defence was that we can often can closer to human truths through good literature than any other avenues. We hope that in some respects at least Serena's story qualifies as good literature. We hope that through this medium it sheds a bright light on the process of school improvement through self-evaluation.

You can start just as easily with the second part, a narrative more grounded in research, more respectful of systematic inquiry, more cautious in value judgement. It begins with the broad canvas (in Chapter 8), with the context of globalisation which creates world markets and shapes the nature of all our lives and all our school systems. With this as a background, the second part of the book moves in to a progressively closer focus on the European project, its *modus operandi* and the lessons that can be learned for schools in any country. It describes the three key elements of the project – the self-evaluation profile, the toolbox of approaches and the role of the critical friends. The penultimate chapter describes case studies of individual schools in Belgium, Scotland, Austria and Sweden.

Whatever sequence you choose, we hope you read both parts of this book, because one sheds light on the other. Each, in complement, refracts, illuminates and deepens our understanding of school improvement in the third millennium.

1 Serena

Serena looked at herself in the full-length mirror in her bedroom. Perhaps she wasn't so ugly after all. Earlier in the week she had overheard her mother telling their nosy neighbour Mrs Reyna that Serena was growing up into a 'lovely young woman'. Serena considered her make-up: her mother disapproved of it – 'at her age' – and especially on school days, but it helped to conceal the last remaining adolescent spot on her lower left cheek while the eyebrow pencil helped to accentuate the deep brown of her eyes. Serena thought she might get to like herself after all.

She moved from the mirror and pulled back the curtain. All she could see through the dark were the Christmas lights of the city in the distance and the illuminated winter garden below her window. This would only be the second time Serena had travelled without her mother and she determined to enjoy every moment of this fairytale city, the Christmas market, the treasures of the Habsburgs, the Royal Lipizzaner stallions.

She returned to the mirror, looking not at her own image but beyond it as if she might catch some reflections of the eventful year which had eventually brought her to Vienna and would, the following morning, require her to speak in front of 300 people on a subject she had known nothing about one year earlier; self-evaluation had become a term full of meaning and association for her in that time.

Serena had just completed her fourth year in 'the big school': this was a term her mother still used as if she was clinging on to those heady days when everything was brand new and Serena was still 'little Serena'. It now seemed a long journey from those first days and weeks many years ago – the exhilaration of new teachers and new subjects, grown-up books without pictures and real homework.

She could bring vividly into her memory her first geography classes where a frail woman with pince-nez glasses had taken them on excursions to places at the other end of the world. Always with their eyes closed – and that was Miss Pebble's one firm rule – she would lead them through some of the great cities of the world. They met and talked to people, mayors, planners, architects, newspaper editors, town criers. They travelled down the Seine in a *bateau mouche* and, with their eyes open again in every sense, discussed what Paris would be like without a river running through it.

Now, four years later, Serena could close her eyes and revisit the places, even the smells and the sounds of the city which Miss Pebble had helped them create so vividly in their minds. In her second and third years of school, after the sad departure of Miss Pebble, geography had become a bore. All the life and vitality had been squeezed out of it. It had become no more than a paper and pencil exercise, drawing squiggly lines to represent rivers she had never heard of, memorising names of capital cities she knew nothing about, writing essays about things she knew she didn't understand. But still she passed the tests and answered the questions when called on and somehow usually got the answers right.

There had been nothing to give Serena hope that her fourth year would be any better. She could recall it as if it were yesterday. She found it easy to travel back in time and without great effort she was suddenly back there at the start of a new school year, at the opening chapter of Serena's story.

The opening chapter

Her fourth year had begun in an equally uninspiring way – some new teachers, many of the old and all-too-familiar faces. Serena saw the weeks stretching out before her in a flat landscape towards the all-too-distant horizon of the mid-term holidays. But there were peaks to look forward to as well, she told herself: the art class was always a pleasure. They listened to music while they worked. They talked to each other and complimented each other on their work. Somebody was always coming up with a good idea and trying it out. Serena tried to think what it was that made that class so special. Perhaps it was because Mrs Hope kept telling them that everyone could be an artist and in that class everyone was.

The walls were decorated with their work. Their strange colourful creations hung from the ceilings and every available surface was covered with collections of jumble – old kettles, bicycle wheels, car hubcaps, ancient coffee grinders. It was the only class in the school where you didn't have to tread carefully between the right and wrong answers, or where you didn't have to find comfort in the fact that there was always someone stupider than you. The art class was probably the only class from which she emerged with something she could take home, something to show for the hours of work, and the amount of 'herself' that Serena put into it.

At home too Serena's pattern of life always seemed to follow a predictable course. She would sit down to watch the television. Her mother would ask her if she didn't have homework to do? Serena would say yes, she had some but she would do it later. Her mother then said she didn't understand why Serena watched that rubbish anyway, and before the end of the programme the phone would ring and it would be her school friends asking about homework or if she wanted to come out.

Homework was usually an after-dinner chore. She went to her bedroom, shut the door and turned on her stereo at full volume, working through each subject in turn. Her mother would usually arrive to tell her to turn the volume down and say she didn't know how Serena could possibly think with all that racket going on and that the homework booklet she had got from the school said she should find a quiet place to work. 'Underline *quiet*, Serena!' Serena would sometimes switch the music off, then switch it back on again five minutes later because she found her thoughts wandering.

The maths was usually pretty routine. She was good at maths and worked her way through the problems effortlessly. She then went on to other subjects, phoning her friends when she needed inspiration, leaving the best to the last, her art homework which she could do watching television: sketching the cat asleep on top of the set, a vase of flowers or her mother's hands folded on her lap.

One of her homework assignments was to read *The Diary of Anne Frank*. History and literature had their brighter moments in year four; both were taught by the same teacher, Mr Ericson, but Serena sometimes got confused with what was what. Mr Ericson had asked them to read *Anne Frank* but now Serena couldn't remember if this was 'literature' or 'history'. She phoned her friend Barbara who said 'It's literature, silly. We have to write a report on what we thought about it. History doesn't ask what you think because it's about things that actually happened.'

Serena lay in bed thinking about what 'actually happened' to Anne Frank. She had seen something on television recently about how they were about to republish the *Diary* putting back some of the bits that had been removed because they hadn't shown Anne in a very good light. She fell asleep wondering if Mr Ericson's history didn't leave out some of the bits he didn't want them to hear. She dreamed an entirely new version of the Battle of Waterloo fought in the streets of Paris with no Seine.

The next day Mr Ericson asked Serena if she had enjoyed *The Diary of Anne Frank*. She said yes, it was a good book.

'What did you like about it?' he asked.

'It was interesting. I enjoyed it,' Serena answered.

Mr Ericson didn't seem very impressed with that answer and Serena felt slightly irritated by his persistence. Why couldn't he just accept the answers and get on with the lesson? And then, to add insult to injury, he would set a piece of homework. If she had given him a better answer, she reflected, perhaps she wouldn't have ended up with 'a short paper, only 200 words' on 'Why *The Diary of Anne Frank* is a good book'.

Yet another chore to keep her in instead of going down to the café with Barbara. After the ritual inquiries from her mother and an awkward dinner, just the two of them, Serena retired to her room and tried to think about the book. She put on some music but she couldn't write more than thirty words. She phoned Barbara who, she was pleased to find, had not gone to the café either but was also writing a book report. Unfortunately, Barbara was writing about a different book and said she couldn't help. Since she still had another three days before her assignment was to be handed in, Serena left it and went on to other work. Maths was routine. She could turn her brain off completely, tune into the music and work mechanically down the page of problems.

The following day Serena told Mr Ericson that she was a bit stuck for ideas and that since the class were all reading different books there wasn't a lot they could do together.

'You did say, remember, that we should share and work together,' she reminded him. 'But it's not easy if you are all doing different stuff.'

'I'm not sure I agree with that, Serena,' Mr Ericson said. Why did he always find some way to disagree? Although, she added in afterthought, it was a nice kind of disagreement. Never content to let a sleeping dog lie, Mr Ericson suggested that the class brainstorm the topic 'What makes a book good?'

'Any book. What makes any book good? Ideas please. What are the rules of brainstorming again?'

Serena knew the rules by heart, although she suddenly became aware that this was the only class in which they ever used brainstorming and, come to think of it, she had never used it when she was stuck with her homework or sitting a test. Mr Ericson reminded them of the five golden rules and as he wrote them again on the board some of the boys joined in the chorus.

1   Just say anything that comes into your head.
2   Everything you say I write down just as you say it without comment.
3   Nobody should criticise anyone else's idea.
4   No laughter; no applause.
5   Let's just get as much as we can down on the blackboard in the space of three minutes.

'What makes a book good?' After three minutes there were twenty-eight items on the board. Serena had contributed five:

- It makes you feel sad.
- You don't want to put it down.
- Anne makes you feel what it must have been like to be in Amsterdam at that time.
- It is clear and easy to read.
- It makes you wonder if that could happen today.

When Serena had volunteered the item about Amsterdam, Hans had said it was silly because it applied to just one book. Mr Ericson had said nothing. He just pointed to Rule 3 of brainstorming on the blackboard and then wrote on the flipchart exactly what Serena had said. It was good to see her own words on the board, just exactly as she had said them. Most teachers had obviously been trained to turn your words into their own more fancy ones and come up with something you had never said or thought in the first place. They probably did it to show how much cleverer they were than you, Serena concluded.

In the end there were twenty-eight items. Mr Ericson suggested they boil them down to about fifteen criteria that could be applied to any book. Then he proposed that they turn them into a checklist, which they could use to evaluate any book they were reading.

The following week Peter, a boy in the class who didn't read much, asked if he could use the checklist with television programmes instead of with a book. Mr

Ericson said it was an interesting idea and Peter came back a few days later and reported what had happened when he tried it out. Some of the items didn't work too well but he had invented some new ones. So the class agreed to test the questionnaire, now named the PETS (Peter's Evaluating Television Survey) on three television programmes over the course of the following week to see how well it worked. After a week of extensive trials PETS was greatly improved and the class felt they had come up with something quite marketable that they might even be able to sell to a television company.

Meanwhile Serena had decided she might like to keep her own diary. It would, hopefully, never be as momentous as Anne Frank's but it would help her remember things that often just slipped out of her mind. In it she wrote about things that happened to her during the day: arguments, tall tales, injustices of wicked teachers, her amazing sketch of a dead frog being put up on the classroom wall, framed by the teacher and signed by her as an original Serena. She wrote about her maths homework and then the chapter Mrs Stein, her biology teacher, had asked them to read for the following day.

Maths. Ten problems. Easy. Finished in less than ten minutes. Read a chapter for biology on termites. Boring.

The next day she wrote a further entry in her diary:

Mrs Stein asked me in class about termites. My mind went blank. Couldn't remember a thing I had read. Very embarrassed! Hans kept sniggering. I could have killed him. Maybe I will!

Tonight's homework. To watch the programme on termites. Thought it would be boring but it was amazing. Termites build this amazing city with tunnels and traffic lanes and ducts and air conditioning. The man on the programme said that termites had brains no bigger than a pin and the queen termite was even pin-headeder. But because they worked together they multiplied their intelligences and did amazing things.

Got out PETS and gave the TV programme full marks. Which made me wonder about the book so I scored it too. Funnily enough it was actually quite interesting when you knew what it was all about. Why didn't I think that the first time round? Is it me or is it the book? Discuss. Ha-ha.

P.S. I think I'd better take out the bit about killing Hans. If he died and the police found my diary I might end up in jail for life.

The next day Serena found herself talking to Mr Ericson about her diary and her thoughts about books on termites. She knew very well that termites weren't Tom Ericson's territory but he *was* interested in books, after all. Literature wasn't history and history wasn't biology but getting all her subjects mixed up like this was actually quite good fun, Serena thought. She was beginning to see some connections after all. She wished she had tried it before.

'I'm very impressed by your question, Serena,' Tom Ericson said.

Serena looked blank.

'The question "was it me or was it the book?" – that's a big question. It is such a big question that philosophers and psychologists and literary critics and historians will probably go on arguing about it for another millennium.'

There was definitely something a bit strange about Mr Ericson.

'Why don't you try this out for homework?' he suggested.

Serena had done it again. She had talked herself into another homework exercise; that was positively the last time she would tell Mr Ericson anything. But when she sat down to it at home that evening it didn't take long, and the next day Serena was able to give Mr Ericson the answer to the question 'was it me or was it the book?'

Me	*The book chapter*
• I wasn't in the mood after doing my maths.	• From the first sentence the writer didn't make me interested in the life of termites.
• It was nearly 10 o'clock and I was tired.	• The layout of the pages wasn't very interesting.
• I kept thinking of other things I was supposed to be doing.	• There were long sentences and some words I didn't understand.
• I wasn't particularly interested in termites.	• The writer didn't explain things very well.
• I wasn't sure why I was doing this anyway.	• It wasn't related to anything I knew about.
• I like to see things and picture things.	• There weren't any pictures.
• I learn best when I can talk over things with other people.	

Luckily Mr Ericson was busy when Serena entered the class and he just took the paper without embarking on another philosophical discussion and another assignment. When she got it back a day later he had written at the bottom of the page:

This is a very interesting piece of work, Serena. I want you to think a little more about how you learn best and how you can make your home study more enjoyable and profitable. Let me suggest a few ideas.

Do you see any relationship between the right and left hand sides of your table? What have you learned about:

- Your own motivation?
- The context (the place and time) in which you learn?
- How you prepare yourself before you start a piece of study (mentally? emotionally?)

- How do you stay focused on the most important things in a text?
- Your 'style' – are you a 'visual' learner?
- How knowledge becomes understanding in your head?
- Why it is important to you to have other people to talk it over with?

And here's a final thought, Serena:
If we got really good at this could we cut homework time down by half and still learn as much? or even more?
And a very, very final thought, Serena. Why don't you discuss this with your mother? She would be very interested and might be able to tell you something about how you learned when you were a baby. It might shed some light on things!

Over the next few weeks Serena kept a more detailed log of how she was learning and began to recognise immediately when her study was most effective. She began to experiment with different times of day for learning, different ways of learning, drawing pictures, working without music sometimes and using music at other times, discussing things with her friends, on the phone or going round to their house, and sometimes even with her mother.

Her mother told her that as a baby she had loved books, especially brightly coloured ones. She had done complicated jigsaw puzzles when she was three. She took things apart and put them back together, broke things beyond repair and then tried to fix them. Well before three she had shown a great sense of rhythm, and could dance as soon as she could walk.

'But you weren't all sweetness and light, Serena, before you get carried away with yourself. You had to be told everything three times before it seemed to penetrate into your brain and your impatience used to drive your poor father crazy. God bless him.'

Serena wasn't too happy about repeating all of this in front of her class when Mr Ericson asked them to 'share with each other' (as he put it) what they had discovered about their childhood. She had no inclination to share anything with too-too-clever Hans, whose stories would always outdo everyone else's. She had no common cause with the morose and turbulent Daniel who, if he wasn't gazing out of the window, would be causing mayhem for those unlucky enough to be in his immediate vicinity. Even the normally composed Mr Ericson didn't seem to know what to do with the totally unpredictable Daniel.

After some coaxing and a little sneering from Hans, Serena eventually recounted what her mother had said about Serena as a three-year-old.

'It sounds to me like you are a very visual learner,' said Mr Ericson. 'Your brain loves colour, you know. Perhaps you are not so good on the auditory side. Just being told things. You obviously learn things much better when you are able to picture them.' That was true. Serena hadn't thought about it before.

'You probably also have a well-developed spatial intelligence … and musical intelligence?' Serena didn't know what the first thing meant but the second was definitely wrong. She hated music in school. But, of course, Hans did know because Hans was an avid reader of newspapers and anything remotely 'scientific'.

'I read in the papers, Mr Ericson ... '

Serena gritted her teeth. She hated his ingratiating ways.

' ... it said that females don't have spatial intelligence and males do. It shows photos of the brain where it is and women don't have that part of the brain.'

Surely he was making it up. Serena determined to find the newspaper, although she would die rather than get the information from clever Hans. She was relieved to hear that Mr Ericson had read the same newspaper.

'Well, Hans,' he said, 'I seem to remember the article saying something about verbal intelligence, that it is much better developed in females. So perhaps that explains why you and I may need some help in this discussion.'

'There are always exceptions to any rule, sir.'

'And there we agree,' said Tom Ericson, who could obviously sense the class's restlessness at this distracting interchange, and so they moved back to the First World War and Serena closed her eyes and imagined the mud and the rain of Passchendaele as Mr Ericson had described it. She couldn't help feeling a little embarrassed about it because this was history and the 'visualisation' belonged to Miss Pebble and geography. She hoped the long-departed Miss Pebble wouldn't have minded.

That evening in the café, the result of a joint decision with Barbara to forget about homework for one night, Serena broke their own first sacred rule – not to talk about school.

'I really get annoyed when those boys, horrible Hans and that creepy little friend of his, say we are wasting our time and we need to get on with the work, don't you?'

Barbara seemed to agree but not with great enthusiasm. She hadn't agreed to breaking the sacred rule in the first place.

'But don't you think it's really interesting when we talk about how our brains work and all that and how we can use our own time better? Don't you think you spend less time on history homework than before because you're understanding it a lot better? Remember that funny little geography lady we had in first year? How you remembered her stuff so well you didn't have to go home and swot it all up? You just learned it.'

Barbara suggested that they bring it up the next day with Mr Ericson. That would lay the subject to rest and they could get back to topics of more immediate concern, like the two boys in the corner who had been looking at them since they came in.

'Yours is the one on the left,' Barbara offered.

Serena did bring up the subject of time the next day and Mr Ericson allowed this small side excursion away from history. Serena explained how she was doing less but learning more and couldn't that be applied to the classroom as well? 'What if, what if, Mr Ericson, you taught less and we learned more?'

'If you could learn in less time they wouldn't have made the school day the way it was. Are you saying you know better than the head and the teachers and Board of Education and the government?' said Hans. Although it was widely agreed that Hans was the cleverest in the class, Serena was beginning to have her doubts.

Serena knew by now that 'what if' questions like this could really get Mr Ericson going. He often called them 'historical questions' – What if we didn't teach history at school? What if there were no schools? What if they hadn't dropped the bomb on Hiroshima? What if Hitler had had a speech impediment? What if you discovered that Anne Frank's diary was a hoax? Would you expose it? Could it still be true? Could a fiction represent a greater historical truth than fact? Stimulated by the class discussion that followed from this last question, Tom Ericson had set them one of his famous homework tasks – 'Could fiction represent a greater truth than fact?' 'Wouldn't it be awful,' Serena said to her mother in one of their rare snatches of dinner conversation, 'if Anne Frank's diary was all just made up?'

'But it wasn't made up, dear,' was Mrs Kaur's reply.

'But what if it was? Could it still be true?'

'You and your what ifs. What if the moon were made of cheese?'

Their dinner descended into a period of silence as Serena mulled over the consequences for the solar system of a moon made of cheese.

On another of Mr Ericson's 'what if' detours he had read them a story from an American newspaper about an old lady who had just died in Connecticut at the age of ninety. In 1942, the year the United States entered the Second World War, doctors had given up hope for her: she was running a temperature of 107° and there was no known cure for her condition. Her family doctor, however, had heard of a new wonder drug and although it had never been tried and had failed to show promise with experiments on mice, it could do no harm to a young woman near death.

Twenty-four hours after receiving the injection the young woman, then aged thirty-three, was tucking into a hearty meal. What if? What if a young Scottish doctor called Fleming hadn't noticed a mouldy dish in his laboratory and what if his curiosity had not been aroused to investigate the curative powers of penicillin? And what if during the remaining years of the war it hadn't been used to save other lives? And what was the connection with an event three years earlier in England, when thousands of children were evacuated from London to the countryside as Britain declared war on Germany? The epidemic of tuberculosis among young children from drinking unpasteurised milk had been kept very quiet by a British government which had already been well warned of the dangers of untreated milk.

Although Mr Ericson's story and the following discussion had taken no more than ten minutes, it was one of those famous 'connections' that Serena's history teacher was so fond of. It had kept Serena puzzling and thinking about it for days after. It had also helped Serena with some of those memory pegs for dates that she was learning about. 1939 and 1942 had a new significance for her.

It was during one of these 'what if' sessions that Mrs Barre had come in and taken Mr Ericson out of the class for a very uncharacteristic chat. A few days were to pass before they were to find out what it had all been about; meanwhile stories had been circulating and growing in authority. The alleged affair between the two was soon dismissed for lack of evidence. The 'truth' was that Mr Ericson was in trouble and would be leaving the school at Christmas. Every piece of evidence pointed in that direction. He looked more troubled than usual. His replacement had been seen entering the school the very next day.

The factual truth, when it came out, proved far inferior to the fiction. A little more animated than usual, Mr Ericson announced that the school had been chosen to take part in a European project. Serena could see that not everyone shared Mr Ericson's excitement. Some were positively deflated. However much they liked Mr Ericson, they preferred their own version of the future, their own 'future history' as someone had called it, Serena couldn't remember who. Daniel alone was oblivious to it all, absorbed as ever by the world beyond the window.

Mr Ericson explained what the project was about and there were a few stirrings of interest. Even Hans seemed to have forgotten his intolerance of time wasting. Serena suddenly became aware that Mr Ericson was asking the class to nominate someone to represent them in the project – and Barbara was already proposing her. Some friend! Serena wanted to climb inside the desk and hide. Someone nominated Hans and there was a loud groan. In the end, with only the two nominations, Serena won sixteen votes and Hans thirteen, with two abstentions. The boys had voted for Hans and the girls for Serena. Three boys, including Daniel, had abstained.

When Serena arrived home that evening she saw that her mother was not yet home from her work. She had preferred the years when her mother was unemployed, even though it did mean less money and not having the things, the designer clothes or the mobile phones, that others like Hans and Barbara had. Serena sat in the window seat and watched two squirrels engaged in earnest conversation in the garden. They were such intelligent creatures; Serena had once seen a television programme in which squirrels were set amazingly complex problems to solve. The ingenious creatures worked at it for weeks but always came up with the answer in the end. She remembered Mr Ericson telling them how James Dyson had made 153 attempts at inventing his new vacuum cleaner before getting it right.

Serena was thinking so hard she hadn't noticed her mother come in. She looked so lonely that Serena felt a sudden wave of guilt; Serena hadn't spent much time with her mother since her father died. His sudden departure had left an awkwardness between them: it had somehow increased, rather than diminished, the distance between Serena and her mother. Mrs Kaur seemed suddenly to have grown older. Her brown hair was now striped with grey and there were new worry lines around her eyes. Serena followed her mother into the kitchen. She said nothing but picked up the tea towel and began to dry the dishes as if it were her normal daily routine.

With both absorbed in their task it was easier to talk and easier to tolerate the long silences in between. Serena told her mother about history not being like a train of lit-up carriages passing in the night.

'You'd better explain that to me,' said Mrs Kaur.

'Well, you know how a train passes and all the carriages are lit up, one after the other, one after the other, all in sequence, all coupled together, passing by in front of you?'

	++	+	–	– –	▲	↔	▼
Outcomes							
Academic achievement							
Personal and social development							
Student destinations							
Process at classroom level							
Time as a resource for learning							
Quality of learning and teaching							
Support for learning difficulties							
Process at school level							
School as a learning place							
School as a social place							
School as a professional place							
Environment							
School and home							
School and community							
School and work							

Figure 1.1 The school self-evaluation profile.

'I get the picture,' said a slightly puzzled Mrs Kaur.

'You must be a visual learner, too,' said Serena. Then, seeing that she had simply deepened her mother's puzzlement, continued, 'Well, Mr Ericson says history isn't like that. It's not all a series of things linked together one after the other.'

Seeing her mother taking a keener interest in the dishes, Serena moved on to new ground. She told her mother about the European project, about being voted on to the student evaluation group and about their first meeting. She described how she had found herself in a group with five other pupils. Two were younger and three were older. The eldest girl, who was the chair, had explained what they were to do and gave out something she called an SEP, consisting of one sheet of paper with a series of boxes. It looked very like one of the questionnaires they had been using in Mr Ericson's class but this was about the school and what they thought of it: academic achievement, personal and social development – was the school very good at this? Good? Not very good? Or pretty bad? How was she to know?

'Here, I've got a copy of it,' said Serena, delving into the depths of her schoolbag to retrieve a crumpled copy of the SEP (Figure 1.1). She smoothed it with the palms of both hands, trying to erase the papery wrinkles.

Serena explained to her mother how Teresa, the 'chairgirl', had asked them to go through it and complete it as honestly as they could without worrying what other people would think. Teresa explained that they could ask questions about what some of the things meant, but what they wrote had to be their own ideas. Serena looked down the list. Academic achievement? Not too sure about that. She tried to think of people she knew. Hans and Michael, they were achievers but there were a lot of others who looked as if they would never achieve anything – Peter, who hardly ever showed up; Daniel, who spent his life looking out of the window or making trouble; and Wilma, who was so quiet up in her chosen corner of the classroom that you would hardly even know she was there. If she was achieving anything you would never know it. Serena put her cross halfway between the plus and the minus: sitting on the fence.

Quality of learning and teaching? That wasn't any easier. Some of her teachers were good but one or two were so boring she counted the minutes until the end of the lesson. Then she thought about quality of learning. It was only in the last month with Mr Ericson that she had felt she was really beginning to get excited about learning. She would be bold and give a minus on this one.

She went through all twelve items and looked at the completed sheet; a zigzag of double pluses, pluses and minuses. No double minuses: nothing was that bad.

Her mother was still listening, the suspended tea towel in one hand, the crumpled SEP in the other. Serena continued her narrative.

The second part was more difficult still. The chairperson told them that as a group, all six of them, they had to share what they had written and agree on what marks they should give the school. They went through the twelve categories again one by one. Academic achievement: no one had given the school a double plus – nor a double minus for that matter. The crucial decision was a plus or minus. A boy in the year above her said his parents wanted him to go to another school because the results in this school weren't nearly as good as other schools, so he had given it a minus. Someone else disagreed because he said eight out of his class of thirty were going on to university and 25 per cent was pretty good for a school 'in an area like this'. Teresa thought that there were statistics available which compared their school with other schools and that she would find out what they showed.

'Does that mean there is a right answer?' asked the boy called Arnold. It was a challenge rather than a question. Teresa looked a little embarrassed then answered:

'Well, I suppose it's *one* source of evidence.' She sat back looking quietly pleased with her reply.

They moved on, but everyone now was thinking 'evidence?' What evidence could Serena offer for any of her views? Pupil destinations, for example. The large numbers of past students hanging around the streets without jobs – was that 'evidence' of pupil destinations? She wondered if there were statistics about what happened to people once they left her school. If this were a really fantastic school would everyone go to a university? Or get good jobs? Or turn into brilliant scientists and poets and musicians?

It was over an hour later by the time they had worked their way through the whole list. Time had gone quickly and there were all kind of questions still left hanging in the air. But this wasn't the end, just the beginning, Teresa explained. Stage two was still to come – the school evaluation group – in which two of the pupils would meet with others, teachers and parents, to go through the profile again. Serena had a mounting suspicion from the way Teresa was looking at her that she was about to be volunteered again, and without much debate she and Arnold were elected! She felt a mixture of dread and excitement. What had she ever done to deserve this? It was all Anne Frank's fault. Keeping diaries and asking questions could get you into trouble.

'So that's not the end of it then,' said Mrs Kaur, clearly disappointed.

'No such luck,' said Serena, 'just when I thought it was safe to go back in the water we had to go through it all again. They called it the school evaluation group.'

The school evaluation group was a bit like a rerun of what they had done before. But there were some big differences. This was like being on stage at La Scala having had a bit part in the school play. Serena was the youngest in the group. The headteacher was the oldest, or maybe it was actually the chair of the board, who looked about ninety. There were two parents and two teachers including Mrs Stein, her biology teacher. One of the parents was the busybody Mrs Reyna from across the road. Serena would have to watch what she said because it would go straight back to her mother, with some fictitious passages inserted by Mrs Reyna to add drama. Perhaps, thought Serena, that is how history gets to be written.

Each of the five groups at the meeting had brought their completed SEP. Serena and Arnold had a copy of the one they had eventually agreed on as a group. How different would it be from what the other groups had come up with?

The chair was one of the two parents, Mrs Larsson, who asked them to call her Diana. Serena didn't think she could do that. Anyway she didn't plan to say a lot. Mrs Larsson wasted no time in getting started. After a brief explanation of the ground rules they were off; Serena hoped that Mrs Reyna had listened carefully to the bit about 'discretion' and 'confidentiality'.

'Academic achievement'? Just as last time there wasn't immediate agreement but this time Serena found herself working a lot harder to keep up with the debate. A copy of the school's examination performance was handed out and comparisons made with other schools. It all seemed to point to a definite minus but her new 'friend' Arnold was having none of it. He wanted to know about 'value added'. Serena decided not to show her ignorance. She would ask about that afterwards.

The chair was having her work cut out giving everyone a turn to speak. Serena saw her looking in her direction and immediately studied her paper intently to avoid making eye contact. It was finally agreed to give a tentative 'minus' to academic achievement but to star this item as one they would come back to and explore in more depth over the coming year. 'A year of this?' Serena said to herself.

The next item caused even more debate: 'Personal and social development'. Serena waited for the sheets of statistics but none came. One of the teachers began talking about there being an excellent programme of social and health education which dealt with drugs, sex and healthy living. Mrs Stein chipped in to tell them how she complemented this in the biology class through teaching the physiology of the human body and sexual reproduction. Putting condoms on carrots, Arnold whispered a bit too loudly in Serena's ear, drawing a disapproving look from Mrs Stein.

Serena had not looked down early enough this time. The chairperson had caught her eye. 'Serena, do you feel that this school has helped you to develop personally and socially?'

The simple answer would have been 'yes' but Serena had learned something important from Mr Ericson at least: to think before answering. She thought for a long, silent ten seconds then said: 'Well, I think I have but, to be honest, I don't think it had much to do with the classes on drugs and all that. I suppose it was mainly from the friends I made and some of my teachers who helped me to know myself better.' She decided that sounded a bit pompous or 'soft', as her friends would have said. She was glad they couldn't hear her now.

These evidence questions were giving Serena a headache. Who was she to speak on behalf of a few hundred students in the school? There was so much, and yet on most things there was so little that everyone could agree on as being good evidence. After an hour and a half they were only halfway down the list. Two items, 'the quality of learning and teaching' and 'time as a resource for learning', had occupied forty minutes. On these two items Serena had felt more comfortable, warming to her subject, realising that she knew a lot more than the parents, the governing board, and on some things more even than the two teachers and Mrs Barre, the headteacher. As Arnold had said, a bit too aggressively perhaps, teachers all taught their own subjects and didn't see the daily cross-section of school life that pupils saw. Mrs Barre visited classes occasionally but when she came in everyone was on their best behaviour, including the teachers. Serena couldn't remember ever seeing Mrs Barre in the classroom before the day she had come in to tell them about the project.

Something else Arnold had said really made Serena think.

'Teachers see time differently from what we do. They kind of think "how much time have I spent on a subject?" and then sort of add all of that up and say "five hours a week on maths". As if that means that for thirty pupils in the class there had been 50 hours of solid learning. For me maybe only thirty minutes in a week is good quality learning, when I feel I have learned something and really understand it. And maybe half of that is what I have done at home in my own time, my own studying.'

To Serena's surprise Mrs Barre, the head – termite-in-chief – was listening and nodding. It had been a pleasant shock for Serena to see how much all the adults were listening and taking the two of them seriously, while Arnold, who had started out a bit aggressively, was now listening to others and agreeing more.

'People were disagreeing nicely,' Serena told her mother, concluding the long story which her mother had listened to patiently but also with interest. But it would not be like her mother not to air her doubts.

'And where is all this taking you? Time as a resource for learning, indeed. Are you telling me all that discussion round a table is time well spent? You must have been missing classes.'

'We'll see what happens next,' said Serena. 'We all agreed we wanted to find out more about three important things – learning and teaching, time as a resource for learning, and home–school relations. So we can make all of these things better. You know what Jean-Jacques Rousseau said, Mum – lose time to save it.'

Her mother gave her a long, dark look. Serena knew that quoting Jean-Jacques Rousseau at her mother was not guaranteed to win her over.

'Home–school relations, mother. Isn't that something you would be interested in?'

'I think things are just fine as they are. Mind you, from what I am hearing now I am beginning to wonder what's going on up there.'

They had come to the end of the drying-up some time ago and moved the dialogue seamlessly through to the living room. 'We'll see,' said Serena. Their conversation was interrupted by a knock on the door. Serena sensed the impending entry of Mrs Reyna. She headed swiftly for her bedroom where homework awaited, re-emerging when the coast was clear and the last lingering remnant of Mrs Reyna had departed.

'The old cow,' she said with feeling, 'I bet she was in here to tell all my news.'

Over the next week they started gathering some data. Five of the pupils from Serena's class were nominated to be 'researchers' and each had a different task to do. On Tuesday Serena made a timetable:

Total times: Tuesday

Movement between classes	17 minutes
Settling in time before lesson begins	21 minutes
Trouble and discipline things	16 minutes
Visitors and interruptions	11 minutes
Giving back papers, checking homework	8 minutes
School announcements, news, things about rules	11 minutes

A week later and Serena had begun to keep some more detailed notes about individual lessons. They agreed they would try a more careful recording of time spent in class together with a judgement of how much of that was 'good learning time', time when they felt they were really gaining important knowledge or skills. Her geography lesson notes showed some of the high and low spots of the lesson.

Geography: Monday

	Class time	My learning time
Settling in before lesson begins	4 minutes	0 minutes
Teacher listens to excuses for no homework	4 minutes	0 minutes
Teacher explains the problem of transport networks in Thailand during Vietnam War	11 minutes	about 4 minutes

Reading a passage and writing answers to questions on it	9 minutes	6 minutes
Getting into groups, discussing what we're going to do	3 minutes	1 minute
Problem solving on building road networks and airports in Thailand for military purposes	8 minutes	about 7 minutes
Report back from first group and class discussion	9 minutes	5 minutes plus 3 **good** minutes
Bell about to go, homework given out and a few questions about it	3 minutes	2 minutes

This was evidence, but Serena wasn't sure it really told her very much except how much time they wasted. This didn't really tell the whole story of what had begun as quite a frustrating lesson but ended up quite exciting. For the first ten minutes or so Serena had written this:

> Listened to the teacher explaining about Thailand's involvement in the Vietnam War.
> Realised I didn't have a clue where Thailand is or what the war was all about. Why are we doing this in geography?
> Wanted to ask a question but didn't want to seem stupid or too smarty pants.
> Teacher asked me a question – what did Thailand use to be called? Didn't know the answer, but Hans did.
> Can't remember what he said. I was too annoyed. Embarrassed?

In the last ten minutes the lesson had come alive for Serena when the teacher explained how they had built the roads and airports and fast communication networks. Serena remembered the termites and had said to the teacher: 'I suppose it's a bit like the way the termites built their city.'

The teacher had looked a little puzzled and asked her to explain what she meant. Hans and one or two others were sighing and making plain their impatience that Serena was once again interrupting a geography lesson to talk about something else. About biology of all things! The teacher was interested, though, and thanked Serena. He said he had learned something he didn't know before and that it was an excellent analogy.

He then went on: 'There is a deeper truth in the story Serena has just told us, isn't there? It is about knowledge and intelligence. It can't be just inside the small brains of the individual termites. It comes out of them working together to create something that none of them knew they could do. Does anybody know a word for that?'

He paused, but not long enough for anyone to come up with answer – everyone knew he was about to answer his own question.

'It's called synergy. A new form of energy bigger than all the individual energies combined. A simple definition of synergy is 1 plus 1 plus 1 equals 5. So now, synergy in Thailand … '

Serena was pleased that she had not only been able to make some links in her own head but had added something to the lesson. Her own contribution to synergy.

Over dinner, she told her mother about synergy. Then she told her about the termites. The way her mother reacted, Serena could tell that she thought it was 'another of Serena's crazy ideas' but she also knew her mother would prefer to hear her ideas, however crazy, than the silence that had lain between them for the last couple of years. They were much closer now.

'Your head is full of termites,' her mother said.

'No, listen to me,' Serena argued. 'You could see a school as a bit like a termite colony. None of us are Einsteins. Not even the queen termite sitting in her office. She is as pinheaded as the rest of us.'

'Serena!'

'What I'm saying is that when we all stop rushing around doing what we're doing and begin to think about it together we could make a better school.'

'I think you'd be better just getting on with your learning,' her mother said.

'But that's just it. This *is* our learning. There's a great word for it our teacher told us. I can't say it. I have to write it down so I can see it.'

Serena wrote METACOGNITIVE.

'It means thinking about your thinking. What we are doing is trying to find out about how the school is thinking about itself. It's called self-evaluation.'

2 Mrs Kaur

Serena's mother

Serena's mother could remember as clearly as yesterday Serena's first day at 'the big school'. She had come home with a long list of things to tell her and couldn't finish one exciting piece of news before she began the next. It was a big school, much bigger than Serena had expected and she told her mother how she kept getting lost. People were helpful and understood she was new to the school, but when she asked some older boys how to get to the maths class they sent her the wrong way. On purpose, she said.

It had a better library than her old school but there were no lockers where you could put your books, so you had to carry them around with you all day. The girls were nice but most of the boys were horrible. She would have liked it better if it had been a girls' school like the one her friend Tamil went to. Boys were such show-offs and took up all the teachers' attention. The girls, like her, just got on with their work.

'Girls are much more grown up, don't you think?' Serena said.

'Well, Serena, that is a biological fact,' her mother told her.

The immediate important news of the school day tended to be put on hold while Serena made a beeline from the front door to the toilet. That was her biggest complaint about the new school: half of the toilets had no locks on the doors and the pall of smoke in the air made her cough. So, with great exercise of willpower, she 'held on' until she was home.

Serena had more teachers than she could name. In her last year of primary she had had only one. She told her mother about her teachers in detail, the ones she liked and the ones she didn't take to. It was a little early to be making rush judgements, Mrs Kaur said, and asked her what it was that made her more positive about some teachers than others.

'Just a feeling,' said Serena. 'You know who the nice ones are.'

When cajoled into being a little more explicit Serena thought that those she liked most had smiled a lot more, didn't talk down to her, and explained very clearly what she was expected to do and what she would learn.

It brought vividly into Mrs Kaur's mind some of the teachers she had had a hundred years ago when she had been at school. She could still see and hear those who had left their mark on her, for good or ill, but she couldn't remember a single one like the strange little lady Serena described who took them on fantasy journeys to faraway places, sometimes to the accompaniment of music. In Sarah Kaur's day that would have not been tolerated. Music belonged in the music class, not in geography.

Three years later Serena's mother was to remind her of those early conversations they had had after Serena had just joined the school.

'Now when you come home and I ask you about school, you just say, "It was OK". Or if I ask what happened today, you say, "Nothing" and then I say, "You can't have spent all day and done nothing" and you say, "Well, nothing happened". End of conversation.' Her mother went on: 'Remember how we used to talk about your homework and you were so eager to do it and so keen to get everything right and please your teachers?'

'That was then. This is now', was Serena's distinctly unhelpful reply. The clear message was 'keep out'.

So Sarah Kaur kept out of her daughter's life. She no longer interrupted her long sessions in her room to check if she was doing her work or was immersed in her music. There was a time when she would open Serena's door and find her sitting or lying on the floor with her books spread around her, as if behind a wall of sound that insulated her from the world outside. She said she worked better that way, but Mrs Kaur was very doubtful of such a proposition since she herself needed total silence to read a book or to think at all. But no amount of persuasion would make Serena change her habits. 'She will grow out of it', Sarah Kaur told herself hopefully.

Sarah was reassured a little when she talked to other mothers. Their children had become equally uncommunicative. From time to time, and only when they felt like it, their sons and daughters would tell their parents about something a teacher had done, or not done. Sometimes, but less and less as they got older, they would ask their parents for help when they got stuck with a piece of homework or when they didn't understand what it was the teacher expected them to do. On occasions their parents would overhear them talking with their friends on the phone – about their teachers, about the injustices they had to suffer, about the boredom of some of the subjects they had to study and the fun that it was to go to certain classes. But parents seemed to be excluded from these intimate accounts.

It had been in Serena's third year at school that the rot seemed to have set in. In two of the subjects she liked most she had had a bad experience. In geography her marks had fallen dramatically and she seemed to have totally lost interest in history.

'History is boring', was all Serena would say.

'But you used to love it', her mother objected.

'That was last year', said Serena, as if that historical fact spoke for itself.

'And what about geography? You were best in the class last year.'

'That's before we got Mr Petit,' said Serena. 'He's hopeless. He can't teach.'

'Well then, we should do something about it.'

Serena looked at her mother as if she had just suggested she take up ballroom dancing.

'Well, I'm sorry, Serena, but this is your education we're talking about. I'm going up to that school to find out what's going on.'

'Don't even think about it,' Serena replied, 'Don't you dare. There is nothing you can do and you'll only make it worse for me.'

Looking back, Mrs Kaur was sorry she had allowed Serena to dissuade her. She had heard tales from some of the other mothers of Mr Petit's inability to control the class.

'The problem is,' said Mrs Reyna from across the road, 'he's such a nice man. He's a gentle soul who would never harm anybody. The kids, well the boys really, make his life a misery. Nobody likes to make a fuss and his wife walked out on him, you know, and he's never really been the same since. It's a shame.'

'How do you know all this?' asked Mrs Kaur, aware that that there was nothing by way of neighbourhood intelligence that escaped the lady from No. 23.

'I had to go up myself and complain about our Claudia. Her marks dropped drastically in a few months. I saw the deputy head who explained all about poor Mr Petit's hard life. I came away feeling heart sorry for the poor man. It was only halfway home I remembered what I had been up to the school for. Our poor Claudia!'

Sarah Kaur had allowed things to take their course. 'Poor Mr Petit' would struggle on and so would Serena. She had wondered aloud to Mrs Reyna what happened when the inspectors came round. 'They hide Mr Petit and all the other bad teachers in a cupboard', Mrs Reyna suggested.

'It must be a rather large cupboard,' joked Mrs Kaur. In fact, from what she could pick up from Serena and the snatches of overheard phone calls, most of the teachers seemed to be OK. But the few bad ones, it seemed, could wreak a special kind of havoc.

'Maybe all the kids are on their very best behaviour when the inspectors call', suggested Mrs Reyna.

'If I was the head, I would make sure the inspectors *did* visit Mr Petit and his likes,' said Mrs Kaur. 'Surely it would be better for everyone if he and his chums were pensioned off. Or couldn't they find a nice job in an office somewhere where he wouldn't be doing so much harm to our children?'

Sarah couldn't believe she had said it. She wasn't used to making bold statements like that but Mrs Reyna's pathetic little story had irritated her. The sad thing was that Serena was so bright. She had flourished in her primary school. 'Too smart for her own good', someone had said then. She played chess and as often as not beat the boys. She was better than most of them at computer games. She did jigsaw puzzles in half the time it took anyone else. She took mechanical things apart and put them back together as if she had been born to it. She struggled at times with classwork and gave up too easily when she hit a problem but on her own she consumed books voraciously. Her enthusiasm and intense curiosity had kept her going through the primary years.

'She is a shadow of her former self,' Serena's mother sadly told Mrs Reyna. 'I feel so helpless.'

'It's hormones you know,' Mrs Reyna explained patiently. 'Did you know that every seven years every single cell in your body changes? You become a new person. Fourteen to fifteen, it's a difficult age for them, you know. She's shedding all the little girl cells and growing woman cells. She is becoming a woman.'

Serena *was* becoming a woman: it was strange, though, that her biological development seemed to follow the rhythm of the school year because now, in her fourth year of school, having left Mr Petit and one or two others behind, there were a few new green shoots of promise. Three weeks into the new school year Serena had come home and, after the ritual visit to the toilet, had given her mother an envelope.

'It's for you to fill out,' said Serena. 'I know what it is. It's a questionnaire about history.'

Mrs Kaur didn't much like the sound of that. What did she know about history?

'It's our new history teacher. He's a bit weird. He keeps coming up with wonderful new ideas. He says he wants us to think but one of the boys, Hans, who's a bit of a smarty, asked him if he didn't think year four was a bit late for that?'

'Well, I hope your Mr Ericson gave him a good telling off for being so cheeky.'

'No he didn't, actually. He took Hans seriously and he asked him why he thought that, and Hans said he was just joking but Mr Ericson said he didn't think it was a joke and eventually Hans said most teachers didn't want you to think. Mr Ericson didn't get angry or anything like some teachers would. That's what's weird about him. It was like he believed what Hans said. So instead of doing history we had ten minutes' discussion about thinking and one or two of the boys got really annoyed because they said it was wasting time and they didn't want to fail their history exam. And Mr Ericson said, "Thinking about thinking is hard work isn't it?" or something like that. And then he asked what Hans thought about thinking historically and Hans just shut up and went into one of his long huffy silences.'

This narrative from Serena was the longest single speech she had delivered, at least on the subject of school, for the last few years. She could hold her own on the subject of clothes for twice that length, but school wasn't a subject to arouse the same passions. Not normally.

Mrs Kaur took the envelope from Serena and looked at the questionnaire. It asked her opinion of history, whether she thought it was important and from where she had learned most history herself. Mrs Kaur did not like this kind of thing. It made her uncomfortable but it was her duty and she wouldn't let Serena or the school down. It didn't take long to fill in and she was glad when it was done and handed back to Serena. Two questions had made her seek advice from her daughter: 'Why do you think it is important to study history?' and 'From what source have you learned most about history?' She left the first one blank and hoped her answer to the second might give her inspiration. She thought about the history she had been taught at school – the Romans, the Black Death, a Seven Years' War somewhere, Columbus in 1492 sailed across the ocean blue. Was that before or after the Renaissance? A date she had once memorised, now suspended in space. What else had happened in the fifteenth century? She couldn't think of anything.

Sarah realised these were all disconnected fragments about which she couldn't have written two coherent sentences. What, from her knowledge of history, did she really understand? She remembered going to see the films *Dr Zhivago* and then *Nicholas and Alexandra* and been so fascinated by Rasputin and the Anastasia mystery that she had read everything she could on the Russian Revolution and persuaded her husband to take a cruise from Helsinki to St Petersburg to see the Winter Palace for herself. Standing in the huge cobbled square in front of the Winter Palace, she could almost hear the hooves of approaching horses and sense the menace it held for the once-imperial family.

It seemed a bit insulting to write down on this teacher's form that the history she knew came from the cinema, books and travel, but Serena assured her that Mr Ericson wanted honest answers. So that is what she did: with renewed confidence she went back to the first question and wrote: 'The best reason for learning history is because when it is told well it is the best story there is.'

Ten days later Sarah had come home to find Serena sitting in the kitchen. She was alone, staring out the window. It was quite unlike her. Normally she would be on the phone, watching television, giggling away with Barbara, or out of the house until, with unerring sixth sense, she would return just as dinner was ready. Serena then did something else quite out of character. Quite of her own accord she picked up a tea towel and began drying the already-dry dishes left over from breakfast. There was a long silence between them while Mrs Kaur pottered around the kitchen and Serena dried and put away the plates. Sarah knew better than to break the spell and ask a question. So she waited, pregnant with expectation.

'How's the new job?' Serena asked. It was not what Sarah expected and she struggled to find something intelligent in reply.

'It's not easy going back to work after all this time. I'm a bit exhausted. I'm just pleased that there's only one more day to go before the weekend. How about you? You're looking very thoughtful.'

'It's school. It's really different this year. Not all of it, but some of the teachers. And the Termite came into our class and everyone wondered what had happened. We thought something terrible. Then Mr Ericson, that's our history teacher I told you about and the one that sent you the letter. The Termite told us about a project – we are going to do a survey of the school and how we learn and things like that.'

'I don't like you calling Mrs Barre the Termite. It's not respectful. Don't you think you should just concentrate on your studies, young lady?'

'That's exactly what we're going to do. Concentrate on our studies instead of studying.'

Sarah sighed inwardly at the usual clever comment that left her without a reply.

'It seems to me your teachers don't have any authority any more. In my day it wouldn't be the pupils who told the teachers what to do.'

It was Serena's turn to sigh. They were interrupted by a knock at the front door. When Serena saw it was Mrs Reyna, she beat a hasty retreat to her room.

Sarah had a curious relationship with the lady at No. 23. Catherine Reyna was one of her few friends, but she could be so irritating that after an hour or so in her presence Sarah would find an excuse to return home. Fictitious appointments, impending phone calls, forgotten shopping or newly invented chores took her back to the silent relief of her own home.

'What did she want?' asked Serena, emerging from her room once she had heard the front door close behind the departing Mrs Reyna.

'To tell me about this European thing. She says they're going to ask her to be involved in it.'

Sarah knew she had said or done something wrong. Without a word Serena went back to her room and when they sat down to dinner together half an hour later Serena said very little except: 'Just like her to steal my news. The old cow.'

Things weren't improved by a second visit from Mrs Reyna not long afterwards. It took her a full hour, with a few interludes for questions and supported by occasional nods of affirmation, to recount the excitement of the important new group of which she had become a part. She called it the school self-evaluation group, which made very little sense to Sarah but she did realise that it had some connection with what Serena was doing and all the rather strange things that had been happening at the school in the last few weeks.

Mrs Reyna's story unfolded in a stream of consciousness. Sarah Kaur had to work hard at picturing the scene and coming to terms with the whys and wherefores of such a strange activity, but it had clearly energised even the normally phlegmatic Catherine Reyna. It seemed Mrs Reyna had emerged as the leader of the group, advancing telling arguments, unfailingly going to the heart of the matter, informing these teachers and the headteacher of the life of a community they clearly knew nothing about. It was, Sarah Kaur learned, that when it came to the discussion of school and home and school and community that Mrs Reyna came truly into her own. All those teachers ever saw of the community was the main road out. How many of them had ever been down their street? Or come into Mrs Reyna's kitchen and seen the incurable dampness that visited her kitchen walls? With a dramatic flourish, with Sarah's kitchen standing in for the notorious Reyna kitchen, Mrs Reyna had produced items of evidence – letters and circulars from the school written in language so incomprehensible Mrs Reyna had to get the help of her daughter Claudia to translate and even Claudia couldn't explain what was meant by 'curricular revision', 'school development planning', 'modular courses' and 'devolved management'.

'And as for the tone,' continued Mrs Reyna, settling into a comfortable cruising speed, 'You'd think we were naughty schoolchildren. Telling us off about attendance and late-coming indeed. My Claudia has never missed a day unless she was sick like with that dreadful flu last year but never once has she been late. Out of the house every morning like clockwork.'

'And you told them all this at your meeting?' asked Mrs Kaur, squeezing in the question not for the sake of formal politeness but from an acute curiosity as to how such information had been received.

'That woman, Mrs Barre, did a bit of shuffling from one cheek to the other and pinkened a bit but didn't say anything and everyone agreed they would look at their letters and circulars and asked my help. They asked me if I thought it would be a good idea to set up a parents' committee to vet the language of documents sent out by the school. The big lad, one of the pupils, said they could call it "jargon busters" and guess who is to chair it?'

Mrs Kaur didn't have to guess, but she did have to excuse herself. She didn't want her neighbour in the house when Serena came home, especially since Mrs

Reyna's saga had reminded her that Serena was part of that very group, although Mrs Reyna's account had treated Serena as a scarcely visible member of the supporting cast.

It was a narrow escape. Serena arrived less than a minute after the delayed departure of Mrs Reyna but somehow she sniffed out the evidence of her recent presence, a lingering peculiar aroma that was Mrs Reyna's legacy of her frequent visits.

'She was here wasn't she?' Serena accused.

Sarah tried to underplay the reason for the visit but she could see Serena was upset that the news of the day had been pre-empted yet again by 'that woman across the road' and so she retired to her room again in resolute self-exclusion. Mrs Kaur would have to wait for the story until the dark clouds had passed over.

When Serena eventually forgave her mother enough to tell the story, Mrs Reyna was cast as a bit player and the other parent in the group, Ms Stern, given the accolade of a quiet thoughtful listener, speaking little but raising questions some of them had never thought about before when she did.

'She said she and her "partner", I guess they're not married or anything, were the most important educators in their child's life. She said you could turn things upside down and see homework like two words "home" and "work", as the really important bit, and school work as what you do to help your home work rather than the other way round. So parents should say to the teachers – have you done your school work today? Isn't that clever?'

It was a bit too clever for Serena's mother. Things were getting a little out of hand at that school. What would they think of next?

'Who taught me to read?' Serena asked her mother.

'Mrs Bett, that nice lady you had in your first class. She was so nice.'

'How long after I started school was it before I was reading?' asked Serena. Mrs Kaur suspected this was not a simple, honest question. Serena was leading her somewhere.

'Just a few weeks of school and you were reading like a ten-year-old. Your dad and I were thrilled at the progress you made.'

'So if I could learn to read in three weeks, why did it take Amanda nine months and Jason two years?'

'Because, Serena,' answered Mrs Kaur looking for a gracious retreat from the advancing artillery, 'because, Serena, you were a very intelligent little girl.'

'No, because for five years I was slowly learning all the things I needed to be a reader and then in school it just happened because all the proper bits and pieces in my brain were in place.'

'Well I still say it's because you were a very intelligent girl. And you still are.'

'But that's the same argument, silly!'

Mrs Kaur frowned at the language being applied to her although she thought it very appropriate for how she felt when she talked to Serena's teachers and more and more when Serena seemed able to tie her in clever verbal knots.

'It's the same argument because it's all connected. I was growing my intelligence and my reading at the same time. Or rather you were – you and dad, and grandmother. Remember how you read to me every night and dad always talked to me about things and gave me long answers to my questions and asked me questions all the time too and remember you told me how you did puzzles with me and I took things apart and put them back together?'

Mrs Kaur did remember one of their most enjoyable conversations being about when Serena was small.

'Mr Ericson told us about how that makes intelligence and what goes on in your brain when you are just little. He said we are the architects of our own intelligence ...' then she added quickly ' ... together with our mums and dads. You did it, mother. It was you and Dad made me intelligent.'

'H'm,' was about the most intelligent thing Mrs Kaur could think of at that moment but it had set her thinking. They *had* been good parents. They had wanted the best for her from the second she emerged on that hospital bed, dark against the whiteness of the sheets, a thatch of black hair, light blue eyes that suddenly one day became almost as black as her hair. But even before then, for the nine months in which Mrs Kaur carried her, she had talked and sung to the unborn child and, when no one was looking and she was alone in the room, she would rehearse out loud the stories she would one day read to her. Sarah began to wonder if, in some miraculous way, Serena had been able to hear those stories. She certainly seemed, even as a one-month-old baby, to recognise the songs her mother sang to her as if she had heard them before somewhere.

'Oh, I nearly forgot,' Serena said, 'another letter.'

'Another one? Is that all they do up there these days? Write letters?'

Serena found the letter at the bottom of her schoolbag. It bore the traces of Serena's lunch.

'I see you left some of the banana for me,' said Mrs Kaur. The letter read:

Dear Mrs Kaur,

Like all our parents you are probably concerned about how well your child is learning and you wish to be reassured that they are making progress and working to their full potential. In order to ensure we are doing all we can on our side to make that happen we are taking part in a European project. Along with 100 other schools in eighteen countries, we are trying to determine what factors contribute to effective learning.

Learning is not only a question of good teaching. Some pupils seem to learn well without teaching and others fail to learn despite considerable instruction and individual help. For all pupils, what they do at home in their own time is vitally important and we would like to know more about how to make homework and study more enjoyable and more useful.

The idea of focusing on the quality of learning and the issue of learning time came mainly from parents and pupils, working together with teachers to identify what we could do better as a school.

But the school does not make it alone. How pupils prepare at home is an important factor in a child's learning. Since we are working toward the same goal we will achieve better results if we support each other in making our children better learners and better able to go on learning after they have left school.

This is the reason why we have scheduled a meeting for 19 October at 19.00. We hope you will be able to join us. We'll serve light refreshments after the meeting.

Best wishes
Jan Barre

'Light refreshments,' said Sarah, 'I hope that means more than a cup of tea and a dry biscuit.'

Despite her previous experiences of school meetings Sarah agreed to go, if for no other reason than not to disappoint Serena.

'This makes a change, Serena. Normally you couldn't care less if I went or not. In fact, you used to tell me it was a waste of time. So what's new?'

'The new Mrs Barre. I think someone has given her a personality transplant; and you'll meet Eric. He's cute.'

Mrs Kaur frowned, but said nothing. Serena's reference to her teacher as Eric was, she knew, a calculated attempt to shock. Perhaps having a closer look at the teacher whom Serena chose to speak about with such familiarity might not be such a bad idea.

And, as it happened, the meeting turned out to be not so bad and there was wine and cheese rather than tea and biscuits. Mrs Barre told them about the European Project, the school self-evaluation group and why they had chosen to focus on home–school relationships. Mrs Kaur had heard it twice before but it was interesting to hear it again from a third viewpoint. She remembered a strange term Serena had been showing off with: 'triangulation'. She now understood what that might mean – a story told by three different narrators, highlighting and selecting what was of most interest to them.

'If we are to understand learning better and make it more effective,' Mrs Barre was saying, 'we will have to look not just at what happens in the classroom, but at home too, and we would really like your help.'

Mrs Barre asked for volunteers to form a small parents' working group on homework and home learning. Mrs Kaur shuffled energetically through her bag in search of some mythical object until the danger had passed. The working group was elected, including a contented-looking Mrs Reyna, who was once again thanked for her commitment to the school.

Mrs Kaur returned home at ten o'clock, tired and a bit reluctant to recount the whole of the evening's events in the level of detail that Serena expected. 'I want to know everything that happened', she demanded.

Tired as she was, Mrs Kaur smiled at the role reversal and began the story. They had come a long way in their mother–daughter relationship. Whatever else this project might or might not achieve, it had done something for them already.

3   Tom Ericson
The history teacher

Tom Ericson used to teach at a medium-sized lower secondary school just outside town before getting a job at Serena's school. He had been happy. Like 80 per cent of teachers around the world he had gone faithfully to school day after day believing that the subjects he taught were important for the future lives of young people and that there was always a way through to at least some of these post-modern kids who seemed to think only of TV, celebrities, the other sex and making money.

When he had first decided to become a teacher he had imagined this would combine his love of history with his love for children. He had seen himself inspiring and enriching their life histories, passing on to them his own excitement in the history of mankind. There was also, he had to admit, the prospect of a tenured position which was more appealing than the unpredictable future of a freelance historian; and then there were the long summer holidays which he had seen simply as an added bonus when he embarked on his teaching career.

These latter benefits had come to weigh more heavily the longer he spent in teaching. Somebody, he couldn't remember who, had given him a copy of a book entitled *Don't Smile Until Christmas* written by young American teachers. In the very first paragraph of the first chapter he had read this:

> I had the idea that teaching English would be a series of extended Socratic dialogues between me and my students. I would lead forth my eager, responsive, naive but (redeemingly) idealistic students from the cave of adolescent mental wistfulness into the clear light of truth upon the verdant and lush fields of literature'.

This teacher's journey from idealism to the real world of classrooms found echoes in Tom's own experience. Now, fifteen years into the job, he couldn't imagine doing without the long break. Teachers in the school called it 'the survival season'. As one of the staffroom cynics had put it 'You need a bloody good break after ten months of generation X'. Generation X, Tom reflected, was a long time ago. It was the generation of his older daughter, now in her mid-twenties and following in her father's footsteps in teacher training, with a passionate desire to teach despite the admonitions and discouragement of her fellow students and closest friends.

'But you are still there, still as much committed to teaching as you ever were,' Christina had said to her father only a few weeks ago, 'Aren't you?' she persisted, as if there was now some flicker of doubt.

He was, of course, although it wasn't easy in a climate where the predominant theme of conversation in the staffroom was the lack of understanding of the job, how it had changed, how misunderstood teachers were. People 'out there', they said, still talked about it as if it were a comfortable sinecure with short working days, long idle holidays and tenured job security. It seemed to them like a concerted campaign to undermine and devalue what teachers did. Newspapers, politicians, other professionals, even people in the school's own senior management, had started jumping on this bandwagon. The head of the mathematics department called senior management 'the enemy within'.

'A few steps up the career ladder and they've forgotten what it was like to stand in front of a class five hours a day!'

The barrage of criticism did serve a purpose. It focused them on their common lot. It created one of the few occasions when all teachers in school seemed to be of the same opinion. They had become the scapegoats of society, getting the blame for everything: economic decline, drug problems, high divorce rates, teenage pregnancy. People acted as if school was not part of the global development but a small world of its own which could be used as a dumping ground for everything that went wrong elsewhere in society. This included people who should know better, politicians and policy makers who found social or economic ills a useful stick to beat teachers with. Governments talked about the 'new money' they were putting into education, but it never seemed to filter down to the teachers.

There seemed to be much more discussion in the staffroom, lunch room and corridors these days but it always seemed to be about problems, and Tom found it difficult not be sucked down into this vortex of self-pity. He could understand it from the inside but then, when he stood outside it and looked in with others' eyes, he saw it as a criminal waste of energy and talent. If anyone from 'out there' could hear them it would no doubt confirm their stereotype of teachers as constant moaners.

Tom couldn't help wondering about how his colleagues taught. Did they take that pessimistic outlook with them into their classrooms or did they leave it at the door? He realised that since coming to this school he had never seen any of his colleagues teach, nor for that matter had anyone seen him teach. How did they cope with difficult situations? How much real learning went on in their classrooms? How much, come to think of it, happened in his?

He had attempted to bring people together for what he thought was an exciting in-service training workshop on new approaches to the teaching of history. He had been sure his colleagues would be enthused by the 'co-operative group learning' which had so stimulated him, but after only one meeting they were suddenly awash with reasons for not being able to attend, babysitters who let them down, sick relatives, tennis partners who were only available at that particular time. The strong parallels with the response of students in his classroom had not escaped him.

'The problem, Tom, is that it was your idea and not theirs', someone had said to him. It had reminded him of a quote that had annoyed him when he heard it for the first time: 'Teachers can sabotage reform efforts with the greatest of ease, and do so either as a calling or as a form of sport.' Perhaps there was some truth in it after all.

The drive to school in the morning had been taking longer and longer over the years. With increasing traffic and people starting work earlier and earlier, what used to take half an hour was now an hour's drive. To alleviate the frustration he had started listening to talking books and audio tapes. One he had ended up throwing out of the window in disgust, but there were others that had set him thinking. Sitting for five minutes in a two-mile tailback he had scribbled down these words from a tape. The author, Margaret Wheatley, was describing her surprise at finding people who, despite a low level of morale in an organisation, 'made meaning':

> They were staying creative, making sense out of nonsense, because they'd taken the time to create a meaning for their work – one that transcended present organisational circumstances. They wanted to hold on to motivation and direction in the midst of turbulence, and the only way they could do this was by investing the current situation with meaning.

Was this a description of himself? He recognised himself and a handful of his colleagues in the quotation, those who made meaning on a daily basis in their relationship with their classes and who drew their energy from one another's commitment and enthusiasm. Tom drew his energy from the pupils; not all, not even a majority, but a gratifying number who seemed suddenly to switch on to history – the 'aha experience' as they had called it in his college days. This was something he had come to value even more highly, those young people who switched on to themselves as learners, with ambitions and goals and self-belief.

'What the hell has happened to Mark Fischer?' a colleague in the maths department had asked him the week before. 'Has someone been feeding him clever pills?'

Mark Fischer was one of those students who suddenly seemed to have come alive after a five-year hibernation. And then there was Serena. What had been the moment when she suddenly switched on the circuitry in her brain? Her new-found enthusiasm had taken him aback. She was becoming a better historian, more interested, more engaged, more questioning. Her previously dormant critical faculties were now being exercised on her own experience of school. This analytic and documentary approach to the present was, Tom rationalised, a historical exercise in a very real sense. But whether or not it stuck to the strict parameters of history teaching, it was certainly taking them on some interesting voyages of discovery.

He had already had one note from a parent asking why they never did any history in his class and used up good teaching time discussing the latest film releases. This must have been a reference to the six-minute discussion of the film *Sliding Doors* which Serena had been to see the night before. The film hinged on an incident in the London underground where a young woman, played by Gwyneth Paltrow, misses a train by seconds because of the sliding doors. The film pursues the question 'what if?' she had been two seconds earlier and had actually caught the train. The discussion had led them into some historical discussion and brainstorming of 'what if' moments in history. The homework which followed from it – everyone to take a 'what if' and develop an alternative historical scenario – had been one of the most fruitful and enjoyable of tasks, and had led them so dangerously across subject boundaries that he could envisage geography's redoubtable Ms Braun knocking on his door any minute. That subject had never been the same since the retirement of the quaint, idiosyncratic but inspirational Miss Pebble.

Tom could see trouble ahead. People in this school tended to guard their subject domains jealously. History was history and geography geography and when someone crossed too far over the line it became a union matter or a debate about professional ethics. But when he had opened up a discussion with his class about their subjects, he found they too had this view of the world. History was what happened in Mr Ericson's classroom and geography was Ms Braun. Ms Braun 'was' geography. No, they said, they didn't take their history with them into the geography room. They didn't take their maths into physics or their art into drama. They were confused enough by Mr Ericson being both their history and their literature teacher. They complained that he kept mixing them up.

But it was through literature that Tom tried to fire a historical curiosity, a sense of history. He read to them from Arundhati Roy's *The God of Small Things*, which described history being like a house with all the lamps lit and the ancestors whispering inside.

'To understand history', he read, 'we have to go inside and listen to what they're saying and look at the books and the pictures on the wall. And smell the smells.'

He realised with a shock how far away their understanding was from his. Perhaps because that was what they had been taught, they saw history as a neat line from the past to the present. It was this that had sparked Tom's idea of sending a questionnaire to parents. What was their view of the subject he taught? Why did parents want their children to be taught history anyway? Or did they? And if so, whose history? What knowledge? Since politicians and authorities were now prone to pepper their speeches with references to the public as the 'clients' and 'sponsors' of education, perhaps it was time he found out what the clients really thought. Tom prepared a questionnaire and a covering letter (see Figure 3.1).

Tom could hardly wait to get the questionnaires back, and it took quite a few reminders through the students to get at least 60 per cent of them returned. At first he was disappointed, but he was reassured by some colleagues that this was quite a good number for surveys of this kind. What surprised him was that it was mostly fathers who had filled in the questionnaires, as normally it was mothers who took care of the home end of all school-related matters; this didn't tally with the small numbers of fathers who attended parents' evenings. European football used to be only on Wednesdays; now it was on Tuesdays and Thursdays as well. Fridays were a non-starter and Mondays not popular either. Tom wondered if the explanation was that history really was a man's domain or if that was no more than

Dear parents,

I am sure you are aware of the present discussions on the quality of education, national standards and international testing. As a history teacher I am trying to make history a subject area well worth studying in school (as all teachers do in their subjects), even in an era when people seem more interested in the present or the future than in the past. Since public opinion is very diverse on this subject I want to get in touch with you, the vital stakeholder in your child's education. I would appreciate if you could give me some guidance from your parental perspective.

1　If you rate history as a subject area to be studied by your daughter or son according to its importance, which interval on the following scale would you mark?

$$+++\quad++\quad\quad+\quad 0\quad-\quad\quad--\quad\quad---$$

Highly important I————I————I————I————I————I————I Not important at all

2　Which of the following points do you think are most important in knowledge about history? Please mark 1, 2, 3, 4, 5 in order of importance (1 = most important, 5 = least important).

___ Famous people in history

___ Important wars

___ Historical thinking

___ Historical facts (e.g. important dates)

___ History of mankind

___ .... (Add your own suggestion)

3　Please give one example for which you gave highest priority in (2). For example, if 'Famous people in history' has the highest ranking, you might write down Napoleon.

....

4　What do you think is most important about knowing history?

....

5　From whom or what did you learn most about history? Please tick only one!

___ Television

___ Books in school

___ Teachers in school

___ Parents

___ Grandparents

___ .... (Add your own suggestion)

6　Any suggestions you have for history teaching in school or anything else you want the teacher to know? Please state!

....

7　Who filled in this questionnaire?

___ Mother

___ Father

___ Mother and father

___ .... (Add other)

Thank you for your co-operation!

Figure 3.1 History questionnaire.

a popular prejudice. It had certainly been true of his relationship with his own daughter, Christina. It was to him and not to her mother that she had come with her history homework, indeed all her homework, and it was mainly Christina's mother who had attended parents' evenings at the school. Christina had discouraged him from going. 'You're a teacher and that will upset them', she had argued, and at the time Tom had accepted the logic of her case.

When Tom started summing up the responses to the questionnaire he became more and more intrigued. It was pleasing to see that most parents rated the teaching of history very highly. He also had to acknowledge, a bit ruefully, that dates, treaties and wars were what parents of his students saw as history. As one colleague had put it, 'a story of events commemorated from the point of view of the good guys who won', and another, 'a progressive unfolding of events towards the inevitability of the present state of things'.

The history curriculum, as most of his parents saw it, were those aspects of their school history that they could remember, or could recall memorising. Yet when it came to the question of their best sources of historical knowledge, school only came fourth in the list: parents, television and cinema all ranked higher! Some parents described watching documentaries and the History Channel on television, frequent visits to the cinema to see war films (*All Quiet on the Western Front, Saving Private Ryan*) and epics such as *Dr Zhivago, Nicholas and Alexandra* and *War and Peace*. Some read historical novels and discussed them with their children. Yet they still wanted from him the kind of homework they got when they were at school. Tom sensed a serious and significant challenge ahead. There were some interesting things to work on from parents' comments. Not all saw history in quite the same way and that was an excellent starting point for a study of history.

'What I like about the history that I read now as an adult is what life was like for ordinary people, how they dressed, ate, spent their time, what they worried about, how they lived their lives.'

'Since I left school I have become fascinated with history because you can see how the story can be told quite differently depending on where you stand. The great hero Columbus, actually was a mass murderer on a grand scale …'

'Both my children enjoy studying history because it enables them to travel to other countries and through time. It is their own personal time machine. The best gift I could hope to give them.'

'I would like to offer you my personal thanks, Mr Ericson. The study of the rise of fascism and immediacy of the wars in Yugoslavia has woken my daughter, Tonya, to the dangers of blaming minority groups for the problems in society. How will they ever grasp what it means to become democratic citizens if they do not learn from history what it is that undermines democracies? What's the use of teaching history if it does not affect the students' further life histories?'

Tom was taken aback by the range of parents' views. He had to remind himself that the term 'parents' was often used as if they were all part of some homogeneous entity whose views could be described under the heading 'parental views'. The government kept telling them 'what parents thought'. Tom realised he knew very little about the parental background of his students. He did know that they included a bus driver, a dentist, two assembly-line workers, two teachers and a number of unemployed single-parent families. As far as he knew, Serena lived alone with her mother, unemployed after the closing of the textile factory. How relevant were such events to their view of history? He wondered how much 'history' Serena's mother could pass on to her daughter about the textile industry, its growth, its union troubles and its rapid decline in the last few years. How could the immediacy of that experience be used to engage a dialogue on globalisation? That was neither on the history nor the literature syllabus, but it was touching all of their lives.

Tom's modest survey had started a chain of thought which intrigued and bothered him. After waking up for the third night running, he decided these were questions he needed to share with his three departmental colleagues. He made a simple graphic of parents' views in the form of a pie chart, inventing a spectrum on which he could place them – at one end those whose views most closely matched his own goals and values; at the other end, those who were furthest away.

It certainly had the effect of producing a lively discussion, if not quite what Tom had anticipated: 'So what if some parents have a screwy view of history? The point is, what do our students think?'

The others tended to agree. Tom's trouble was that he read too much, that was the general consensus. It had been a mistake, he realised, to quote Peter Coleman's book of which none of them had heard and which, coming from a Canadian academic, did not immediately commend itself to them. The subtitle of the Coleman book was 'The power of three', describing the triangle of influence – parent, student, teacher – and demonstrating through research the powerful role of parents in shaping attitudes, however subtly and unconsciously.

Their concern was with what happened in the classroom and, ironically, there was a temporary alliance with government spokespersons who claimed that it was good classroom teaching that made the difference and that teachers should not be distracted from their main concern.

'You'll be wanting us to teach history to parents next, Tom', teased one of his colleagues.

It was an opportunity Tom could not resist. He read out a comment from one parent:

'Your question, "From whom or what did you learn most about history?" offered five options including parents and grandparents. You missed the most important source – children. Speaking personally, I have learned so much from, or should I say *together with*, my son, Thomas, that it has changed my view of the world completely.'

'Changing your view of the world. Perhaps we have forgotten that was what we came into teaching to do', someone said before they moved on.

The comment led them back to the discussion of how they could influence their students' view of the world and they agreed to pursue the question, 'What do our students think?' because it was one they weren't all sure they had the answer to.

'*Do* they think?' one of Tom's colleagues had asked. It was a serious joke.

The question opened the door to another survey. Why didn't they put the same issues to the students and then they could triangulate three sets of answers – parent, teacher and pupil views. It had been a circuitous route but it brought them back in the end to the power of three.

Tom didn't see much of Mrs Barre, the headteacher. He couldn't remember her ever visiting his class in the three years she had been there. So when she walked in halfway through the lesson, probably at the worst possible moment she could have chosen – a smell of rotten eggs had just escaped somewhere in the vicinity of Peter and three or four of the boys had bolted with exaggerated alarm to other desks – Tom was temporarily unable to say anything coherent or sensible.

'I've been asked if we would be interested in joining a European project on school self-evaluation,' she began, apparently oblivious to the mayhem that had prevailed only moments before. 'My first instinct was to say "no" but I was aware of the very interesting work you were doing and I thought, well hold on, why not? If Mr Ericson is game, that is.'

Tom wondered what 'self-evaluation' meant. Or, more precisely, what it meant to her, or to the policy people in Brussels. He would need to know a lot more before committing himself to some bureaucratic exercise. He had visions of more mountains of statistics, standardised tests, distributions and disaggregations.

Mrs Barre gave him some background papers and suggested that if there was any interest they would have a staff meeting and see what 'the troops' thought of it. Tom had a pretty good idea what they would think of it – another distraction from the job, another way of keeping 'Eurocrats' in jobs!

Tom's scepticism began to evaporate, however, when he started to read the background papers; it was so close to what he had been doing in his own class. It involved pupils, and teachers, and parents, asking questions and looking for evidence. Wasn't that exactly what he had been doing? If that was what they meant by self-evaluation he was all in favour. If they really meant what the paperwork said, they could use this opportunity to address all or at least some of those issues which were bubbling under the surface of school life, sapping people's energies and the vitality of the school itself.

In the event, at a hastily convened staff meeting, there had been opposition. There was the kind of long adversarial debate which some teachers seemed to thrive on – the reconditioned reflex of dissent. Four different reasons had finally persuaded the opposition. It was, for some, an opportunity for getting back at management and the world in general. A larger number welcomed the opportunity of just having their voice heard. Some agreed to go along because it was voluntary and they didn't have to be involved. Then there were a dozen or so like Tom who thought it just might breathe some new life into the school.

Mrs Barre had been taken aback by the staff's willingness, if not enthusiasm, to go ahead. She had thanked Tom profusely for the part he had played in persuading them, although in truth he had said very little and had tried not to influence them one way or the other. If it was not entered into voluntarily, it would not work. He had learned that much. Mrs Barre's hard sell was generally counter-productive and Tom could see that she appreciated the power of his 'softly softly' style.

Over the next few weeks the project had been driven more or less by Tom and a small group of enthusiasts with Mrs Barre an interested spectator, sometimes anxious, sometimes excited. Whatever reservations he might have had about her management style, she was giving the project her support and endorsement.

Tom took no direct part in the school self-evaluation group but Serena, who was a pupil representative, reported in full to the class, indulging in a bit of role-playing of the various characters in the group. With the aid of a colourful overhead transparency and dramatic effect, she built up the SEP profile stage by stage, through to the final profile of the school. Could this be the same Serena who had been so conspicuously bored when she joined Tom's class at the beginning of the year?

Serena explained that three areas had been chosen for further investigation – the quality of learning and teaching, time as a resource for learning and home–school relationships. A few of the students were clearly a bit bemused by what this meant and Serena got herself into some deep water trying to answer their queries. Tom came to the rescue, drawing a triangle on the board with each of the themes at the three corners and adding connecting arrows between them.

'The quality of learning is about what you learn and how well you learn it. It depends partly on the time you have to learn, class time and home time.' Tom drew a connecting arrow between 'quality' and 'time'.

'I nearly said "your own time" but actually *all* your time is your own time. Our job as teachers is to help you use it well in the classroom and the job of your parents is to help you use it well at home.' He drew in the third connecting arrow: the power of three.

'So, what we can find out through this project is how well we – you – use your time so that we improve the quality of learning. For me as your unfortunate – I mean fortunate – teacher, you can help me to use my teaching time better and, if we really get good at this, it will help all teachers in the school.'

'Does that mean Mr Petit as well?' Hans asked, affecting total innocence.

Tom decided to sidestep the question, knowing what lay behind it. But if this project was going to work, not just for this year but in the longer term, they would have to tackle some pretty tough issues such as Claude Petit's consistent failure to engage or challenge his students.

A week later, staff agreed on what evaluation tools they were going to use. There were thirty tools suggested in the European Guidelines, one of which was peer observation. Tom, one of eight volunteers, found himself paired with Tony Campos, a physical education teacher. He couldn't think what they had in common at a personal or professional level. For the first time he was beginning to have his doubts about the project and whether this was a good use of his, or Mr Campos', time.

Two weeks later, Tom did his first observation of physical education and found it hard to give critical feedback because he had been so impressed. Up until then he had had no idea what happened in the physical education class, nor shown any interest in it, but it was a model Tom thought he could probably apply to history. How would it fit?

The physical education period had started with the eighteen students seated on the floor around the teacher. Tony Campos briefly reviewed where they had been and outlined the purposes and goals for that day's session. He asked for four or five of the class to describe what they had done at home over the last three days to meet their personal targets. The following six minutes were spent in setting targets for the coming session and then discussing these in pairs. Students then spent the next thirty minutes working on their routines in pairs and giving one another feedback. The final five minutes were spent in writing up an evaluation of the session against their initial targets. The final minute, timed immaculately to the end of period bell, was given to setting homework.

Before Tony Campos' return visit to Tom's class, the two met together to agree a focus for the observation. Tom asked if Tony would look specifically at time devoted to girls and boys and to probe a little deeper to see if there were qualitative differences in his interactions between boys and girls. Did he, in any ways he was unaware of, treat them differently?

Tony Campos' observations contained two unexpected shocks. At the end of the lesson he asked Tom to estimate how he thought he had divided his time between the girls and boys. Being very aware of that as the focus of the observation, Tom replied that, if anything, it was slightly in favour of the girls – 55–45, perhaps. Tony's calculations, however, showed a boy/girl split of 58–42 in favour of boys. Tom had, apparently, addressed about as many questions to the girls as to the boys but the verbal exchanges with the girls had been shorter and, most disturbing and revealing to Tom, qualitatively different. Tony's analysis showed the following:

	Positive	Neutral	Challenging	Negative
Boys	39	2	28	31
Girls	42	28	5	22

It appeared from this analysis (which could surely not be true) that Tom was both more positive and less negative in his conversation with girls but consistently less challenging of their ideas. Was this because their ideas were better to begin with? Or (he hoped not) because he patronised the girls more and was more afraid of confronting them?

Tom lost more sleep. After so many years of teaching and all his experience, could some key aspects of teaching and learning still be operating below his level of consciousness? Tom decided to see what his students made of it. After all, it was their data. To his relief – or was it even more worrying? – they too had been unaware of it. One student claimed she had felt something 'funny', 'unfair', that she had never been able to put into words because Tom Ericson was such a nice, fair and considerate teacher. But now with their antennae sharpened and knowing what to look for, Tom found that their evaluations of his teaching and their learning had a sharper cutting edge.

'Wouldn't it be funny,' someone said, 'if one of the least sexist teachers in the school ended up being accused of sexism?'

Tom thought it was the least funny thing he had heard all year, but it did provoke some thoughts about historical parallels. 'This self-evaluation journey can cut deep, and deeper still', Tom heard his own voice say to him one night as he was slipping into sleep. It woke him up.

'Yes,' he replied to his own voice 'but it can also stay at a very superficial level too.' He had recently read an article by an American writer, Bruce Joyce – it had been given to him by Ursula, the critical friend appointed to work with them on the project – which described the doors to school improvement. He fell asleep and dreamt about opening a door behind which was another one and then another one and another – an infinite series of doors.

In the six months that followed, many doors that had been previously closed were now open. Some still remained tightly shut. However positive this project, it did seem that the school was a more uneven place. It was less aligned. The distance between the missionaries and outright opponents had increased rather than decreased. But those in the middle, the free-floaters and undecided, were being pulled towards the positive end of the spectrum. Tom was replaying the Margaret Wheatley tape in his car with a new level of understanding.

Although chaos theory had its application in history and that's what the *Sliding Doors* discussion had been about, it had previously seemed to him like a rather pretentious notion when applied to organisations such as schools. Attractive to academics who never had to deal with chaos in the tranquillity of their ivory towers, he had thought, the first time he had listened to the tape. But now it seemed to make sense to him that it was through turbulence that order emerged and that a new 'order' would only be a temporary and inherently unstable state. Tom decided it was probably not wise to share these thoughts with his colleagues.

The peer observation, which had started with four pairs, had now grown to eight. Two teachers had switched pairs, mutually agreeing that they were not working well together. On two occasions the sixteen teachers involved had met as a group to pool their findings. They agreed on four ways in which their awareness of learning and the effectiveness of their teaching had improved:

- Balance of whole-class teaching, small group, paired and individual work
- Questioning skills
- Pacing of activities and use of time
- Use of homework and study.

Feedback from his 'internal critical friend', Tony, showed that Tom was now spending less time on exposition, injecting more pace into his lessons, cutting time on paired and small-group tasks so that students were required to be sharper and more on their toes. He had raised the level of challenge in what he asked of them and the questions he put to them. He spent more time on probing and open questioning, allowing more time between question and answer. The class had made a game out of the 'Q and A indicator'. Hans, who loved anything statistical, had calculated an average increase of 1.2 seconds between teacher question and student answer over the last month, from 2.9 to 3.7 seconds. Hans was creating his own turbulence by using his technique on other staff. Mr Andersen, he reported to Tom Ericson, had been less than amused to be told his average Q and A 'thinking time' was 1.1 seconds.

There was a buzz about the school. People were talking more about learning and about education. There was not perhaps the greater level of harmony Tom had envisaged; more differences and disagreements among staff were beginning to surface. But it seemed much healthier than what had existed before. The disagreement was more vocal, more studied, more engaged, people were asserting positive things and arguing their corner. And over the weeks Tom began to notice a greater and greater tendency for people to ask for evidence, not simply to accept things at face value or to counter assertion with assertion.

Two weeks into the New Year, Tom was surprised to receive a visit from Ms Braun. She had been in the school for two years but their paths had rarely crossed; their relationship was one of polite and professional distance. Ms Braun had something to show him. It was a force field evaluation she had done with her third-year class. She handed Tom the sheet of paper with the collated results (see Figure 3.2). Tom was impressed by the perceptiveness of the students and the usefulness of the data. Clearly Ms Braun was, too.

'I was intrigued by the comment "it helps when you understand the history of somewhere". That's why I came to see you. What do you think it means?'

'I could guess,' said Tom, 'but it would be only a guess.' Ms Braun waited patiently – an unspoken 'well, guess then!'

'My guess would be that when places becomes real and vivid to our students, through stories and characters, visiting them in their imagination, the geography of those places gets an immediate and easy open sesame into memory. It has meaning.'

'I liked this one,' Tom went on, pointing at the item 'when we can put it into our own words'. 'That's another important way in which it gets to have meaning. It's a kind of translation process in their heads which makes it their own.'

Ms Braun was listening. Tom felt a bit embarrassed. He didn't want to lecture her but he was warming to his subject and she seemed interested. 'David Perkins, the Harvard psychologist, talks about "knowledge coming on the coat tails of thinking". A lot of people laugh at that, but it is absolutely true. Our students create knowledge in the process of finding the words, the contexts that make sense to them, and when it is connected into somewhere meaningful it becomes knowledge.'

'I suppose it's quite close to this,' said Ms Braun, pointing at the item 'when you teach someone else you understand it better'.

'Remember that saying, "How do I know what I think until I hear what I say?" As I understand it, it works like this – I have some idea in my head; I try to explain

Working in different ways	When things are not well explained
Variety	Sometimes we have no idea of how to manage our portfolio
Summarising written articles in our own words	Some texts are too difficult
Using the library to find out things	Sometimes we don't have books because other classes need them
Working in the media room	
Having time enough for reading	It's hard to put things in your own words sometimes because you don't understand
Having thinking time to answer teacher's questions	Some people don't like learning and interrupt you and you can't concentrate
Being shown where you have gone wrong	When the teacher doesn't listen to your ideas
Working in pairs with someone who can help you	Putting things on maps when you don't know what it's for and you don't really know the places
It helps you when you understand the history of somewhere	When you have to just memorise things
When you teach something you understand it better	

Figure 3.2 The collated results.

it to someone else; I am struggling to make sense of it, realising what I don't understand about it, and I hear my voice – out there – and it is fed back to me and I reformulate it in my head. It's true – the best way to learn is to teach. I think our students understand that.'

'So what next?' asked Ms Braun.

'What's next is: adapt your teaching. Take on board what our students are telling us.'

Ms Braun was shaking her head, not aggressively but doubtfully. 'That would be like stripping me away, what I am. I have been teaching for twenty years and it's like reaching in and stripping away what I am as a teacher. This is me, Mr Ericson. I can't be someone else.'

'But you can strip away the surface things, the superficial things that don't affect the core of what you are as a teacher. Small things.'

'Like?'

'Like setting exercises which ask students to put things in their own words. Paired work where they teach each other something. Talking to them from time to time about how they are learning.'

'You've been doing some work with Tony, haven't you?' she asked. Tom nodded.

'Would it be an imposition – would it be possible, just for a one-off, to observe in my class and see if you could give me some suggestions?' Ms Braun tailed off.

Reluctantly, Tom found himself agreeing. He wondered what he had let himself in for. It had come so suddenly, an overture from Ms Braun! He wondered if there was a hidden motive but expelled the thought from his mind as quickly as it had entered. He decided her overture was pure and purely professional.

'On one condition,' Tom replied. 'That you come and observe me and give me feedback. Fair exchange?' Ms Braun looked at Tom as if to say 'what could you possibly learn from me?' but what she actually did say was 'OK then, that's a deal.'

4   Mrs Barre

The headteacher

When Mrs Barre had opened the letter and read that they were being invited to take part in a European project she was so shaken she had to sit down before she could read on. Hers was not a lighthouse school; in the three years she had been there it had been an uphill struggle and were it not for a core of good committed staff she would have thrown in the towel a year ago.

But it was those very committed staff who had attracted the attention of the authorities, in particular the self-evaluation work going on in the history department. Mrs Barre realised to her shame she had hardly exchanged more than a dozen words with Tom Ericson: she had heard good things from parents, but she had never passed these on to him or congratulated him on the colourful mind maps, models and drawings that had begun to appear in the history corridor.

Her reverie was interrupted by the phone. The firm that was supposed to repair the toilet doors would not be able to do it for two weeks. She had hardly put down the phone when there was another call, from the council, informing her that the 'new build' project had been cancelled. That was a blow. It had been a top priority when she arrived, but since then the number of pupils in the school had been slowly, but consistently, decreasing. It was no reflection on the school; the population of the area was getting older. People were moving out to the suburbs. Houses were being demolished to make way for car parks and small businesses.

She couldn't quite come to terms with why she reacted so dismally to the cancellation of the building project. She tried to reason with herself: 'Jan, you should not be so irrational: what is important is what the children learn, not how many there are'. But she knew in truth that it was a quite rational response to a declining role. It was bad for morale, and on a personal level it was bad for her. And she couldn't help but feel frustrated at the long hours she had put in over nearly three years to get the new wing. 'All that time, and for what?' she said to herself out loud.

Jan Barre was an experienced principal. This school was her third and by far the most challenging. So much of what she had practised successfully in her last two schools didn't seem capable of being translated into the rocky soil of this neighbourhood, into this school with its chequered history, with its staff who had been there too long, with a community whose expectations were too low, with a building that should have been demolished and rebuilt a decade ago. In that long career, school self-evaluation had never been on her agenda, and certainly not in the way it was being proposed in this European Commission document, involving not only teachers but parents and pupils too. Maybe Tom Ericson could make it happen for them.

Jan was pleased and relieved to get a positive response from Tom. She had called a staff meeting to sell the idea but it had not been a totally pleasant experience. It was seen as another management ploy; a plot to undermine them, to bring yet more pressure to bear on overworked teachers. They had had enough of indicators, performance data and value-added tables.

'They tell us they're to help us but we know they are only to control us.'

'They drown us in data but don't tell us what to do or how to change things.'

'What we need is additional resources, and pupils who come to school better prepared and wanting to learn.'

'If you think that we're not doing a good job, tell us and let's talk about what we can do to improve.'

Tom Ericson had picked up on the positive in this last statement and moved the discussion into a more forward-looking frame. Jan was grateful to him for stepping in to lead the discussion: she admired his skill in not reacting to or arguing with any of the points made, but waiting until they had exhausted all the negatives. He acknowledged how they felt and agreed with some of their grievances – he was, after all, one of them. He stated the terms on which he would become involved – if the project belonged to them as a school and if there were clear ground rules about confidentiality and ownership of the data. He declared himself quite open to ditching the whole idea if the staff didn't support it. Not everyone was an immediate convert but after listening to Tom a majority agreed that the project should go ahead. This was something of a victory in itself. After the meeting Jan Barre thanked Tom, commenting that he had taken a big risk in offering them the opportunity to abandon the project.

'I knew at that point they wouldn't,' he said, 'but anyway they have to make the commitment otherwise they would grumble forever after that you, Mrs Barre, imposed it on them against their will.'

Happily, things had taken a turn for the better after that. Although it was a voluntary commitment, almost all of the staff had turned up at the introductory meeting for the project. Jan introduced them to the school's new 'critical friend', Ursula, ignoring the audible asides from the cynics' corner. Most of the staff had, however, warmed to Ursula as she explained her role as 'critical friend' and what she hoped she could offer without interfering in their work. That had gone down well, added to the fact she was personable and had a quiet air of authority. Her explanation of why self-evaluation was so important made people wonder how the school had survived for so long without it.

Over the following weeks Ursula had steered them through some of the rockier shallows, and meetings of staff, pupils, parents and the governing body had all gone off much more smoothly than expected. Getting representative groups of pupils and the governing body had presented no problem; parents had been a tougher task and in the end Jan had to settle for those parents who were a) willing to turn up; and b) confident enough to have a say in proceedings. At least out of the six parents she had been able to include one whose picture of the school was not at all a rosy one. Staff had also been a little tricky. Although they were all volunteers, Tom and Jan had worked hard at getting a balance of staff, not just the positive people. Tom Ericson had brought with him a diagram he had found in a book. It classified staff into 'missionaries, true believers, lip servers, freewheelers, outright opponents, underground workers and emigrants'. It had proved a useful set of categories for inviting staff to participate but one, Jan thought, unwise to discuss too openly, certainly at this stage. Perhaps in the fullness of time, when self-evaluation became a reality, people would be honest and trust one another enough to share their true feelings.

Teachers met in three groups of four and went through the self-evaluation profile trying to reach agreement on each of the twelve items. One group finished it in just under an hour. The two other groups took close to an hour and a half. The following week the three staff groups met as one large group with Ursula in the chair and came to an agreement, eventually, as to their rating of the school. On one or two items they had agreed to disagree and the staff version of the self-evaluation profile eventually looked like Figure 4.1.

Two members of staff were then nominated to go forward to the school evaluation group where they met with representatives of the parents, the governing body, the pupils and Jan Barre herself: nine people in all plus the critical friend. Before the event Jan had harboured her doubts about the contribution that pupils could make, especially one as young as Serena, but during the discussion of the SEP both pupils had more than held their corner. The discussion of quality of teaching and learning had opened her eyes to things she had never thought about before. She had read some of the literature on learning for understanding – Gardner, Perkins, Entwistle – but here was the theory being realised in practice. Arnold spoke knowledgeably and eloquently about learning styles and with remarkable insight into his own learning. She had to stop him at one point when he started to differentiate among teachers who helped learning and those who actually hindered. He clearly knew more about it than Jan herself, who was glad when the discussion moved on to safer ground although she recognised, with a considerable degree of discomfort, that the big challenge for them as a school was in taking a long, hard look at the quality of teaching and learning.

There had been a quite intense discussion on parents and homework. One of the teachers had claimed that parents failed to help their children with homework and it caused daily hassles for them in chasing up assignments not done or done half-heartedly. One of the governing body had said that if they were going to look at time as a resource for learning it would have to concern itself with the quality of

	++	+	–	– –	▲	↔	▼
Outcomes							
Academic achievement		X			2	8	2
Personal and social development		X				X	
Student destinations	X					X	
Process at classroom level							
Time as a resource for learning		2	7	3	6	6	
Quality of learning and teaching	X					X	
Support for learning difficulties	X				X		
Process at school level							
School as a learning place		X				X	
School as a social place		X				X	
School as a professional place		7	4	1	7	5	
Environment							
School and home		X				X	
School and community		2	10			X	
School and work		X				X	

Figure 4.1 The completed profile.

what pupils did in their own time and what parents did to support them. The parents seemed both surprised and flattered to discover how important they were.

Although the European Project Guidelines had suggested five areas of focus, staff had agreed to move forward on three fronts only; that seemed plenty to go on. There had been a lot of discussion before finally agreeing on those key areas. They had explored relations with parents, relations with the local council, personal and social development with some enthusiasm. It was a surprise to Jan, whose previous efforts to emphasise these things had been met with total indifference and even hostility. They decided in the end to work on three interrelated areas – the quality of learning and teaching, time as a resource for learning and home–school relations. Although there had been a strong push for academic achievement to be included, given the high government priority for this, one of the two pupils had been able to persuade them that the quality of learning and teaching would necessarily have to focus on achievement.

The meeting had lasted well over two hours and even after it broke up people stood around chatting in small groups. Neither of the two pupils were in a hurry to return to their classes – they were still engaged in animated conversation. From their body language Jan Barre couldn't help wondering if Arnold wasn't perhaps showing too intense an interest in the young, and undoubtedly beautiful, Serena. Both of the parents came and thanked Jan and said it had been the most interesting and informative meeting they had ever attended.

Jan went home that evening with an exhilaration that she hadn't experienced for a long time. Her husband – a Director of Human Resources and Quality Assurance in a large private company – had even emerged from behind his paper to comment on the irony of having to say 'I told you so' to an eminent educationalist.

'Trust people. Trust the process. Engage them with what is important to them. Allow them to speak for themselves. Tolerate ambiguity. Don't be afraid of conflict and disagreement – it's healthy. Go with the flow.'

'Easy for you to say', had always been Jan's stock response, but now she had experienced it for herself. She had experienced the 'flow' her husband had gone on about for so long. She might, after all, read the book *Flow* which Leonard was perpetually waving in front of her, although she thought Mihaly Csikszentmihalyi was not the most promising of names for an inspiring author.

'You are always in such a hurry,' Leonard would say to her, ' You know where you want to go. You see vision as something that is yours and you want to pull people along behind you. You will be surprised by the talent and intelligences that emerge when people are allowed to commit themselves.'

Leonard always used the plural of the word 'intelligence'. Jan had yet to be convinced. She had a pretty good idea of what the singular meant and the teachers and pupils who fitted, and didn't fit, that particular label.

Over the next few weeks Jan found herself talking more to her husband. 'If nothing else comes out of this, at least it will have done something for our marital relations', she told him; his newspaper on that occasion had not wavered for even a microsecond from its upright position, obscuring the entire top half of the Leonard Barre frame. For all his people-centred principles, Leonard was uncomfortable with such intimacies.

As they began to discuss how they would proceed, Jan discovered in her husband a resource she hadn't known existed. She found out, although she wouldn't admit it to him, that he knew more about learning than she did, at least more about learning organisations. For the first time she found herself taking, and even acting on, his advice. In his company they had practised upward – or 360° – appraisal for five years. Leonard's performance was evaluated by his own staff and, after a few rude shocks in the early days, he was now quite used to getting this kind of feedback.

Jan didn't think she was quite ready yet to be evaluated by her teachers or her pupils. She decided to talk to Ursula about it; Jan had been impressed by her sensitivity and insight. She arranged to meet with Ursula at 3 p.m. the following Wednesday in her office.

At three exactly Ursula was knocking on her door. Jan served the coffee and waited for Ursula to start.

'Let's start by talking about the school and how you see it.'

That was an engaging opening. Jan could talk about her school all day and halfway into the night, as her husband could testify. Ursula listened without interruption. It was at least fifteen minutes before she spoke.

'It sounds hard. You've put a lot of energy into the school, a lot of investment but without a lot of returns. But there must be positives too, things you can build on.'

Jan Barre realised she had been entirely negative so far in her account. Problems, dilemmas, weak staff, lack of support from the authority, badly behaved kids, uncontactable parents, a curriculum that didn't seem to engage with these pupils and their everyday lives.

The pluses were more difficult. But there were so many nice kids, by far the majority. There were supportive and committed teachers, not many missionaries but half a dozen true believers. While only a minority of parents turned up at parents' meetings, there was a core of committed parents who always wanted to help and could not do enough for the school.

'Where two or three are gathered together …' Ursula interjected, leaving the rest unsaid.

Jan remembered the biblical aphorism well from her childhood and a passage from a tape that Tom Ericson said he had been listening to in his car. The disequilibrium created by three or four people in an organisation – 'positive attractors' – could be such a powerful source of energy that it could be used to reconfigure the organisation. Tom, and the lady on the tape no doubt, had said it more eloquently and used the analogy of physics to make the point, but Jan recognised the possibilities it held for the school.

'Releasing energy. Turning negative energy into positive', Ursula had repeated thoughtfully as if this was the first time she had thought of it. 'That's just what it is, I suppose. Wouldn't it be wonderful if we could do that?'

Jan was struck by the 'we'. She remembered something else Tom had given her, another extract from the tape which he had written down. She rummaged in her desk drawer for a minute then retrieved a crumpled piece of paper with an almost illegible scrawl, written in Tom's car during a Monday morning gridlock.

> For many years, the prevailing maxim of management stated, 'management is getting work done through others'. The important thing was the work, the others were nuisances that needed to be managed into conformity and predictability. Managers have recently been urged to notice that they have people working for them. They have been advised that work is done by humans like themselves – each of us with strong desires for recognition and connectedness. The more they, we, feel part of the organization, the more work gets done. This, of course, brings with it a host of new relationship-based problems that are receiving much notice. How do we get people to work well together? How do we honor and benefit from diversity? How do we get teams working together quickly and efficiently? How do we resolve conflict?

Ursula read the piece of paper that Jan passed to her. 'That puts it rather well,' she said. 'How about telling me a bit more about yourself, about you in your job? What does it mean personally to be a headteacher?'

Jan told the story. She didn't avoid the negatives but it was a better story than it might have been an hour or so beforehand. It was past 7 p.m. when they finished. Jan had done most of the talking while Ursula had mainly asked questions, not in an inquisitorial way, more like a friendly dialogue in which Jan had gradually felt more and more comfortable about opening up some of the most private concerns about her work.

Ursula said: 'I get a sense that being a headteacher is a very lonely job. You can't really confide in anybody because you are their manager and you need to be strong, in charge. But yet that you would like to if you felt you had the support to take risks?' It was really a statement but she phrased it as a question with a rising intonation at the end.

'It's no different in a way from when you start teaching,' replied Jan. 'You have to be seen to be the boss. You can't admit to any weaknesses because as soon as you do you will have lost control.' Ursula nodded. 'And yet as you develop your relationship with the class you can relax a bit, open up a bit, show you are human and that you can learn from them. And that you're not good at everything.'

Jan remembered an occasion a couple of years ago when a young French teacher had asked her to come into the class and be quizzed by the pupils in French. 'But my French is terrible,' Jan had objected. 'I know, that's why I want you there; so they can see that even headteachers make mistakes and that, possibly, just possibly, they might know more than you do.'

After Ursula had left, Jan sat for about ten minutes thinking about how much she had learned, about herself, about the school, about self-evaluation. Self-evaluation had not been mentioned once in the course of the conversation but that was what it had been – a long, hard and critical look at leadership. She also had a very much clearer grasp now of what 'critical friend' actually meant.

Jan took another forty-five minutes to make some notes – Ursula had left her with some 'homework'. She was to keep a diary for a day, noting in it what she did, who she spent her time with, what she learned: time as a resource. The starting point was how she used her time. She realised already that it was not going to show an optimal use of time. Where she should be and wanted to be was with pupils and teachers but much of the day was spent behind the office door coping with crises.

Jan jotted down her first responses to Ursula's questions:

- What do I want to achieve from this project?
- Where are the growth points to build on?
- What am I going to do next?

The answer to question number one was 'increased academic achievement'. She would like to be able to show one year down the line that pupils were getting better results – but she'd been pushing that for years without any demonstrable gain. Was Leonard right? Was she pushing too hard? Or in the wrong direction?

'You know the definition of insanity?' he had asked her one evening without even lowering his paper. It was a rhetorical question to which he was about to tell her the answer so she waited indulgently.

'Insanity,' he said, lowering the paper to savour the moment, 'is keeping on doing the same thing but expecting different results.'

Jan smiled at the memory and how she had dismissed it at the time as another of Leonard's cute quotes from his endless repertoire. She returned to her note-taking but now wondered if, after all, there was something fundamentally true in what Leonard had said. If the school had a reputation for being a place where pupils and teachers worked together to improve learning in a positive atmosphere, wouldn't that be a good way to attract new pupils? Parents wanted good academic achievement, but they also wanted conviviality, good relationships between teachers and pupils, an outgoing, confident and competent staff. Above all, they wanted their children to be happy and fulfilled. If she could succeed in raising achievement through a really rigorous self-evaluation, through stimulating a real dialogue about learning and teaching, through good hard-headed investigation of how they used their time and how they could use it better. If ...

She came to her second point on the balance sheet. Jan knew that, as the headteacher, she would not be judged by exam results alone, nor by the conviviality of her school, but because the school 'ran well', avoided newspaper headlines, kept good discipline, was strict about homework. This initiative, as appealing as it was, could be risky. It could open up a can of worms It relied on some key people to make it work. She realised for the first time what that overworked phrase, 'shared leadership', really meant. 'Trust the process', Leonard kept saying to her until it had become a weary cliché. But this project wasn't just about her, and it would only work if she was willing to let go. So far the self-evaluation process had already demonstrated that there was a vitality and a willingness to take more responsibility. The only puzzle was why Jan had never seen it before.

Third point: Jan realised they had taken on something for which they needed a lot of skill and guidance. Self-evaluation would necessitate some form of classroom observation and that couldn't be undertaken lightly. She knew that researchers used trained observers for this kind of work and even then the validity of it was open to debate. Their research findings tended to end up on dusty library shelves where, as one of her most cynical members of staff had said, 'they were chewed over only by cultured mice'. Classroom observation here was something of a quite different order. It was about real people with tender feelings and years of investment in their craft. There were many teachers who would object to being observed by her because she was the boss; by pupils because they were after all just pupils; by parents because who knows what they would report to the neighbourhood grapevine; by inspectors because promotion might ultimately depend on it. In fact, anybody at all would be a disruptive influence and in the end arrive, at best, at a partial and limited view.

These were questions for Ursula. Then, on second thoughts, why not questions for the staff, for all of them to grapple with? To share such concerns: that was, after all, part of the learning process they had embarked on. The meeting was held after school for interested staff only, but Jan knew there would be some 'underground workers' there to defend their interests.

She went into the meeting less prepared and forearmed than she had ever done before. Someone had told her in her early years of headship never to go into a meeting without knowing what the outcome would be. That rule was about to be well and truly shredded.

Faced with an open question and eventually convinced that there was no hidden or predetermined agenda, staff got to grips with the question, 'How are we going to conduct observation in a way that is revealing but not threatening, challenging but supportive, useful but not too time consuming?'

'Why do we assume that we should use observation?' asked Simone, one of the newer members of staff.

Jan realised it was a question she hadn't even considered. The answer would, hopefully, lie in the Self-evaluation Guidelines furnished by the Commission's 'experts'. She had photocopied pages, enough for people to share in twos or threes. They now flicked through it, studying the different approaches. The Guidelines listed thirty different methodologies. Some they rejected immediately as too complex or too simplistic and, after nearly two hours of discussion, two decisions were reached. One, it would be for volunteers only. Two, they would use four strategies – peer observation, shadowing, focus groups and the force field.

The force field was included only after some debate about its purpose and usefulness and, in a moment of spontaneous inspiration, Tom Ericson had proposed they take five minutes in pairs to try one out. He proposed the subject, 'our school – brakes and accelerators on improvement' and passed out sheets of blank paper and demonstrated the format on the overhead projector. In the plenary, literally five minutes later, Tom did a quick round of the room, taking one item from each pair. His composite list looked like this:

Accelerators	*Brakes*
Committed staff	Cynics and well-poisoners
Concerned and supportive parents	Disruptive pupils
Critical friends	Hostile press
Helpful colleagues	Lack of resources
In-service courses (good ones!)	Too much paperwork
Enthusiastic pupils	Lack of time
Self-evaluation	An overcrowded curriculum

The ensuing discussion had to be cut short. Tom suggested this could produce a lot of material if used by students to focus on what helped them learn and what hindered their learning. Apart from two members of staff ruefully shaking their heads, there was general agreement that this would be worth trying.

Eight teachers volunteered for peer observation, working in pairs to agree a focus within the general rubric 'learning and teaching', and how they would report back. They paired across subjects: physical education with history; science with geography; art with English; and mathematics with technology. Six senior students volunteered each to shadow a junior student over the course of a full school day with a set of questions to be answered for each lesson in turn on time as a resource for learning. A series of three focus groups, consisting of parents and students, would be arranged, to examine home–school relations. Ursula agreed to chair these groups. The force field, it was agreed, could be used in each of these three contexts with a different focus for each.

Jan had left the meeting early to attend to another crisis. Toilet doors, broken windows, security alarms, upset parents, inquisitive newspapers looking for a good story – these were the things that occupied her time for the next few days. And as days stretched into weeks, Jan realised that that the self-evaluation project was going on without her. She was brought back into focus by her diary entry: an impending visit from Ursula, her friendly critic. She had agreed to keep a one-day diary logging her time, and to report back on progress of the evaluation. She needed an update on progress. Jan headed for Tom Ericson's room.

Tom was teaching, so Jan stood outside the door and waited. He was absorbed in what he was doing and hadn't seen her through the glass of the door. After about a minute she ventured inside; it was during a moment of complete quiet. Tom Ericson was standing, head to one side as if waiting for an moment of inspiration or an answer to a profound question.

'Because, sir ...'

Jan recognised the dark-haired girl who was speaking as Serena, one of the pupils on the self-evaluation group. She blushed inwardly at the thought that she knew so few names of the pupils in her school. Serena was, in fact, volunteering the answer to some profound question.

' ... because I don't think there are any facts. Well, I suppose there must be, like Columbus *did* cross the Atlantic in 1492, but it's all the different versions of the story that you get that are really interesting because he made such a terrible mess of things and ended up in disgrace but he is still a great hero. We visited his house in Gomera last year on holiday, and anyway the Vikings were there about five or six centuries before him so it wasn't like he "discovered" America. So that's not a fact.'

Tom Ericson waited until the speech was over and turned to speak to Jan. As they walked over to the door together one of the pupils got out of her seat and came to the front of the class and took over where Tom had left off.

'They're used to it,' said Tom as they went outside into the corridor. 'They're getting very good at it too. Lots of potential there for recruitment in the future.'

Jan asked him for an update on the project. 'From your point of view, that is. I'm told there are no facts.' She hadn't been able to resist the small irony and Tom took it in good part.

'Well, from my point of view, which is of course the factual one, some really good things have been happening,' Tom began. 'The paired observation has been brilliant. Well, for most of us. One or two people didn't really click with the people they were paired with. But I have been doing a little paired work recently with Miss Braun, sorry Ms Braun, well actually, Margaret ... and we have begun to develop some interesting ideas about team teaching. The kids have been throwing in some good ideas too and I think Margaret is really getting a lot out of it. As am I. For me the biggest thing is getting to see the strengths in someone I might just have written off. I've learned a lot from her.'

Qualities of leadership	Major strengths	More strengths than weaknesses	More weaknesses than strengths	Major weakness
Commitment				
Up-to-date knowledge				
Ability to initiate				
Ability to direct				
Communication skills				
Manages staff effectively				
Delegates effectively				
Models good teaching				
Creates confidence in others				
Inspires others				
Has a positive influence on practice				
Ability to evaluate others effectively				
Demonstrates breadth of vision				
Takes decisions effectively				
Maintains good relationships with staff				
Maintains good relationships with pupils				
Maintains good relationships with parents				
Involves others in policy development				
Disseminates information promptly and efficiently				

Figure 4.3 The self-evaluation form.

Miracles are still possible, Jan thought to herself. She hadn't meant to show Tom the paper she was clutching in her hand. It was for her meeting with Ursula, but on impulse she found herself handing it to Tom to have a look at (see Figure 4.3).

'It's a self-evaluation form I got from a book Ursula gave me. I have been scoring myself on it. I was wondering ... ' Jan hesitated. ' ... I was wondering what would happen if I gave it to the staff and asked them to evaluate me.'

'That would be very brave,' Tom said. 'But could I suggest you don't do it yet? Give it a couple of months, nearer the end of the project.'

Tom was being diplomatic. Jan knew very well what he was trying to tell her. To do it now might give her a bit of shock, but if she was to achieve a lot in the next few months and take a real lead in the success of the project, then she might ask staff to fill it out. In a few months' time she might just get a much better result.

'I think that's good advice,' replied Jan. 'Thank you, Tom.'

5   Ursula
The critical friend

Ursula listened intently to what Jan Barre was telling her about the school and her role in it. Listening was hard work, trying to catch the nuance of expression, the feeling that lay behind the words. She was trying to look at the school through Jan Barre's eyes, seeing it with the emotional content that it had for Jan.

As the story unfolded it became an increasingly personal account. The conversation had started matter-of-factly, warily, all about structures and procedures, roles and responsibilities. It had a detached quality, as if Mrs Barre was talking about somebody else. But as Ursula listened, probing gently, and the defensive layers began to be peeled back, Jan Barre the person began to reveal more of her real feelings about what it meant to be the head of a large and complex organisation.

Jan Barre had obviously invested much of herself in the school. Its triumphs were her triumphs, its disasters her own. The European Project was important to her because it could provide the catalyst the school needed to move it forward, to jolt it out of its routine, to take a thoughtful look at itself. But it was not a process she was viewing with undiluted delight. On a personal level she could see fingers being pointed at her; she had not been the kind of principal she would have liked to be. She was not as charismatic as some of her colleagues; she didn't have their confidence or ability to fill a room with her presence. She was not as efficient, not the complete time management expert, planner or strategist. She wasn't a great talker or raconteur, with a fund of anecdotes about her pupils to be told with embellishment and a keen sense of what an audience wanted to hear. She wasn't as well read as she would have liked. She wasn't an innovator, a break-the-mould person, a risk-taker or an entrepreneur.

'It doesn't leave much, does it?' Jan had said to Ursula in a self-deprecatory moment. Ursula did not try to deny or reassure. The relationship, only two hours old, had already progressed far enough for Ursula to accept that this was a real expression of how Jan saw herself and, perhaps, how others saw her too. She did wonder, though, to what extent these could be said to be traits that 'belonged' to Jan, characteristics of her or, on the other hand, reflections of the environment in which she found herself. She wondered it out loud and Jan mulled over the idea before replying.

'I've been here ten years and in a funny kind of way I think maybe the school has moulded me in its image. I'm not a missionary or an innovator but maybe I could have been in another school. I suppose there are a quite few things there I could learn to be. I suppose there are things I have become because of the kind of school this is.'

'What I sense,' Ursula said, 'is that you give a lot of space to other people. You allow your teachers to develop and you give them your support to do their job well.'

'I think that's being a bit generous,' Jan replied, 'I think that is what I would like to do. That would be my preferred style of leadership, but I haven't really done it. I was aware of lots of good things going on in the school – Tom Ericson in history and literature, for example – but I have never given him the support he deserves, I suppose because I have attended so much to the sick and destitute. ' She smiled at her own metaphor. 'I mean it's hard to cope with the constant crises and just keep on top of things day to day.'

'The tyranny of the urgent?'

Jan recognised the quote from Steven Covey, whose book her husband had given her. *The Seven Habits of Highly Effective People* had made her even less confident of her own abilities. But Covey had hit the nail on the head in one respect; she was a victim of the urgent. Time to attend to, and build on, the good things was what she needed. She remembered somewhere else reading 'don't water the rocks', but yet she continued to do so. She continued to try and coax life out of barren soil rather than tending to the green shoots of growth.

Ursula gave Jan a cutting she had taken from the journal *Managing Schools Today*. It was headed 'The Swamp' (see Figure 5.1). It depicted a headteacher standing on dry, solid ground with a swamp in front of her. At the far end of the swamp there was thick impenetrable sludge. Nearer to land the swamp waters became progressively less murky and at the nearest point to land there was soft, nearly dry, ground. How many of Jan's staff could be said to be on the high, dry ground; on the soft sand; in murky water; or beyond reach in the deep sludge?

Although it was concentrated work, Ursula found the time together had passed quickly. They had covered a lot of ground and opened a succession of doors. They finished with an agreement that as part of her self-evaluation Jan would fill in the matrix at key points in the day, recording the nature of the decisions she was making and the classification of those decisions as (1) important and urgent; (2) important but not urgent; (3) urgent but not important; (4) not important and not urgent. Jan's task over time, as she and Ursula agreed, would be to move more actions and decisions into the second quadrant, 'important but not urgent'. Jan had also agreed to keep a more detailed one-day diary recording how she spent the day, with whom and with what purpose in mind. Ursula would return in two weeks' time to review and discuss what Jan had done.

Her time with Jan Barre had been valuable for both of them. For Jan, Ursula seemed to have offered a listening ear in what was very evidently a lonely job. For Ursula, it had taught a lot in a very short period about the nature of school leadership. She would be more careful in future not to generalise or pontificate about the competences of leadership as if they could be listed, assessed and injected in formulaic quantities into prospective leaders.

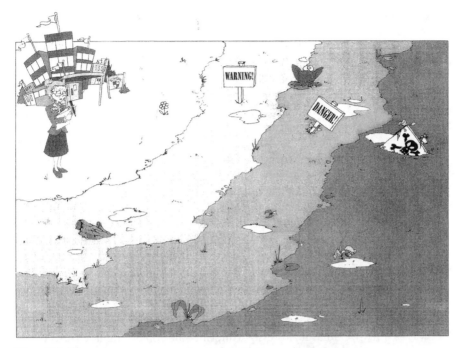

Figure 5.1 The swamp.

Their new closeness had also created a problem for Ursula. Jan had obviously adopted Ursula as her critical friend. Ursula, though, saw herself as a critical friend to the school, to the staff, to the students and to the parents. It was important for her not to be too closely associated with the head because that might inhibit the trust she was hoping to build with others. Ursula made a point of spending time with teachers, eating with them at lunch time, visiting their classrooms when invited, trying to view the school through different lenses.

It was a quite ordinary, unspectacular school. It followed its routines with an almost mechanical predictability. The self-evaluation group had been the first disturbance to that routine, and had released a trapped source of energy. Ursula imagined coming in with a thermal imaging camera and photographing the energy flows, the cool and hot spots around the school – the icy blues, the oranges, the reds. She imagined the places of the school captured in vivid colours. She wondered if some classrooms would show positive streams of energy flowing between teachers and students, in and among students.

The process of change. It was what could be called, in a sense, bottom-up/top-down. The 'disturbance' had come from a few teachers and a few students. In the words of a Spanish teacher she was to meet in Luxembourg, 'it spread like a channel of oil'. It was an apt metaphor for the gradual seepage into consciousness, the way in which self-evaluation worked and what it could achieve.

Bruce Joyce's metaphor of 'doors' to school improvement was more than metaphorical. Doors were opening in a physical and professional sense. Teachers were not only admitting their colleagues into the inner sanctum of their classrooms but into the private places of their thinking and beliefs. Some teachers were positively welcoming the evaluation of their teaching by their classes, while others had begun to cautiously experiment, encouraged by the enthusiasm of their colleagues who had discovered that it was an enlightening and formative experience.

One teacher had shown her the results of a questionnaire which she had given to six different classes. It had provoked such a stimulating discussion that Ursula had immediately recorded it in her diary. She had written:

> I felt I was at last being accepted when Roberta came to me for advice. She was concerned that the standard questionnaire she had used with six different classes had not produced uniform results. Three rated her teaching very positively. Two were generally positive and one was mixed, with some negative ratings. She said she had studied reliability and validity in her university course. Did this invalidate the instrument? What should she take from it? We discussed her relationship with these classes. Which did she look forward to? Which did she get most satisfaction from? It became clear quite quickly that the positive results were from the classes she enjoyed most. I asked her if she thought she might be a different teacher with different classes. She was puzzled at first and then surprised me with a statement that was as unexpected as it was insightful. She said something like this: 'I suppose I am not the "same" teacher with every class. Some people would say Mrs Kohl is a good teacher and I am, but sometimes and with some classes I'm not. It's a bit like being a good wife. It depends where your vantage point is, my children, first husband or my second husband. They would give me a very different quality report.'

> It reminded me of something I had read about 'polyocular' and 'monocular' knowledge. The idea is that a single pair of eyes sees something which you might take to be an objective reality, but many pairs or eyes would see quite differently – different angles, different perspectives. The whole truth is always in the process of being discovered. I found this quote which I find very reassuring. I have sent it to Roberta. I should send it to some of our policy makers and inspectors!

> 'The Japanese had no word for objectivity. It had to be invented once Westerners began talking. The word now used is *kyakkanteki*, literally "the guest's point of view" (while *shukanteki* is "the host's point of view" or "subjectivity"). There is surely a hint of reproach in the first of the two terms. The guest is not simply an outsider and a stranger, but is probably naive about the non-visible relationships of the family being visited. The guest "sees" a number of separate people and, unlike the host, cannot know the pattern of dynamics within the whole.' (Hampden-Turner and Trompenaars p.113)

> And ...

' ... the problem with "objectivity" is that those who claim to have it believe they need to look no further, need listen to no one else, and never alter their convictions. They have the "data" or the "givens". But those pursuing polyocular knowledge will never be satisfied, never know enough.' (pp. 114–115)

A few days later Ursula received an email at home from Roberta. It read:

Yes, but ... there is a saying in Iceland about the 'visitor's view', meaning that they see things you can't see because it is all so familiar to you. Have you ever come home to your house after a long time away and everything looks different, as if you are seeing it with new eyes? Is this the guest's view, too?

Ursula had set in train a dialogue that was to continue for a number of weeks and challenge her own thinking as well as that of the teachers who gradually joined in their small website conference. This new-found enthusiasm for reflection and debate was, of course, by no means true of everyone. The 'emigrants' had emigrated even further and the outright opponents were, in the main, still opposing. Many of the floating voters, though, were being pulled towards the eddies of activity. And the missionaries, few as they were, were being less messianic, as if drawn in and tempered by the moderate and pragmatic approach of their colleagues.

Luxembourg

It wasn't until the first conference in Luxembourg that the European character of the project had come home to Ursula. She had arrived in Luxembourg on a dismal, foggy November day. As an introduction to this quaint duchy it had been disappointing; the glass building where the conference was to be held looked forbidding in the grey morning. The conference room was vast and impersonal. Every European flag, half of which Ursula couldn't identify, hung across the back wall. The high ceiling and the glass walls added to the grandness of the room, while the banks of microphones and translators' booths convinced Ursula of two things. One, there was no way she was going to speak in that intimidating forum. Two, something important and far bigger than the school was happening.

The first morning had been a succession of speeches from people who had to be given their place on such a grand occasion. Important people spoke importantly. The talk that had impressed her most had been from the European Union of Students. 'Students know best' had not only been the title of the talk but the headline of a garish poster which the student, Maurice, thrust into her hand as she exited the hall. Was it really true, that students know best? Ursula wondered what Serena was making of it all. It was, to be sure, a mixed ability group: politicians and policy makers, teachers and headteachers, parents and governors, researchers and academics, bureaucrats and Eurocrats, critical friends – and Serena.

Thrown together in workshop groups, they exchanged experiences in a dozen languages, people translating for one another – Italians, Spaniards and Portuguese trying to find a common language, separated by a dozen different idioms and vernaculars but with the common bond of the activity in which they were engaged in their schools.

The language barrier had all but disappeared in a workshop Ursula attended on photo evaluation. She had not until then appreciated the power of the visual medium to transcend language. Working in small groups and armed with cameras, they had captured salient moments in other workshops, frozen-in-time transactions between participants, framed aspects of the environmental 'wallpaper' that would otherwise have passed by unnoticed. They arranged their photographs in telling juxtaposition and pinned them to walls of the hallowed Commission foyer which, Ursula was sure, had never witnessed such irreverent images.

Over coffee she drew Tom and Serena's attention to the posters and described the photo evaluation process to them.

'One for our repertoire?' she asked.

'How do you think that would go down with our lot?' asked Tom.

'Don't see why it shouldn't go down well,' answered Ursula, 'as long as you ignore the siren voices in the wings.'

'Let's do it', said Serena, already projecting on to her brain wall the kinds of pictures she would take of her school and classrooms, not to mention the toilets.

Ursula, who was keeping a diary of the project, wrote brief notes at the end of the first day, identifying issues and putting questions to herself:

- Huge variation in where people are with self-evaluation in different countries.
- Attitudes (excitement to caution to scepticism) seem to reflect national characteristics and systems.
- 'Hard' measures v. 'the tin opener school' (data as an impetus to dialogue).
- Question: can we bring these two schools of thought together – 'from the tyranny of the *or* to the genius of the *and*?
- Question: what do we need to do to bring in the doubters and sceptics?

Clearly the critical friend plays a key role in this. Backgrounds and styles of critical friends vary so widely:

- From directive to non-directive.
- From facilitative to interventionist.
- What works best and does it depend on history and context?
- Can I be interventionist in one school and non-interventionist in another?
- How much is determined by the expectations people have of me? and how far must I go in meeting those expectations? exceeding them? or in confronting/changing them?
- Is changing expectations an important part of my job?
- Intrigued by reports from two schools in Iceland whose experiences of critical friends were quite different. Yet both had the same person. But … is the critical friend the 'same' person in two very different contexts?

Best bit of this morning's presentations – man from Department for Education and Employment (DfEE) in England. His overhead transparency cartoon:

> I taught Stripe (the dog) to whistle.
> Why isn't he whistling then?
> I taught him. I didn't say he learned it.

Ursula liked this so much she asked Bill Clark, the official from the DfEE, if she could get a copy. She would use it to introduce her session at a whole-staff meeting to which Jan Barre was urging her to contribute.

March: a whole-staff meeting

The first whole-staff meeting Ursula was to address took place just before the Easter break. It was an intimidating prospect. Her one experience of talking to an entire staff had been far from pleasant. It had made her wary of that collective 'teachers' and their potential power when harnessed to the negative. While that experience was three years in the past, Ursula felt she had needed all of that time to recover and pluck up the courage to try again, to see if that latent energy could be deployed in pursuit of the positive. Before the meeting she had scribbled down a few 'vital signs' of her own progress as a critical friend:

- People say hello and smile, some call me by my first name.
- Some teachers ask me questions or ask for suggestions of books to read.
- Some teachers join me for lunch.
- The deputy head asked for my opinion on a tricky ethical issue.
- A teacher invited me in to observe and give feedback in her class.
- Invited by head to give feedback on my observations to staff development session.

Ursula's part of the meeting was to be a 15–20 minute slot to give some feedback on what she had observed in the six months she had been associated with the school. In the event the session lasted twice that time.

   She had started by taking the three areas they had chosen for their focus of development, asking for some brief comment on progress in each of these, then she gave her own assessment, emphasising its tentative and subjective nature, describing for them the guest's point of view, asking for comment on the extent to which they thought she was getting it right. She suggested three or four things under each heading.

Time as a resource for learning

- Teachers and students are generally conscious of time and how it is being used.

- There is evidence that some students (perhaps a small minority) use their homework/study time more effectively.
- There is some evidence of teachers pacing their lessons better.

Quality of teaching and learning

- A much wider awareness of the differences between teaching and learning.
- A wider interest in how learning works.
- A more informed debate about quality.
- Beginning the development of a learning policy.

Home and school

- Greater awareness of the role of parents and home learning.
- More involvement of parents in evaluating learning.
- More critical attitude to homework practice.

These suggestions provoked considerable discussion. Ursula was pleased to find a general consensus around her observations, with one or two voices of strong dissent. What did please her was the level of debate. People seemed more open and less defensive in their arguments. Even the dissenters seemed a little less strident.

The most satisfying outcome of the meeting, however, was the decision to develop a learning policy for the whole school and to set up a working party of volunteers. The policy would place learning at the centre and plan whole-school strategies which would be used in the coming session to promote learning for all. The working party agreed to a sustained monitoring and co-ordination of learning in four contexts:

- Classroom
- School
- Home
- Community

Equally pleasing for Ursula was the change she had seen in Jan Barre. The project had been good for the headteacher: it had brought her a new confidence, an openness, a willingness to allow leadership of others. Tom Ericson was an obvious example, but there were others too. Tony Campos, the physical education teacher, seemed to have a new lease of life and was volunteering for things he would previously have gracefully declined. A parent, Mrs Stern, had galvanised a group of parents into action over homework and set up an after-school study club. Perhaps, Ursula reflected, she should encourage Jan to use her self-evaluation instrument after all. It would be evidence that the staff had seen a change in her, too. And if the results weren't altogether positive, Ursula was sure Jan would now be better able to handle any negative feedback.

What Ursula was confident of were the tangible signs of improvement to demonstrate at the second European conference to be held in Vienna in November. That conference would be under the auspices of the Austrian Presidency with Serena, Tom Ericson and herself as delegates. Ursula was sure they would have a good story to tell.

6   Coffee with the professor

Serena took one last look in the mirror. She was late for their meeting but she wasn't going to go until the last straggling bit of hair was in the right place. She was the last to enter the room and felt uncomfortable weaving her way through the legs. The chairs were arranged in a circle but some of the students were sitting on the floor. Most of them looked older than her and far more serious, she thought. She counted twenty-four in all, including herself.

'We're not just here just to make up the numbers', someone was saying as she squeezed herself into a space on the floor. It was Roel, a delegate from The Netherlands. He and Serena had got off to a bad start at the last meeting when he had cut across her and made her case on her behalf as if she wasn't competent enough herself.

Her wandering thoughts came down into the circle. The Norwegian girl, Hanne, was speaking in her no-nonsense way, lively, fast, fluent and with total conviction in what she was saying. She was obviously equally impatient with Roel's arrogant style. Her ability to deal with people was clearly a product of her experience with the European Organisation of School Students, OBESSU.

'I think we should grab the opportunity to talk to these guys,' she was saying. 'I think we might learn something and it would be good to publish an article in our magazine Q saying what we think. The student perspective.'

'Interview them about what?' asked a German student.

'About what their research has to say about the self-evaluation of schools. And about the role of students in it.'

Serena realised that Hanne was referring to the 'experts' who had been talking to them in the morning session.

'Well, it's pretty clear from everything we've heard here in Vienna so far that the policy makers are keen on self-evaluation', Hanne said. 'It's going to be a big policy issue and that goes for every one of the eighteen countries here. But there's no guaranteeing that it will be worthwhile for us, for school students, unless, of course we do something about it ourselves. Roel's right in one thing: we're not just here to make up the numbers.'

'But why should we go and talk to *them*?' said Roel, waving his hand dismissively in the direction of the invisible experts.

'We need to talk to *them*,' said Hanne, borrowing Roel's emphasis but adding an inflection of her own, 'because what they say and what they've dug up from their research studies may end up having a big effect on us and our schools. And, by the way, I think you'll find them very simpatico.'

Some of the group looked sceptical, dubious that anything of practical value could ever emerge from such a discussion.

'They've sold out to the policy makers,' argued Roel, who was unwilling to be brushed aside so easily. 'If the policy makers don't like what these experts come up with they just ignore or ask them to change it. And if the experts don't fall in line they won't use them again.'

'I think that's very unfair,' Serena interjected, surprised at her own boldness. She had liked the look of the French professor and couldn't envisage him selling out to anyone. She was able to tell at a glance that he was someone of obvious integrity. He looked wise and eccentric, just like a French professor should look, bald but with luxuriant black curly hair protruding from each side of his head.

Her defence of the professor was taken as an act of volunteering and without much further discussion Serena found herself, along with a French boy, Arthur, and a Greek girl, Zoe, nominated to interview the professor.

'That's what happens to people who come in late', Hanne said to her afterwards, but in a such a nice way Serena couldn't object. She could forgive anything in someone with the skill to deal with obnoxious boys like Roel.

'What are we interviewing them about?' Serena asked, embarrassed that she didn't know but feeling it might be a useful starting point.

'About school effectiveness and what it has to say on the subject of school evaluation,' Hanne replied.

Serena regretted even more her long reverie at the bedroom mirror. The other students had set off into the city to do some early Christmas shopping. Serena, Zoe and Arthur would have to carry the burden of the group's homework.

The interview

The professorial interview took place at the end of the afternoon. It was a crisp November day with a pale winter sun illuminating a corner of the bar where the professor was sitting. His papers were laid out in three neat piles on the round coffee table. He held a cup of coffee in his left hand but it remained poised between table and mouth as if he had forgotten it was there, so concentrated was his attention on the paper he was reading. A packet of Gauloises sat on the corner of the table as a reminder of his national identity. As the three students approached he rose with exaggerated old-world courtesy and beckoned them to three preordained chairs.

Serena couldn't help thinking how awesome it was to interview this patently scholarly man sitting before them. Arthur had been chosen to kick off because he could set out the ground rules in French, more to put Arthur at his ease than the professor; the professor spoke fluent English with hardly a trace of the guttural 'r' or the comic 'z' which so many of his countrymen substituted for the English 'th'. Perhaps to cover his own nervousness, Arthur began by asking the professor to be clear and to the point.

'Just what, on one famous occasion, a student said to Jean-Paul Sartre when he got up to give a speech at the General Assembly of Students at the Sorbonne, in May 1968 : "Sartre, sois bref!" I will try to do likewise,' he said.

It was a challenge the professor had met before in his rather abortive attempts to explain the nature of his job to his own children. 'So, who's going to begin?'

The professor scanned the three young people seated in a semi-circle around him: the homely Greek girl with her round owlish glasses; quiet intense Serena whose name seemed so patently to capture her presence; the tall, studious-looking Arthur with a plume of hair that he kept sweeping back nervously from his face. Arthur made the first overture.

'Is self-evaluation a good thing?' he asked. It seemed to him, as he asked it, a rather lame question. It wasn't quite what he had meant to say.

'Yes,' answered the professor. 'Is that a short enough answer?'

The three smiled in response to the professor's enjoyment of his own joke.

'Professor, your special field is school effectiveness. We're not too sure what that really means but perhaps you could explain it to us and tell us how it ...' Zoe tailed off. Serena finished her sentence for her:

'How it ... well, what it has to do with self-evaluation.'

'Well, what it will *not* tell you is how to go about self-evaluation. That is something for each school to decide for itself. But what I'd like to propose is that we talk about what school effectiveness is and how that can help you decide what it is you want to evaluate. What do we mean by "effectiveness" when we are talking about a school? What kind of "outcomes" are we talking about? What are the characteristics that have been found to be linked with effective schools? These are the questions.'

Zoe already had a slightly glazed look; Arthur wondered why the professor was asking the questions when that was their job; Serena wished she had gone shopping after all. She wanted to buy something special for her mother who had been so patient through the hard times and the bad years. Since the death of her husband this would be the first time Mrs Kaur would be alone in what they always called 'the family home'. Serena realised with a flush of embarrassment that the professor was looking at her and waiting for an answer to his question: 'Would you agree with that proposal?'

The three students studied each other for a moment. There seemed little option but to accept the proposal and, with the most enthusiasm they could muster, they gave their guarded assent. Arthur switched on the cassette recorder. Serena assumed her most serious expression and began.

'So, professor, what do you mean when you talk about effectiveness?'

'Well, there is actually a definition of an effective school, and that is: "a school in which the pupils progress further than expected".'

'Than expected by whom?' Zoe and Serena chorused and then looked at each other sheepishly.

'Than expected by ... ' the professor tailed off, looking for a better starting point for his answer. 'Well, let's put it this way. I'm sure you've noticed that the best students at the beginning of the year are pretty often also the best at the end ... '

As this seemed to meet with general agreement, he continued. 'You have probably also noticed that children from, say, workers' families are often not so good at school as children of teachers or doctors or, or well any group we could call "middle class"?'

The three said nothing, but they were all listening a little more closely. Serena looked doubtful. She could think of at least three people in her class who didn't fit that description, including herself.

'So, how well students do by the time they leave a school does not depend just on how "effective" the school is, but also on what they know or can do when they start school. This is what we call "cultural or social background", and what we know from all the studies that have been done is that this has a big influence on how well students will perform at school. So, on this basis, we *expect* some students to do better than others.'

The professor sensed the growing impatience with this answer and raised the palm of his left hand to the vertical, a signal that he hadn't yet finished his story.

'But, if I read you rightly, there are a lot of people like you who don't like this idea. They feel it's too sweeping, too fatalistic, as if school made no difference at all and it was all down to what your parents were and what social class you were born into. So ... ', the professor paused to see if his three sceptics were still with him. Serena had said something almost under her breath but the professor had caught it and repeated her words:

'"The ends of all stories are contained in their beginnings",' he repeated, 'from the English poet T. S. Eliot I believe', letting this hover in the air with a mixture of self-satisfaction and studied admiration for the girl who had voiced the thought.

'Very pertinent,' he said, 'because what school effectiveness researchers set out to do was to see if some schools did actually change the state of things. Were there schools in which children from whatever background could go further, could do better, could achieve more than expected? If so, as I said earlier, we could call such schools "effective".'

'Effective because their students did make more progress than might be predicted from their social and cultural background,' repeated Arthur to demonstrate that he, at least, was listening.

'So,' said Zoe, 'my school is what you would call an effective school because my dad worked on a farm but I did well at school, better than all the people in our village expected me to.'

'If that was true for a lot of other young people like you in your school, Zoe, then yes, you are right, it would be an effective school.'

'But,' Serena interjected, 'if it was only Zoe who did well and all the other farmers' children did badly then it wouldn't be ...'

' ... an effective school,' said Arthur, filling the unspoken space at the end of her sentence.

'Then it wouldn't be,' agreed the professor. 'It's quite a complicated equation. How many students do better than expected is really the issue. There would have to be a critical percentage of the total student body. But a really effective school is one that is effective for all its students.'

'You keep on talking about "doing better", professor,' said Zoe, a little more aggressively than she had intended. 'What does "doing better" mean?'

'Well, as I say, doing better than you might have predicted from background factors, or, if you want to take this bothersome social class issue out of the whole equation, better than what could have been predicted from what the student could do when she first started at the school. This is what we normally call a "measure of prior attainment".'

'But better at what?' Zoe persisted.

'You're not going to let me off lightly are you? You three are too clever for your own good. Well, when we say "better", we're talking about achievement. And it has to be achievement we can measure in some way.'

'You mean tests and exams and things?' asked Zoe.

'Yes, certainly. How well students perform in exams is something we can measure and compare. It is important. Don't you agree?'

The three inquisitors looked at each other to see if there was any dissent. Arthur nearly got as far as opening his mouth before the professor continued.

'But that's not the whole story. We aren't interested solely in what we can measure by tests and exams. There are other things equally important: for example, personal development; sociability; citizenship, and lots of other things too – and, yes, you are now going to ask me how we measure those things, aren't you? And the answer is they are not easy to measure and not easy to compare but that hasn't stopped researchers trying to do just that, and some of the best studies include all these aspects.'

'You make it sound very mathematical,' Arthur ventured. 'But I don't see how you can add all these things together. You can't add them all up and do a calculation and that's it. The most important thing for me is whether I like being there and like the teachers and want to learn. Do you know what I mean?'

'I think I do,' said the professor. 'Wellbeing? I think that's what it's called. It's something we French researchers take very seriously. And you'll be pleased to know that we've learned from these studies that schools which are academically effective are often also schools where students are happy, enjoy school, get on well with their teachers and believe that their teachers want the best for them. It is, of course, a little more complicated than that, but let's just say that it makes a lot of sense that these things together – feeling good and doing well – are a powerful combination.'

Arthur was still not happy with the reply. 'So who is it that decides what is going to be measured? Who says what effective is and effective isn't? Why don't you ask us? Us students? We would tell you if a school was good or not because it's us that have to sit in classrooms for five hours every day.'

'Funny you should say that,' said the professor, waving with his coffee cup at the other side of the room. 'See that man over there? He would agree with you because he asked students like you to tell him what made an effective school and what made effective teachers and he then used these as criteria for the school's own self-evaluation. The interesting is that these criteria happen to be very close to what sophisticated research describes as the characteristics of the effective teacher. In some research I carried out with an eminent colleague of mine, on wellbeing at school, we found that the criteria of wellbeing were very much the same for boys and girls and for children from high and low socio-economic backgrounds.'

'It seems you always just want to complicate things all the time,' said Zoe a little impatiently. 'Why don't you just talk about good schools?'

'Yes, I think we do get a little tied up in our language,' agreed the professor, smiling. 'Right, let me see if I can shed a little light on this. I would say that a "good" school ... ' he made little air marks with his forefingers around the word 'good', ' ... is a much broader notion than an "effective" school. The term "effective" has been used to narrow things down, to help us focus on some of the things we can all agree on as important. And things we can measure. It's just as much a value judgement as the notion of good, but it's more easily manageable.'

'So, a school could be effective without being good?' said Arthur.

'In theory,' agreed the professor, 'but then you would have to define your meaning of "good"' – more air marks – 'very carefully for me.'

Serena had been quiet for a while. She was chewing over something which she finally found a way of putting into words. 'I don't think it's really like that', she said eventually.

The three others looked at her expectantly.

'I mean good schools and effective schools and wellbeing and all these things you were talking about. I don't think it's like that at all. In my school I am sometimes totally bored and fed up and sometimes I really enjoy what we are doing because it's a good teacher or a good subject like history. But biology is just really boring most of the time. You are talking as if school was all the same thing all the time.'

'Of course, Salina has put her finger on the big problem with all of this.'

Serena wished someone as clever as a professor could remember a simple thing like her name, but she decided not to correct him because he was now in full flow.

'In an effective school, you would expect to find that all subjects were pretty good. In statistical language there is a positive correlation among subjects. But, of course there are very few schools where all subjects and all teachers are good, if you will permit me to use that word, Arthur. I suppose there will always be differences between subject departments as long as teaching is left to human beings. So in biology, let's say, students don't do so well and may even fall short of expectations while in history students do better than expected – exceed expectations.'

'So it isn't really the school which is effective, but the teachers,' Serena suggested.

'This is getting more and more difficult. Let's see. You do ask complicated questions, you know.' The three students, who thought that professors were paid to answer complicated questions, waited patiently.

'All right. Three things,' said the professor. 'First, your progress in history or biology will depend on how effective your teachers are. And, as Salina says, that counts for more than the effectiveness of the school you are in. If I may be allowed a little research jargon, "teacher effects are stronger than school effects". But –

and here's the but – it is also true that how effective your teacher is will depend in part on the school he or she is in. So, Salina, your wonderful history teacher might not be such a wonderful history teacher in another school.'

Serena was weighing this up and trying to picture Mr Ericson being a bad teacher. She wondered if that could possibly be true.

'And, furthermore, let's mix in another ingredient here. Your history teacher will probably have a very different relationship with a class where everyone is very good at the subject and wants to do well, or a class in which most of the students have difficulties or are badly behaved. And not only do teachers perform better where they have good classes, but students also do better if they have others in their class who are doing well too. And if a teacher is in a school where his or her colleagues perform well – that is, where the bulk of the teachers are effective – he or she will be pushed to be more effective themselves.'

He paused and took a sip of cold coffee. He grimaced and continued. Zoe stifled a giggle.

'Moreover, when teachers meet difficulties in their classrooms, some schools help them more than others. An eminent colleague of mine describes this as "nested layers": the pupils learn, teachers help them to work well, and the school also helps the teachers to work. So the school itself has an indirect effect. But an important one.'

Arthur wanted to ask about the nested layers. Serena was trying to picture the eminent colleague, while Zoe was still fixated on the cold coffee which the professor was absent-mindedly stirring as he spoke. She wondered if her physics teacher was right: that if you stirred coffee long enough and hard enough, the molecules would create heat. It seemed unlikely, looking at the cold coffee.

'The third thing is this. The size of the teacher effect and the school effect vary depending on how much co-ordination or collaboration there is among teachers. If there is no co-ordination, especially if teachers have no idea of how the pupils perform in classes other than their own, the school effect will be weaker and the teacher effect will be greater.'

Zoe had missed the last few minutes of the conversation. She had drifted off from a Vienna winter to her school outside Athens where there would be a warm, rather than a cold, sun. She looked at her watch and imagined her school friends pouring out of school, racing for their bicycles, anxious to put in the distance as soon as possible between themselves and the school building.

'Zoe. You look deep in thought.'

'I was wondering if that means if I had gone to the school in the next village, rather than the school in my village, I might have done better?' she replied.

'Well, in that case, you probably wouldn't be here today, Zoe,' said the professor. 'But you are certainly asking the right question. Let's put it this way. Let's say that at the end of your primary school you had a test in maths and that you were 500th out of 1000 pupils. Then you had a choice of two middle schools. Chances are that one would be more effective than the other. If you attended the more effective of the two you might rise to 420th out of 1000 after two years in this school while if you went to the second of the two schools you would be about 580th.'

'That's not so bad,' said Serena.

'Not really a big difference,' said Arthur.

'It *is* a big difference,' said Zoe, '160 places of a difference.'

The professor chuckled. He seemed to be enjoying himself. 'You sound just like a group of school effectiveness researchers arguing over whether the glass is half full or half empty. It all depends on how you look at it, I suppose. It's not such a dramatic difference on the face of it but it could make the difference between going to university or not, or getting a good job or not.' The professor used his hand again as a stop sign. He hadn't finished and Serena's objection would have to wait.

'And, Zoe, if your neighbouring school happened to be one at the very bottom of the heap – a particularly *in*effective school compared with your own village school, which is particularly effective – the difference could be between a ranking of 680th compared with 320th.'

'Three hundred and sixty places different,' said Zoe admiringly and perhaps a little smugly, too, at the swiftness of her mental arithmetic.

'More mathematics,' objected Arthur. 'It just sounds all a little too neat for me. I don't think your statistics can take everything into account about human beings and how they are. I mean we are so unpredictable ... '

'You're right, of course, Arthur. We are not dealing with tins of beans here. Our basic ingredients are people. Boys and girls, different from one another, different year to year, and in different combinations year to year. Teachers talk about a "good year" and a "bad year" – more air marks – 'referring to the students of '98 or the students of '99. But as researchers we have to deal with this somehow, so we talk of all of these factors as inputs.' Then, noticing Serena's rather dismayed expression, he added, 'Yes, I'm afraid in this statistical world, Salina, that is what you are, an input. In the real world you are, of course, a totally unique being, but if we are going to get anywhere in this world of school effectiveness we have to reduce you to a numerical cocktail which we can then play with, if you don't mind me mixing my metaphors – sex: female; age: 16? 17?; social class background? mobility (how many schools have you been to before?) and so on. And however inadequate this is, Salina, to capture the radiant qualities that make you *you*, it helps us to see how significant these various factors are.'

He paused for breath, resisting a Gauloise that they all knew he was keen to light but at the same time trying to be a good role model. Serena could swear that he had winked at her and couldn't help wondering if fifty-year-old professors ever had improper thoughts about sixteen-year-old girls, then chastised herself immediately for having allowed such a thought to enter her consciousness.

'So,' continued the professor, barely pausing to catch his breath, 'things change, people change, so we have to try and account for what happens over time. We find some very distinct differences between the performance of boys and girls in different subjects but we also find these change the longer children stay in school. Some studies have shown that in maths girls are behind boys at a certain stage but then catch up and overtake boys. Some studies show the gap between working-class and middle-class students growing larger over time. In some schools it may narrow. My own conclusion, with which some may, of course, disagree, is that effective schools are not all the same. Some will be particularly good for one category of students, let us say girls, while in others boys will do particularly well. But whoever you are, it is always better to be in an effective school than an ineffective one.'

There was a sudden silence. No one was volunteering a further question. The professor resumed. 'And that is why school effectiveness is such an important study, boys and girls. That is why self-evaluation matters. Because if schools themselves don't know how good they are and whether or not they are getting better or worse they will be pretty helpless and then it is easy to blame all sorts of conditions – bad students, inadequate parents, poor resources, lack of funding from the government. But with the knowledge of where their strengths and weaknesses lie, and with the tools to evaluate themselves, even the worst schools can improve.'

'Well, that's the answer then,' said Zoe, as if to conclude the session. She was looking studiedly at her watch and the professor could see that his students were coming towards the outer limits of their attention span.

'Yes, Zoe, there is some evidence that self-evaluation helps to make schools more effective.'

'So that means,' said Zoe interrupting him, 'that our schools, the schools here at this conference, should be more effective.'

'*Pas forcément,*' said the professor almost to himself, as if collecting his thoughts in French before passing into English. 'Not necessarily. Not necessarily.'

'Because some schools could do any old evaluation and it wouldn't make any difference to what the kids were learning', suggested Serena, anticipating his thought sequence for him.

'I couldn't have put it better myself,' said the professor. 'Even the most state-of-the-art evaluation won't guarantee that students will learn. It is what you do with it that counts. But we can come back to that. Let's take stock and see where we've got to.'

The three young people looked at their notes and Arthur began.

'Well, if all schools were equally effective, there would be no point in trying to evaluate them. But they're not. Research shows that there are differences, sometimes quite big, and that there is always room for improvement.'

'Top of the class, young man. One of our favourite sayings is "everybody can learn". But bear in mind that there are different reasons for evaluating schools, not just because we want to compare them. So, what else? Salina?'

'Effectiveness varies according to the subject, or "domain"?' she paused on a questioning note. The professor nodded encouragement and Serena continued. 'So, if you want a complete picture of a school you need to evaluate all the domains – or subjects.'

'*Prima,*' said the professor. 'Not necessarily *all*, but all that matter. Or should I say, more precisely, all that matter to the school stakeholders. Hence the importance, which we have seen very clearly in this project, of an agreement of all stakeholders, especially of teachers and pupils, on those areas or domains which are to be evaluated.'

'Anything else?' he inquired. And, as the three young people remained silent, he said, 'then will you allow me to draw you a few other conclusions?'

'That's what we're here for,' said Zoe.

This prompted a momentary hesitation from the professor, trying to interpret the tone of the statement and deciding that in cross-language communication much latitude has to be allowed for misinterpretation.

'Three things, then. First, as effectiveness is not very stable from one year to the next, evaluation should take the form of in-built, ongoing monitoring. This means having a retrospective record of previous evaluations. Second, remember what we said about nested layers: that is, the object of the evaluation is not only the school as a whole, but also classes and teachers. That is why, in this European project, we made a point of having teachers evaluated by their peers, or by pupils, examining how they learn and are taught in their classes. This provides the opening, the common ground if you like, for pupils, teachers, parents, to speak together about issues, problems, opportunities. Evaluation doesn't have to be very technical or take the form of "heavy" procedures. It can be a conversation, a story. As soon as somebody says to someone else, "I think that could have been taught better", they are already evaluating.'

'So all of this isn't new. Everyone's doing it anyway,' said Arthur.

'Yes and no. It is said that teachers are natural evaluators. In fact, aren't we all? But we need the evidence. You've heard of the PHOG equation?'

They clearly hadn't, although they nodded in unison.

'PHOG: Prejudice, Hunch, Opinion, Guesswork. You can go a long way on these. They are very useful human skills, but they need to be tested with more solid evidence. Wars have been won and lost on hunch and guesswork.'

'And the third point?' asked Zoe, both reminding him of the second shoe still to drop, and hopefully accelerating him towards a final conclusion.

'The third is more hypothetical. It is really more of an impression I gain from the research on effective restructured schools.'

'Hunch and guesswork?' asked Zoe.

'An impression, yes, but seasoned with a little bit of logic and evidence, Zoe. There seem, in these schools, to be some more enduring characteristics of effectiveness. These are ethos, culture and habits of effectiveness, if I may use such a phrase. These don't seem to be the result of quick interventions but come more from the ongoing application of sound principles.'

The three were beginning to take on a rather distant look. The professor pressed on to his final point.

'This leaves me wondering if evaluation shouldn't be twin-faceted. What I mean by that is: on the one hand, a broad-brush evaluation, looking at the school as a whole, a kind of overall health check – blood pressure, heart rate, cholesterol level – vital signs if you like; then, with more delicate instruments, to probe a little deeper. To mix my metaphors, a finer tuning, at the classroom level, allowing us to look more microscopically at the small details, little perturbations as they appear day-to-day.'

Arthur, a keen physicist, liked the scientific metaphor.

'Tell you what,' suggested the professor, 'why don't we meet again at the end of tomorrow afternoon's workshop? I'll invite my other colleagues to join us. They may give you a different slant on things. After all, my good young people, you don't want to take my word for it. That would not be a good way of getting evidence, would it?'

Seeing the twinkle in the professor's eye, Serena couldn't help wondering, with a sudden frisson of dismay, if the whole conversation had, after all, been a nice piece of fiction invented entirely for their benefit.

7 The professor revisited

Serena, Zoe and Arthur were first into the bar. It wasn't altogether to do with eagerness for the meeting, they agreed among themselves, more to accelerate the process so that they could squeeze in some Christmas shopping. Reluctantly they confessed to one another that they had actually enjoyed their previous session with the professor. Arthur was now the proud owner of a document that had been distributed at his workshop. He placed it ceremoniously on the table and the three scanned its contents (see Figure 7.1). Serena was pleased that she had mastered the art of upside-down reading.

'Meet my eminent colleagues.'

The three students had not noticed the entry of the professor with his two companions, the grey-haired man they had seen yesterday in the bar and the tall Austrian whom they recognised from his speech the day before.

'The three wise men,' whispered Arthur to Serena, but not quite quietly enough, because the Austrian professor turned and nodded conspiratorially.

'I have a document of my own,' said the professor, placing a single sheet on the table beside Arthur's. 'It is from research on French middle schools.'

Five people now studied the two lists (Figures 7.1 and 7.2).

'But these are quite different,' said Arthur, with obvious dismay.

'Hold on,' said the French professor. 'Look more deeply. A researcher must always exercise restraint and patience. If you look more closely you'll see that there are quite a few common points. In both you see the importance of parents, structured teaching, evaluation of pupils, high expectations, maximisation of learning time and others ... But it is true that in the French one you won't find "collegiality" and "collaboration" of teachers, or the role of the school head.'

'Because you don't believe in such things in France?' suggested the British professor mischievously.

'More probably because they aren't as significant or they are less well developed in our country. But then you won't find "academic emphasis" either, but that's not because it isn't important for us – indeed, quite the opposite.'

'Why is it not there, then?' asked Arthur.

'Precisely because it is so important and commonplace. In France there is a detailed national curriculum, so there are no strong differences from one school to

---

Professional leadership
Firm and purposeful, a participative approach, the leading professional

Shared vision and goals
Unity of purpose, consistency of practice, collegiality and collaboration

A learning environment
An orderly atmosphere, an attractive working environment

Concentration on learning and teaching
Maximisation of learning time, academic emphasis, focus on achievement

High expectations
High expectations all round, communication of expectations, providing intellectual challenge

Positive reinforcement
Clear and fair discipline, feedback

Monitoring progress
Monitoring pupil performance, evaluating school performance

Pupil rights and responsibilities
High pupil self esteem, positions of responsibility, control of work

Purposeful teaching
Efficient organisation, clarity of purpose, structured lessons, adaptive practice

A learning organisation
School-based staff development

Home–school partnership
Parental involvement

Figure 7.1 Variables associated with school effectiveness: British and North American schools (from Sammons *et al.*, 1995)

the next. Remember, in all this school effectiveness work we are focusing on things that differentiate one school from another.'

'But the curriculum could be taught very well or very badly,' said the Austrian professor. 'You can have all the academic emphasis you like in the curriculum, but that doesn't guarantee good teaching or effective learning.'

'Do you know what the longest distance in the world is?' asked the British professor. Then, answering his own rhetorical question: 'The longest distance in the world is between a state curriculum policy and what goes on in a child's mind.'

Serena realised that what was going on in her mind at that precise moment was something that the three professors would never, and could never, know. Her attention had been caught by the tall Dane who had entered the bar and seemed to be observing them from a distance. She was searching around in her memory banks, constructing an identity for him based on people she had met in the past. The professorial interchange had faded to a background buzz and she had only been brought back to the matter in hand by those arresting words.

	French	Maths	Civic attitudes	Sociability
Context				
Parent support	++	+		
Parents' high expectations	++	+		
Peer motivation	++	+		
Class level variables				
Pupils say teachers are competent and fair	+	+	++	++
Teaching is seen as structured	+	+	++	++
Good relationships with teachers	+	+	++	++
Good discipline and little time lost in classes	+	+	+	+
Opportunity to learn	++	++	+	
Formative evaluation	+	+	++	++
School level				
Importance of support for learning	+	+		+
Careful monitoring of truancy	+	+		+
Punishments for misbehaviour are clear and well known	+	+	+	
Teachers regard the school as having a good reputation		++		

Figure 7.2 Variables related to effectiveness: French middle schools 1990–94 (adapted from Grisay, 1997)

'Is that what self-evaluation does?' she asked. 'Try to find out what's going on in your mind?'

'Yes,' said the British professor.

'Mmm,' said the French professor.

'Maybe,' suggested the Austrian professor, 'maybe we'll be able to do that one day. The technology already exists to photograph activity in people's brains, so we may not be able to tell what you are thinking but we can tell how you are thinking.'

'What do you mean?' said Arthur, leaning forward with new interest.

'It's called thermal imaging. It photographs the hot spots in the brain, the kaleidoscope of patterns changing every second or microsecond. Thermal images can report on you, like lie detector tests, whether you are emotionally involved, bored, half asleep, or buzzing with creativity.'

Serena was reminded of something they had read in the literature class. It was about the brain described as 'the Enchanted Loom', perpetually weaving a picture of the world, tearing down and reweaving, inventing new worlds in the mind. She had never forgotten those words and the powerful image they carried.

'My eminent colleague is, as usual, three or four steps ahead of the rest of us', said the French professor. It sounded to Serena like a mixture of admiration and admonition. She was pleased to see that experts could have their disagreements too.

'The point is simply this,' said the French professor, 'if we want schools to improve we can't just take all of these effectiveness characteristics off the shelf and ask people to apply them. They shouldn't be like some kind of iron collar. We have to find out for ourselves what matters in our own schools. We have to dig deeper and we have to do our own digging. But the research gives us a very helpful starting point, a useful framework.'

Serena was still captivated by the thought of these multi-coloured patterns inside her brain. It was a frightening thought that some day someone might open up her head and look inside.

'Have you ever seen that book, *The Seven Habits of Highly Effective People?*' the British professor asked. They all shook their heads.

'It's a very interesting book,' he said. 'You probably wouldn't argue with the importance of any of the seven habits. But having them all might not actually make you effective and certainly we would find very effective people with only a few of those habits. And we might find some very "good" people with none of those habits. We will probably never, as long as human beings are human beings, be able to reduce human life and human interaction to a simple formula. But that doesn't mean that we can't learn, that we can't find some general principles.'

Serena was finding herself more absorbed with the body language of the two 'eminent colleagues' than with what they were saying. The British professor was slowly retreating to the back of his chair while, as if in concert, the French professor leaned forward. It was if they were reading one another's unspoken signals – my turn to speak; OK, I'm just finishing.

'Imagine if we could take all the eleven or twelve effectiveness characteristics from our two lists and just impose them in an authoritarian way, in the hope that we could guarantee greater effectiveness. But in the process we destroyed the good relations among teachers, and diminished their capacity to face new situations together or share in problem solving. You might possibly increase effectiveness in the short term, for a year, say, but certainly not in the long run.'

'Isn't this the nub of the problem?' added the British professor. 'If you treat these characteristics each as somehow having a life of their own, then you reduce a school to a number of separate parts. As if discipline was one thing and quality of learning and teaching another and relationships something else. So we often end up with a kind of "bits and pieces" approach to school improvement. We end up with discipline policies and homework policies and equal opportunities policies and so on. We should really be thinking about these things as an interconnected series of levers. Pull one and they all move.'

He pulled a length of string from his pocket. 'You know what a cat's cradle is?' he asked.

Three heads shook simultaneously. The professor asked Zoe to put out both hands and he began to construct a web between thumbs and fingers. Serena, who had never known it by that name, immediately recognised the game she had played many years ago with her father. She leaned forward and plucked two of the interconnecting strings, transforming the web into a new, more intricate, design. Zoe, who now also recognised the game, responded with a deft movement of thumbs and forefingers, transforming the web again into another configuration. Arthur looked on in amazement as if it had all been rehearsed.

'The cat's cradle,' said the British professor, 'is a pretty good metaphor for school improvement, don't you think?'

Serena wasn't too sure she saw the connections but hoped that all would soon become clear. The British professor continued: 'Well, one way of looking at school improvement is to have a set of criteria, just like the ones we've been talking about, and use these, over time, to assess whether or not you are getting better as a school. That's what you did with the self-evaluation profile isn't it?'

Three heads nodded.

'But I guess you found that it was hard to separate each of these twelve criteria. Or to do something about them, because you pull one and everything else moves.'

'When we looked at the quality of learning and teaching we found we were also talking about time as a resource, academic achievement, school as a learning place', Arthur agreed.

'In other words, it's a dynamic process,' said the professor. 'That's what I understand by school improvement. It starts where school effectiveness leaves off but it can't move far without it.'

'Like Siamese twins,' suggested Zoe.

The Austrian professor laughed and added 'great!' Serena judged it a nice laugh. She liked the way he listened intently to what they were saying, as if it was important.

'But remember this,' said the British professor, 'just as school effectiveness has fifty-seven varieties, so does school improvement. It means different things to different people. For example ... '

He stopped and stroked his beard as if he might find there the example he was looking for. Serena wondered what patterns were weaving in his brain, what kaleidoscope of colours was forming and reforming at that precise moment.

'An eminent colleague of mine from Cambridge,' he began, winking at Serena complicitly as if he knew she would share the joke, 'argues that school improvement is what we can measure in terms of so called "value added" over and above the natural progress that all schools make year on year. Standards are rising generally, but in improving schools they stay ahead of the expected, or average, increase in attainment.'

'That's a very limiting definition of improvement,' said the Austrian professor. 'It's about improvement in a sense, of course, but it doesn't say anything about the capacity of the school, about the school as a learning organisation.'

Seeing the students' puzzlement, he continued: 'It simply means an organisation in which everyone is a learner. And as everyone learns and shares their learning, the organisation itself becomes a learner, too. So if you can think of your school as having a high IQ, constantly learning from its mistakes, constantly becoming more intelligent, you could justifiably call it a learning organisation.'

There was a short silence. Arthur seemed to be turning this over in his mind; Zoe was thoughtfully studying her shoes; Serena's attention had been taken by the tall Dane who was now standing at the end of the bar. She wanted to go over and ask him to join them. She switched her thoughts from background to foreground. The British professor was speaking.

'That word "capacity" is frequently used by school improvement people. It describes improvement not so much in terms of student outcomes as in terms of improving the capacity of the school to go on getting better, to handle change, to plan, to deal with crises and problems. Let me take an example: here we have an Arthur – that is your name, isn't it?'

Arthur nodded.

'Well, one way of finding out if this Arthur is improving or not is by measuring his attainment at the ages of nine and eleven and fifteen and saying yes, we have definite signs of improvement, over and above what we might have expected of Arthur at each of those ages. He's clearly an improving student. That is one valid way of describing improvement. There is another, but it is considerably more difficult to get a handle on. We could, if we had such a thing as a capacity measure, try to ascertain how Arthur is going to be able to go on learning in the future once he has left school – when he is twenty, twenty-five, fifty-five. That would tell us something more important than the here and now. It would tell us about something enduring, an inner resilience, an inner capacity. Remember that overhead transparency from the speaker this morning – "it doesn't matter how many A-Levels they acquire, it is the capacity to go on learning once they have left school that matters" – remember that?'

They did remember it, and nodded agreement.

'So, by analogy, we might apply the same argument to the school as an organisation. Has it learned enough to equip it to go on learning? Is there a strong seed and a culture to help it grow? That word culture is used a lot, in fact it's a bit overused, but it's a good word because in its biological sense, it describes the conditions for growth.'

Serena was suddenly back with Mr Ericson and his story of the Scottish scientist who had left a culture in his laboratory and it had grown a furry fungus which gave the world penicillin and saved the life of a young woman in Long Island when all hope had gone.

'We have to think of improvement in all these ways,' said the professor. 'It isn't easy to get real proof of the link between culture and outcomes but we have strong reasons to believe that there is a link, don't we?'

The professor looked for confirmation and support from his French colleague, who had been uncharacteristically silent for some time.

'Indeed, we believe there is such a link or we wouldn't have embarked on this project. And it's stronger than just a belief. Culture, or ethos, is one of the characteristics that emerges most consistently from all the studies that have been conducted all over the world. I have some findings from a study which may throw some light on this. Here we are – I made three copies for you.'

Schools	Management	Teachers	Teaching	Pupils
Ineffective	Aloof relations with teachers (e,f) Lacking or purely administrative (f) No coherence among the management team (e)	Difficulties are said to come from external factors (e,f) Conflicts among teachers (f) High absenteeism (e)	Quality of teaching very different in 'weak' and 'strong' classes (e) Discipline is seen as a precondition for teaching and learning (e)	Discipline is maintained through punishment (e) Teachers criticise the pupils' work or achievement (f)
Effective	Management team share the same goals (e) Participative (in low SS schools) or *laissez-faire* (in high SES schools) (f)	Teachers agree on the purposes of schooling, share the same spirit (e,f)	High expectations, interest in academic performance and in instruction (e)	School has good relations with parents (e,f) Discussions between staff and pupils as soon as a problem appears (e) Praise and reward culture (e)

Figure 7.3 Differences between very contrasting schools (adapted from Cousin and Guillemet, 1992 and Sammons *et al.*, 1998)

The professor solemnly distributed the papers to the three students (see Figure 7.3). 'Sorry there isn't one for you,' he apologised to his fellow experts. 'This paper compares high schools which were ineffective over a period of several years with others that were very effective. They belong to this little group of either very effective or very ineffective schools. It draws on two studies – one French and one English – in both cases using interviews in a small number of schools. You will see a small "e" where it refers to the English schools and an "f" where it is the French. You will also see that the results are rather similar, even if the dimensions which were investigated were not exactly the same. For instance, the French study does not investigate the teaching dimension.'

'What I think this shows', said the professor, 'is quite marked differences between schools at opposite ends of the spectrum of effectiveness. For instance, agreement, coherence, interest in pupils and emphasis on teaching appear to be characteristics of the very effective schools while the very ineffective ones are at the opposite end. From a school improvement point of view we don't know what are consequences and what are causes, but it does point us in some useful directions, doesn't it?'

'It must be pretty bad to be in those really ineffective schools,' said Arthur. 'If teachers are in conflict with each other how would they ever agree on how to do evaluation and if they couldn't do that, how could they improve?'

'There is the problem in a nutshell,' answered the Professor. 'If all the problems and difficulties are seen as coming from somewhere else, from the outside, it won't be easy for staff to agree on what needs to be done. That's why these schools may need some external pressure as well as support if they are going to improve. In these schools self-evaluation will not be easy, at least not without a lot of help, and it may not even be sufficient.'

'But,' objected Arthur, 'aren't these just people's opinions about what is "good" or "effective"?' – borrowing the professor's air-mark technique and clicking his fingers in space around the spoken words.

The French professor replied, punctuating his deliberative statement with bold underlining: 'But don't forget … go back to what I was saying earlier about the French study. Pupils say teachers are competent, teachers say the school has a good reputation … These are opinions, yes, but they are still valid measures. We have found that the judgement of the students was pretty much right, perhaps even more right than the judgements of any of the other stakeholders. In other words, when the students said that their teachers were effective, the measurement of pupils' progress confirmed that. We concluded that students' judgements, perhaps not on every single teacher, but on the global quality of teaching, are a valid and important part of how we go about evaluation procedures. And we have learned that evaluation has to address the question of how pupils learn, how they value their life in the school, the kind of support they receive, the relations they have with their teachers. It is only as we struggle to understand these processes, and how to affect them, that we will be able to improve our schools.'

The French professor suddenly looked tired. He had drunk three Austrian coffees which weren't of the strength he was used to – he hadn't wanted to order a beer in front of the students. He moved swiftly to the benediction.

'I hope you have answers to your questions, young people. I hope you will take these ideas, these research findings, more as pointers, a set of suggestions rather than as prescriptions. There are a lot of things we don't know. But that's the fun, finding out.'

The three youngsters were also tired. As the male present, Arthur offered thanks on behalf of the three, assuming that prerogative.

'Thank you very much, professor. We have learned a lot. We have some answers and a lot more questions. Thank you, sir. And thanks to your two eminent colleagues', said Arthur, trying hard, but unsuccessfully, to conceal the mimicry.

Out again in the hotel lobby, Serena turned to look back. There was something the professor had said that she wanted confirmed. She retraced her steps and found the professor about to order his long-awaited beer.

'Is it true that, we, the students, are so important in evaluation?'

The professor smiled.

'Oh, yes. You are the ones who are doing the learning, aren't you? All that we can do, your teachers as well as us as researchers, is to find ways of helping you do it better.'

'Thank you,' said Serena, 'I enjoyed it'.

'Goodbye, Serena,' said the professor.

She had hardly taken two steps when the professor called her back.

'You might like to read this paper,' he said, holding out an eight-page document which looked like a chapter from a book. Serena read the title out loud – *A Change of Story*. 'See that man over there by the bar?' said the professor, pointing towards the sole occupant of the long, polished oak counter. Serena recognised the tall Dane.

'You might like to go and talk to him about it,' he suggested.

A Change of Story. Serena sensed the opening of a new chapter. She settled down to read the paper.

The professor ordered his beer.

8 A change of story

The story is told of the time traveller from the last year of the nineteenth century visiting his hometown one century into the future. Bewildered by the scale and nature of the social landscape, he finds a reassuring stability when he visits a school. Many of the structures are familiar; teachers and students occupy familiar roles and the curriculum contains much that is known to him. Most changes are mainly superficial and his delight is enhanced by learning of the 'back to basics' movement and the public nostalgia for bygone times when there was rigour, discipline and a commitment to standards. He is, however, bemused to discover, despite the scale of social upheaval, that the school has come to occupy a more and more central place in the society of 2000. He is also puzzled by a heightened expectation on schools and teachers to compensate for the perceived failures of church, family and social services.

The time traveller might well be bemused. We now expect more of teachers. They are required to cope with and adjust to the needs of children and young people growing up in an environment and with a set of social pressures which they themselves struggle to come to terms with. At the same time, and from a different direction, they have to deal with the demands of policy makers, politicians and media to do better, to raise standards, to demonstrate value for money, to add value where other agencies have failed.

In evaluating the effectiveness of schools and teachers we have to be acutely aware of these two sets of prevailing forces, the downward pressure from the policy context and the upward pressure from the pupils who carry with them into the classroom the anxieties, aspirations and limitations that are their social and economic legacy.

A world fit for young people?

In July 1999 three English teenagers were sent to jail for intimidation, extortion and drug dealing. They had built an extensive network of debtors – children and young people of their own age – trapped into becoming pushers to pay off their escalating debts to the gang, too afraid to tell their parents, too scared to alert the police, not so much because of the consequences of the law as because of the retribution they might face from their terrorist peers. When parents eventually became aware of their children's deteriorating school grades and declining physical and psychological health they joined the conspiracy of silence because they shared their children's fear of the authorities on the one hand and the adolescent enforcers on the other. The leader and inspiration of this network, Rocky Roberts, had started pushing drugs at the age of thirteen and within five years had made £300 000 from his expanding drug empire. It respected no boundaries of class, race, gender or academic ability and reached into the lives of the most and least privileged of families.

This story could have been told in virtually any European country, community or school. The drug culture is simply one facet of a society into which the children of the new millennium are being introduced. But the culture, if indeed there is a singular term to describe it, is multi-faceted. It is kaleidoscopic in character and might be characterised as a materialist or consumer culture, a designer culture, a hedonistic 'me-first' culture, a fast track culture, a virtual society – but none of these would be adequate to describe the world which children and young people have to make sense of and attempt to come to terms with. And, because it is 'grown-ups' who conduct the research and write the journal articles and books, the adolescent world is necessarily viewed and described from an adult perspective.

We can in part shed light on youth culture through a perusal of the statistics: hours of television watched; what money is spent on; where and how young people spend their leisure time; employment and unemployment statistics; the job market with its changing profile of needs and the changing demands of employers; the disparity between the richest and poorest; the rising incidence of teenage pregnancy; instances of sexual, racial and sectarian violence; suicide.

The local context

While we can, to some extent, evaluate the youth culture in such quantitative terms, we also need the qualitative, 'thick' description of a typical European classroom with its cast of characters, sharing a common culture in one sense but with widely varying experiences of, and response to, that culture. We may take as exemplars three young people, who could be found in any European school.

Serena, sixteen, lives with her mother, a lone parent since her husband's premature death. Both parents took a close interest in Serena's development in her infant years and she started school articulate and keen to learn. Shortly after the death of Serena's father, her mother became unemployed when the local textile factory closed down, but she has struggled for five years to provide Serena with what she needs to be able to keep material pace with others in her class – designer clothes and adolescent toys. She has so far resisted Serena's urgent need for a mobile phone – 'like all her friends'. As Serena moved from primary to secondary school, a gulf opened up between Serena and her mother as Serena held more tightly to her independence and 'adult' status. From her mother's point of view she had grown up too fast; at fourteen already sexually mature but, her mother prayed, not yet sexually active. But she recognised how vulnerable Serena's innocence and undoubted attractiveness made her. On the other hand, the darkness of her skin had made her subject to racial abuse and harassment and forced her into a constant battle against the expectations of others that, as an Asian girl, she would not progress far beyond school, would be required to marry someone she had never met and settle down to a life of subjugation.

Serena has had to cope with being cast in other people's moulds and to try to change their conceptions of who she is and what she wants to become. She has to work hard at bridging the worlds of school, home and community. There are worlds in which Serena lives which teachers never see and from which they are carefully and consciously excluded.

Hans is a classmate of Serena's. He has a brother two years younger than himself, a mother who runs her own company and a father who works for a large multinational company as a human resources manager. As a child Hans enjoyed the close attention of his mother and the occasional visits from his father, but for the last five years, since his mother started her own company, he has seen less and less of either parent. His mother sometimes does not return home until 8 p.m. at night and his father's presence at home is erratic. Reluctantly, Hans looks after his younger brother and sometimes has to provide him with an evening meal – four minutes in the microwave. Hans is conscientious about his homework, using his state-of-the-art PC that he also uses for many hours to surf the Net. Some of what he finds he puts into special locked files accessible only with a password. In his father's presence he is careful never to put a foot wrong because he has been trained from his earliest years to respond reflexively to authority, and to a father who expects him to excel with no excuse for failure. Now at sixteen, with less and less surveillance, Hans is beginning to find more scope to escape the watchful eye of his father and has become skilled at persuading his mother of his honesty in all things. He has successfully convinced his teachers that he is simply a diligent, hard-working and thoroughly obedient student.

Daniel is in the same class as Serena and Hans. His father and mother separated when he was eleven. For two years after the split he stayed on and off with his father, but since his father remarried and moved further away he has seen little of him. His mother has enjoyed a series of 'boyfriends', one of whom drinks heavily and hits Daniel's mother when she speaks to other men or displeases him in some other way. He once hit Daniel, too, after which Daniel stayed away from home for three days, spending the night in shop doorways until picked up by the police and returned home to his hysterical mother, who expressed her deep regret and asked Daniel for forgiveness, treating him to expensive presents.

After that incident Daniel stayed out of the house when his mother and her boyfriend were drinking, wandering the streets or staying overnight with people he met. In his third and fourth years of secondary school Daniel's attendance became increasingly erratic, sometimes missing school for a week a time. When the school wrote numerous letters and eventually phoned Daniel's mother she promised to ensure Daniel's attendance but her good intentions were never sustained for long and appointments made for Daniel's mother to visit the school were never observed. When Daniel did come to class he remained absent in spirit and even his best teachers found it impossible to engage his interest for long.

Although it was a matter of much speculation in the staffroom, Daniel's inner life remained a largely inaccessible mystery.

Typically, teachers in European schools have not only three, but twenty to thirty pupils in their classroom, with a diversity of social and psychological backgrounds, making the term 'homogeneous grouping' a term of minimal usefulness, relevant only to a highly specific and temporal context.

The policy making context

The class in which Serena, Hans and Daniel meet and pass through on their way to different economic destinations seems a world away from the national and European seats of power and influence. Yet they are intimately, if often obscurely, connected. In Prague, Budapest and Tampere, European ministers meet to discuss their common concerns and address how to move their respective systems forward. Simultaneously, high-level officials are meeting in Brussels, Copenhagen and London. In Luxembourg and Vienna, within the context of one European project, policy advisers meet with headteachers, teachers and students and take back powerful messages to their respective governments. Serena is one small voice, but one thing she said about her school experience will be quoted in ministerial speeches in Lisbon, Rome and Reykjavik. The student perspective is one with an increasing appeal to policy makers and politicians because of its compelling and authentic character.

The past few years have witnessed frenetic activity around the globe to exchange information and ideas, and to come to terms with the concept of quality and standards in education. We can identify three key reasons for these issues becoming a priority for discussion on an international scale. These may be described as:

- The resource argument
- The social inclusion argument
- The knowledge society argument.

The resource argument

The quest for quality in education has been driven in part by numbers, by swelling percentages of students using the education system for longer and longer periods of their lives. This has required a commensurate increase in resources devoted to schools and to further and higher education. These have increased in all industrialised countries during the last thirty years. At the same time, international surveys in the field of education, such as the Third Mathematical and Science Study (TIMSS), International Educational Assessment (IEA), Key Data on Education in Europe (EURYDICE) and Education at a Glance (OECD) have gathered data on resource provision and expenditure, linking these to structures and outcomes of education systems. The international perspective which these surveys has brought has made it possible not only to compare specific indices but has opened a cross-border debate on a whole range of educational issues. All European policy makers now want to know the relative performance of their own national system. The debate serves to focus public and political attention on how one's own country is faring internationally at key stages within the education system, at eleven, at sixteen, or at entry to higher education. A low score raises concerns about continued prosperity and economic and social development. It focuses priorities and drives policy. It demands that action be seen to be taken.

The social inclusion argument

Another reason for the high priority given to education is that in many countries it is seen as the solution to problems of employment and social cohesion. The argument runs like this.

National economies are becoming more and more interdependent within a global economy in which trade between countries is blossoming. Developing countries are becoming more and more efficient producers of industrial products – steel, ships, cars, and so on. Salaries in these countries are substantially lower than in developed ones; free trade makes it possible for developing countries to market their products in the developed world, hence people working in directly competing sectors have to become more efficient or face salary decreases and lay-offs. Writing on the dangerously insidious effects of global capitalism, Haq and Kirdar (1986) warn 'Poverty can wait, the banks cannot'.

In developed economies, as in countries most vulnerable to new market forces, politicians have to react to the dilemma posed by the global economy, and their principal answer is education. Reflecting a tendency in many Western countries, the three priorities of the political programme of the New Labour government in Britain are 'Education, Education and Education'. The rationale for this policy was that only by educating people can they be made less vulnerable to the forces of globalisation. Only by equipping them with marketable skills and competencies can countries avoid the squeeze of the global economy, and keep their societies from breaking apart.

The knowledge society argument

A third reason for the intensified focus on quality and standards is the knowledge explosion. Societies are becoming increasingly complex, information rich and technocratic. Robert Reich (1991) develops a scenario in which he describes three economic boats: one sinking rapidly, one sinking more slowly and one rising rapidly. The first – sinking – boat contains the routine producers; the second contains the in-service workers; the third, the rapidly rising boat, contains the symbolic analysts, the people who identify, solve and broker problems in the world of new information.

The flow of new information and the rise of international co-operation make for a rapidly renewing civil and working life. Through education, individuals need to adapt by assembling their own qualifications, building blocks of knowledge through the formal education system, on the job or in a more informal way. Learning throughout life becomes the key to controlling the future on a professional and personal level, allowing people to take part in societies as active, and proactive, citizens.

There appears to be wide agreement that good quality in the education system is of vital importance for the survival and development of national economies. But what is 'quality' in education and how is it to be achieved? There is no simple answer, no easy consensus, no secret formula.

The definition of quality in education is a matter for political debate and part of the democratic process. The debate is about objectives, means to achieve those objectives, economic priorities, knowledge about what education is, the learning processes which underpin it and the contexts in which these can most effectively occur. It has to take account of the needs and expectations of the wider society but at the same time educate those needs and expectations. The education that people experienced a generation ago is not the education that will best serve their own children.

What are the central elements of this political debate? What are the objectives of the education system and what are some of the means by which these objectives can be realised? How do we go about quality evaluation at school level, and what is the purpose and role of self-evaluation?

Education for work

An objective of the education system, increasingly predominant in the minds of policy makers, is to prepare pupils for the labour market. The structures and requirements of this market are changing rapidly and there is great uncertainty about the qualifications that will be needed in the future world of work. At the same time, there are doubts as to whether rationalisation in industry and commerce will leave enough employment opportunities for all. Knowledge is becoming outdated at ever-shorter intervals: it is estimated that about 80 per cent of the technologies applied today will be obsolete ten years from now. This makes it problematic for education or enterprise to identify and define what should be learned, at what stage and what the most appropriate place for learning is.

One response to this is to accept that the education system should focus on general skills of learning to learn, on the capacity to go on acquiring and reformulating knowledge long after school days are past. Linked to this, a case is made for social and life skills which are applicable in a range of human contexts: co-operation; team working; information handling; problem solving; decision making; adaptability and so on. This line of argument focuses on the competencies that the individual should possess in order to adapt to and contribute to changes in society. It is stressed that in the current and in the future workspace, more and more work will take place in teams. When problems and solutions are addressed and shared in teams, communication and negotiation skills come into their own. Other skills at a premium include the ability to accept criticism positively, to give credit to others and to be able to accept responsibilities within the team. This is in stark contrast to what frequently happens in schools, where the focus is on individualistic skills. Co-operation is often discouraged, particularly in the exam situation, preparation for which is such a driving force for so much of the work of the classroom.

A study group instituted by the European Commission in 1997 specifies these skills somewhat further:

> The current period is one of the development of autonomous and fully-rounded persons, who possess key competencies founded on basic knowledge and social skills. The social skills include, in particular, methods for learning with a view to adaptability, being conversant with information technologies, communication skills, the capacity to work as a part of a team and to develop partnerships as well as to take individual responsibilities … Most simply, these skills involve making the familiar strange and strange familiar: being able to switch between standpoints and identify positions, and between empathy and critical distance. Learning these skills is to some extent a matter of using techniques and of training observational–analytical capacities, but it is also a matter of having the confidence to switch position – in particular, to regard oneself critically and to tolerate personal and social ambiguities and contradictions.

Another line of argument focuses on standards in core skills and subjects – reading, writing, mathematics, science and languages. This argument rests on the premise that there is a growing number of young people unable to master the simplest skills and that, as a consequence, these pupils are excluded from society. It is argued that in a time of major changes where future skill demands are not certain, the very least the school system can do is to ensure that all pupils have reached an acceptable level in key skills and knowledge. The advantage of focusing on basic skills is that pupils have a clear idea of what is expected, can acquire necessary basic proficiencies, and so have a better opportunity of participating in the labour market on equal terms. From this viewpoint it may be argued that co-operative skills, reflective skills and competence in problem solving can be developed through reading, writing and other subject disciplines. A further advantage of focusing on these skills is that they are relatively easy to measure and therefore politicians, local/municipal authorities, schools, school leaders and teachers can be held accountable for pupils' performance.

The discussion on how to best prepare pupils for the labour market is, however, in danger of advancing down blind alleys, since research into the learning processes has still not been able to say with confidence how and where pupils learn best and how schools can most effectively support their learning. Nor do we know what knowledge and skills young people actually put to use in their day-to-day work or leisure. As school systems all over Europe continue to fail a substantial minority of their pupils, there is an urgent need to re-examine the what, how, when and where of learning.

Education for life

Entry into the labour market is not the sole or even primary objective of education. Education has always pursued broader personal, social and academic goals. Changes in society and particularly in the role of the family as a social institution have sharpened the focus on those wider, deeper, timeless goals for education. Parents (or a lone parent) are no longer at home full time, and they are therefore not able to provide education and socialisation to the same extent. Schools have had to take over larger and larger parts of what was previously considered a task for the family. The objectives of education in many countries may therefore include the following aims:

• To contribute to the mental, physical, artistic and social development of pupils.
• To prepare pupils to take active part in a democratic society, that is, enabling them to take on responsibilities, to understand rights and obligations and to contribute to the peaceful development of their society.
• To develop understanding of their own and other cultures, and an acceptance of other ways of organising societies.
• To give them the 'tools' for leading a successful life in every sense of the word.

In most European countries it is significant that pre-school education is becoming more and more commonplace. While the nature of pre-school education is an area for debate, most governments and experts agree that early childhood experience has a crucial determining influence on intellectual and personality development and subsequent social integration.

How to achieve objectives in education?

In the following section, we will focus on simply a few of these policy or 'political' instruments, namely the instruments of decentralisation, external evaluation and self-evaluation, all three of which are closely interconnected. The interrelationship of these within a legislative framework is illustrated in Figure 8.1.

Decentralisation

Decentralisation has been described as a 'mega trend' (Caldwell, 1993), an overriding force, impelled less by educational considerations than by financial and political imperatives. Many European educational systems have experienced great changes during the last two decades, involving more autonomy, accountability and responsibility for schools. In The Netherlands and the United Kingdom schools have the greatest degree of autonomy, but in Belgium (the Flemish community), Denmark, Finland and Sweden most decisions are now also taken at school level. In Italy, a reform which involves a great degree of school autonomy has been mooted since 1997. In Austria, reforms in 1993–4 enhanced the autonomy of the schools.

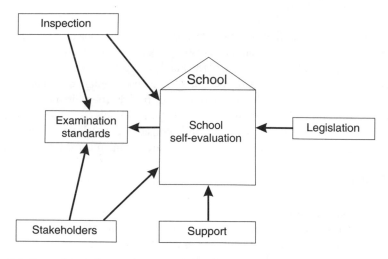

Figure 8.1 Interrelationships within a legislative framework.

The process of decentralisation means that a larger degree of decision-making power is devolved to lower levels of the education system. It may be seen as an instrument for bringing the political debate on quality into the arena of school and classroom.

The tendency to decentralisation keeps company with the lack of trust in the state's capacity to provide an adequate answer to each and every need of an increasingly demanding population. Stated differently, it acknowledges that there are no right answers and that people most affected by the decision should have a role in taking those decisions.

Decentralisation may be used to empower people who have the least power, making them responsible for defining what they understand by quality in education and giving them 'ownership' and a stakeholding in the education system. The process of decentralisation is often seen not only as inevitable but also as positive. However, it poses problems, too. Since it is the responsibility of the state to ensure that quality education is for everyone, it has to assure itself that at every level this objective is being met. Decentralisation can lead to differences in standards between schools within a country, so making it incumbent on national or regional bodies to monitor standards; to ensure that inter-school differences do not deny opportunities or hinder pupils from achieving their full potential.

If the driving force of decentralisation is political rather than educational, it is incumbent on educators to respond proactively, with measures that are primarily in the interests of pupils, teachers and parents. Quality evaluation at school level is one strategic mechanism that can inform governments, raise awareness and support schools in the management of decentralisation.

Quality evaluation as a counterbalancing force

The evaluation of quality is not new, but it has assumed a significantly higher pro-file as a consequence of decentralisation. It may be defined as the endeavour to understand educational processes and products, to monitor and assure that those processes are congenial, user friendly and effective; to ascertain that not only do they produce the desired outcomes, but are of themselves educative, both in the present and in the longer term. There are essentially two main approaches to qual-ity evaluation, namely external and internal or self-evaluation.

External evaluation

External evaluation may be justified on the grounds of need at centralised level to control and guide schools. This is at a higher premium in systems which are decen-tralised. Centralised systems which prescribe and control inputs (curriculum, form, content and so on) and have a high level of standardised practice, tend to place less reliance on monitoring and external evaluation. In decentralised systems, on the other hand, with less emphasis on control of input, greater emphasis has to be given to the monitoring and control of output. As schools become more autonomous in the financial, managerial and sometimes the curricular domain, there is a commen-surately greater need for checks and balances.

External evaluation, whether by central government or at a more localised level, whether through inspection or other quality assurance mechanisms, attempts to ensure that quality education is provided, that schools use resources efficiently and that they provide value for money. It has the task of ensuring that differences in school standards are not too discrepant and that agreed outcomes are met. External evaluation also raises the public's general awareness of quality issues by publishing reports on the general health of the education system or of specific schools. While external evaluation is driven primarily by a need for accountability, it may combine this with an improvement perspective. It can give impetus to school improvement by providing comparative data which can then be used as a management tool for focusing on a school's performance in comparison with others. External evaluation can offer feedback to schools on their strengths and weaknesses, drawing up action points, offering support or resources to meet their targets.

Of all the member states of the European Union, it is in The Netherlands and the United Kingdom that schools have the greatest degree of autonomy at primary and lower secondary level. It is therefore no surprise that the external evaluation system is most developed in these two countries. In both there has also been a con-certed move to implement self-evaluation and to find the best kind of balance between the internal/external relationship.

Self-evaluation

Self-evaluation is underpinned by a different rationale. While it also has an accountability purpose, its primary impulse is developmental. It is an intrinsic feature of effective schools and professional practice but acquires an extra urgency from decentralisation. From a policy perspective, self-evaluation is viewed as a mechanism for empowering schools themselves to improve quality from within, helping them to monitor their progress and to report accurately to their external constituencies – parents and the wider public. It is seen as contributing to the democratic debate as to what constitutes quality at school and classroom level and complementing the work of external agencies. From a school perspective, self-evaluation has a more immediate purpose. Dialogue is focused more on the internal stakeholders and their contribution to planning and improvement at classroom, school and community levels. To achieve this effectively requires the involvement of all relevant actors, and access to instruments which can best support decision making, learning and teaching.

We could describe self-evaluation, then, as having two primary functions:

1   To stimulate dialogue on objectives, priorities, and quality criteria at school and classroom level; and
2   To achieve objectives through the use of appropriate and easily accessible tools.

Self-evaluation is an intrinsic and necessary component of school improvement. As it develops within a school, the systematic gathering and judgement of information becomes a routine and integral aspect of planning and school development. Self-evaluation is based on the premise that collectives and organisations can learn – not just individuals. Like individuals, organisations are proactive and reactive: they lose and gain energy, and they acquire and learn intelligence.

We find it difficult to think of 'intelligence' in different ways from those we have been brought up to. We are accustomed to thinking of intelligence as if it is something that exists inside people's heads; we tend not to conceive of intelligence as lying 'out there' in the environment, in between people. But, as many theorists now argue, intelligence is created in the interaction between people and between people and things. The psychologist David Perkins (1996) talks about 'distributed intelligence' and 'people-with' intelligence. This may be a group with a flipchart or a set of cards or a computer, engaged in creating something which is new and unique and evolves out of the interaction between them and the tools they are using.

Organisations, business enterprises, schools or universities become more intelligent by virtue of having at their disposal tools which can help them to see more clearly; tools which provide different lenses through which to understand the world of classrooms and the inner life of students. Intelligent tools are those which teachers can use to test and challenge beliefs, values and knowledge – their own and those of the school. A tool may be nothing more than a few words on a few lines of paper, not particularly intelligent of itself but powerful when brought into play to focus people's thinking; and, as thinking becomes spoken, emerging knowledge is available to be questioned, challenged and refined. As they use powerful instruments of evaluation, people modify their words, reorder their

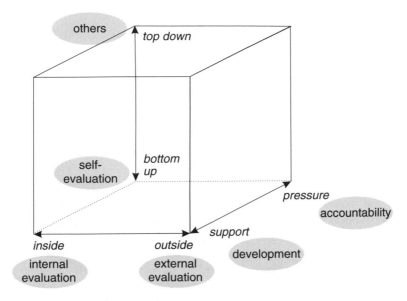

Figure 8.2 The cube model of evaluation.

thinking and look for evidence to support their ideas: this is called learning. This is intelligence in the making, and this is what Perkins means when he writes about 'smart schools' (1996).

In conclusion

The successful and lasting marriage between internal and external evaluation is the goal towards which European systems are striving. All countries can place themselves somewhere within the cube model (see Figure 8.2). The cube has three dimensions, which we can define as internal/external, pull/push and bottom-up/top-down. Within these three dimensions we can find one particular point which defines the nature and describes the process of evaluation. Finding this ideal point of balance is the challenge for all systems which seek to evaluate quality in a way that enhances the capacity of schools and teachers. Top-down approaches need bottom-up responses. External expectations have to meet internal needs, and pressure will not work without the push of some internal direction or vision.

To achieve their objectives for the education system, politicians and policy makers have a whole range of means at their disposal. They can use 'softer' strategies such as persuasion, enthusiasm, incentives and rewards. They can regulate through laws, and they can create institutions that guide, advise and control. They can draw on a repertoire of strategies in order to achieve what they consider the highest quality return for resources invested. They cannot, however, progress without the commitment of teachers, students and parents who 'are' the system and who have their own personal stake in quality, standards and improvement.

9 Self-evaluation
The power of three

When and how does self-evaluation begin? In response to the announcement of external inspection? With a management decision to audit quality and standards? Or with the entry into a project such as Evaluating Quality in School Education? The answer is in fact 'none of these', since self-evaluation can never be something entirely new. It should never be viewed as an imposition, as onerous or time-consuming, but as an essential and integral element of good teaching, meaningful learning, effective leadership and evidence-based management.

Schools are places of learning and teachers are natural evaluators of learning. They are trained to ask questions and to seek answers. They discuss their teaching and reflect on their triumphs and failures. 'That went well today' or 'that lesson was a complete disaster' are day-to-day evaluative comments. Teachers routinely assess the progress of their pupils; sometimes at an informal, intuitive level – 'She's learned nothing in the last year', 'She has come on in leaps and bounds' – or they may assess more formally through tests and examinations. The successes of their pupils are the benchmarks by which teachers judge themselves and it is only the most cynical of teachers who would regard pupil performance as having nothing to do with the quality of teaching.

In a real sense, therefore, self-evaluation has no beginning; it has no end, either, because it is always growing and improving. The task for the school is to continuously seek to make it better, more systematic, more rooted in reflection and evidence. Mature self-evaluation is so embedded in the day-to-day life of the school that it is invisible and indivisible.

Because self-evaluation is built into the ongoing life of the school, grounded in its unique history and individual context, there is no simple or single recipe for it. There is no magic solution; it can be approached through many doors. The American researcher, Bruce Joyce, uses the metaphor of interconnecting doors to describe the process of school improvement. It is a very helpful one in understanding how self-evaluation works. Self-evaluation is located in many places and takes many forms but it becomes systematised when it makes the connections, through a process which transforms a random maze into a sequenced and structured pattern. It builds on what is already there rather than trying to impose something entirely new.

There are many aspects of a school that may be evaluated, but, of course, all domains are not equally significant and some aspects assume more significance than others at a given time or place. Some aspects are, however, perennially important. Academic achievement will always be more important than the quality of the school grounds and buildings, and the critical nature of conditions for learning and wellbeing is universally recognised. Self-evaluation must, therefore, find the balance between the important and the peripheral, the universal and the specific, the ephemeral and the everlasting.

It has also to be mindful of the micropolitics of the process. Ernest House reminds us of the importance of multiplicity:

> The field of professional evaluation has faced a formidable problem of multiple values, criteria, methods, measures, and interests. After considerable experience and debate, a key development has been that multiple methods and measures should be used to collect data, and that multiple values and criteria are needed to judge a program's success, that multiple stakeholders might have different interests in the program, so different views and interests should be represented in an evaluation. (House, 1995: 33)

School life is a composite of multiple perspectives and the choice of an evaluative approach therefore requires a sensitivity to the complexity inherent in every aspect of school life. Complexity not only varies from country to country but also from school to school. Using evaluation methods with a view to reducing complexity is always a sensitive process with a 'political' underpinning and an implicit (and often explicit) power relationship. There is always the question of 'who decides?' For example:

- Who (what) defines the quality criteria?
- Who owns the data?
- What will the consequences be?

Collecting and handling information in self-evaluation is always an intervention of some kind and therefore a potential interference with people and the social situations they are in. So, applying methods in a self-evaluation exercise is not only a matter of working one's way through a certain procedure (for example, collecting data, interpreting data, presenting data), but also a continuous process of interpretation and negotiation (see Schratz, 1997: 17).

Comprehensiveness and selectivity: finding the balance

Schools do not have the time to evaluate every aspect of their operation and to do so would be a distraction from their main task. Selection of what to evaluate has therefore to be undertaken with care. It would be unhelpful to evaluate a domain in which things were going well and neglect areas in which things were going badly. It may be damaging to the morale of the majority to evaluate an issue of interest only to a small but powerful group of stakeholders. It could be misleading simply to evaluate innovative aspects of school life or to focus on one area to the detriment of another. There is a real danger in investing energy in some politically high profile areas of the curriculum at the expense of others. An increase in mathematics achievement, for example, might imply less time for geography; the question then for the school is 'Do we value improvement in maths enough to accept regression in geography?' Aware of the dangers in the American situation, Elliot Eisner (1991) counsels:

> We are all too impatient about attaining the educational ends that really matter. The press for accountability pushes us towards short term goals. We are too eager to settle for what is quickly demonstrable. We need to learn how to take a longer term view. (p. 23)

If self-evaluation is to be for school improvement, then it must be a participative process. Since it is designed for teachers, pupils and parents it should involve them, or their representatives, as far as possible at each stage in the process. It is important to reach agreement on what is to be evaluated before proceeding further. That was inherent in the purpose and rationale for the Socrates project 'Evaluating Quality in School Education' which was the stimulus for this book and helped significantly to shape our thinking.

The project involved 101 schools from eighteen countries, each one with a different starting point and prior history. They had widely differing structures and diverse national and cultural backgrounds. Some were quite advanced in their thinking about self-evaluation, some less travelled down that route. In some schools self-evaluation was already formalised while in others it was informal or embryonic in development. All schools, however, joined the project to learn more and made an agreement to employ a common instrument and work with a common set of tools. How they went about it and where it led them differed immensely, but it was that diversity and ownership of the process that gave the project its inspiration and impact.

The project had a number of important dimensions – a European substructure and imprimatur; direction and advice at national level; plus three key operational features:

- A self-evaluation profile
- A set of guidelines containing a wide repertoire of evaluation tools
- The support of a critical friend.

While together they comprise an inseparable trinity, each had a unique part to play and contribution to make.

The self-evaluation profile

The common instrument was known as the SEP or, to give its proper name, the self-evaluation profile. It is a very simple instrument, designed to help schools select for further evaluation and improvement those domains which matter most.

	++	+	–	– –	▲	↔	▼

Outcomes

	++	+	–	– –	▲	↔	▼
Academic achievement							
Personal and social development							
Student destinations							

Process at classroom level

	++	+	–	– –	▲	↔	▼
Time as a resource for learning							
Quality of learning and teaching							
Support for learning difficulties							

Process at school level

	++	+	–	– –	▲	↔	▼
School as a learning place							
School as a social place							
School as a professional place							

Environment

	++	+	–	– –	▲	↔	▼
School and home							
School and community							
School and work							

Figure 9.1 The school self-evaluation profile.

It consists of a set of twelve areas of school life which can be used to open up discussion about its quality and effectiveness. These are shown in Figure 9.1.

The twelve areas were chosen after lengthy discussion and examination of the literature on school quality and effectiveness. In a sense the SEP may be seen as a 'multi-level model', encompassing processes at individual, classroom, school and community level. The areas are by no means sacrosanct and spaces have been left on the SEP for people to add their own categories. It is significant, however, that in so many different countries and school systems the twelve categories proved to be relevant and robust.

In short, the SEP aimed to:

- Promote serious and purposeful discussion among all stakeholder groups, helping to create a culture for further inquiry and ongoing self-evaluation.
- Get a picture of the school as seen through the eyes of staff, students and parents.
- Help to identify and prioritise areas for deeper inquiry.

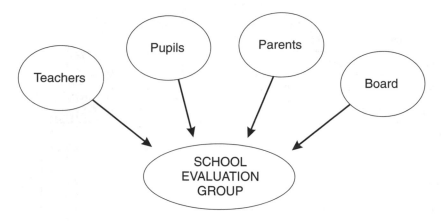

Figure 9.2 Stakeholder groups.

How it worked

For the purposes of this project, the systematic process of self-evaluation began with all schools filling in the SEP. Groups of stakeholders – pupils, teachers, parents, school management, governors, school boards or councils – all took part, making their own judgement about the school across each of the twelve domains. Some schools organised discrete groups of students, parents, teachers and so on. In other schools mixed groups were preferred. In both cases, however, this was only the first stage preceding the school evaluation group which, at a later stage, brought together representatives from each of the smaller groups to make up one large composite group. This consisted of eight to twelve people, drawing representatives from all constituencies. This is illustrated in Figure 9.2.

The school evaluation group was chaired either by someone within the school or by an outside 'neutral', such as the critical friend. His or her task was to lead the group through the twelve areas one by one, allowing time for discussion and debate. The group's task was to seek consensus wherever possible but to avoid compromise and to respect disagreement. It was also charged with constantly pressing for evidence, questioning grounds for assertion, considering where valid and reliable information might support the group's judgements.

The end result of this process did not provide a definitive statement or hard evidence but served as a 'door opener' to further systematic search for evidence in some specific areas. Schools were asked to choose five areas for further in-depth inquiry, one from each of the four main domains, plus one other. Some schools saw this as too much and selected fewer areas – in some cases only one, as, for example, in a Scottish school, which selected 'time as a resource for learning'. Such flexible decision making by the school was an important precondition for overall success at both project and individual school level.

The area, or areas, for further inquiry were chosen on a number of different grounds, for example because:

- There was a wide divergence of opinion on the issue.
- There was an apparent absence of evidence.
- It was an area of conspicuous weakness in the school.
- It was an area of good, or promising, practice on which the school wished to build further.

The self-evaluation was not an end in itself, but only the beginning of a process. What it managed to achieve was an opening-up of discussion, often in a way that had never been experienced before. It provided a forum in which headteachers, teachers, students and parents could express their views on an equal footing, 'leaving their position and status at the door'. Many schools reported that this was 're-freshing', 'challenging' or 'illuminating', because it offered new perspectives on long-standing problems, and gave a voice to people who previously had no medium through which to channel their views or openly express their real feelings.

Evaluation tools

Having chosen areas for further inquiry, the next step was to find the most appropriate tools of evaluation. There are many sources from which schools can draw, from research literature and a growing body of self-evaluation manuals. In times past these were researchers' tools, often jealously guarded and enveloped in mystique. Within the last few years these have become more readily available to schools and access can be had through libraries, bookstores or the Internet. Most schools are already using evaluation in some form – attainments tests, questionnaires, observation or interviews, for example. More and more, teachers are discovering how to use and customise tools, seeking support in, say, questionnaire design or in ensuring the reliability and validity of instruments used.

Schools in the European project were provided with a set of guidelines including a wide range of tools. Many of these could be used in different contexts and for different purposes and most schools used a variety of methods, adapting them to their own context, in some cases inventing new tools for themselves. However, experience has shown that tools should not be selected randomly without thought being given to the nature of the instrument and to the scope and limitations of its use. Before embarking on the choice of tools it is, therefore, useful to consider a number of questions. Figure 9.3 suggests some questions which can help in choosing the most suitable method for self-evaluation.

Figure 9.4 illustrates a simple framework in the use of the SEP from the selection of an area, to identification of evaluation criteria, devising of indicators and finally the selection of methods as appropriate to the task.

An example

This is how it worked in one school. Teachers, students and parents went through the SEP, looking in turn at strengths and weaknesses in the twelve main areas. After considerable discussion, the group identified 'Quality of learning and

Aim	What do you need it for?
Consequences	Who will use the results?
Side effects	What might the unintended consequences be?
Feasibility	Can you do it?
Practicality	Can it be put into practice within your existing framework?
Time	Does it fit the time constraints in your situation?
Balance	Does it cover depth or breadth?
Data	What are the expected data?
Involvement	Who will be involved in the process?
Time lag	How long will it take to get feedback?

Figure 9.3 How to choose the best method or instrument.

teaching' as the area in which there was most disagreement and which offered most scope for further inquiry. They went on to identify criteria for success in this area. For example:

- Pupils are helped to test their understanding of what the teachers are teaching.
- Teachers give prompt and helpful feedback on pupils' work.
- Homework among different subjects is distributed evenly across the week.
- Standards of marking are clear to everybody.

With these criteria as a guide, they considered appropriate indicators which would be transparent to teachers and pupils, framed in a way that would enable everyone to judge whether or not the criteria were being met. Examples of such criteria include:

- Provision is made for pupils to evaluate their understanding within each lesson sequence.
- Days for submission of homework tasks are agreed and observed by all teachers.
- Standards for the assessment of pupils' work are written down in each subject area and made available to pupils and parents.

Having agreed on indicators, the next step was to find appropriate methods to measure their success. The school decided to use the following methods:

- Working together, pupils and teachers develop a self-evaluation form for a pupil peer review. Pupils complete it in pairs.
- Pupils fill in a homework grid illustrating how they divide their time and balance subject demands at home.

Area	
Criteria	
Indicators	
Methods	

Figure 9.4 A simple framework in the use of the SEP.

- A questionnaire is developed and used with each year level to find out the standards teachers use in assessing pupils' work in their subject area.

When a school engages in this systematic process, it helps everyone involved to agree on where they are going and how they are going to get there, ensuring clear signposting en route. While this process can be short-circuited, it may lead to problems later on. We have found that people very typically proceed on the assumption that everyone shares the same understanding of terminology, uses or purpose. Misunderstandings can be avoided if time is taken to go carefully through the sequence of stages suggested above, clarifying meanings and resolving ambiguities. The process is likely to pay off in a deepening of understanding, refining and making explicit what might previously have been implicit or simply taken for granted.

The critical friend

One of the most valued aspects of the European project was the support and challenge offered by the critical friend. These friends were appointed to, or selected by, the school, and brought with them a wide variety of expertise from professional or lay backgrounds. They came with a simple mandate – to be a friend and critic of the school – but demanding a high level of sophisticated skills. He or she had to operate in a number of different arenas and with a variety of tasks. Some of those tasks included:

- Setting the scene, clarifying the purposes and creating the climate for the project.
- Helping to smooth the passage through the SEP.
- Advising on the selection and use of tools.

- Advising on data collection.
- Participating in the interpretation of data

One of the first things that a critical friend must appreciate is what Theodore Sizer (1984) has described as the intensity factor. The pace, demands and intensity of school life make it difficult for people to be reflective and objective, to extract themselves and stand back from the pressure of daily routine, to suspend the tyranny of the urgent and restrain the imperative of the unexpected. In the intense world of schools there is often only time to act and respond, to record or to use recordings to gain a perspective on your actions and reactions. Pressures to gather data may actually simply intensify other pressures and leave even less time for considered reflection and attention to what really matters. It is in this sense that Highett (1996) describes many schools as 'data-rich but information-poor'.

This is where critical friends have much to offer. They can help people to consider what is a real priority and what is within their own control. They can help to remind people of their core values and see for themselves the congruences and incongruences in their own behaviour. They can support heads and teachers in following their convictions and taking risks, breaking with precedent, making courageous decisions. They can give access to more systematic tools and strategies. They can share the burden of responsibility and lend a listening ear.

One of their most important roles is in helping people to engage with the data. Dealing openly and creatively with good data in a supportive climate can prove to be a motivating and empowering process. As we have learned, creating the space for management and teachers to stand back and review the school is a challenging, and at times disconcerting, experience, but it serves to open doors in thinking and in practice. The critical friend plays a crucial role in this, particularly when the data are ambiguous, and even more so when the data are unambiguously bad news.

The critical friend is a powerful idea, perhaps because of its inherent tension. Friends bring a high degree of unconditional positive regard. Critics are conditional, negative and intolerant of failure. Reconciliation of these Janus faces depends on a successful marrying of unconditional support and conditional critique, demanding, as Sarason (1986) argues, an 'exquisite sensitivity'.

There are many traps awaiting the outsider who is unaware of history and context, who can all too easily fall foul of hidden agendas and power struggles. It is a delicate and difficult role but potentially a very powerful one, as we have learned from this project. It is the 'third leg' which has to be present to balance the other two.

In the following chapters we deal with each of these three supporting legs in turn.

10 The SEP

What it is and how to use it

The Self-Evaluation Profile (SEP) (Figure 9.1 on page 97), consists of two components: a formal description of the schools in twelve areas; and a methodology for discussing which of these twelve are the most relevant for evaluation in the specific situation of an individual school.

Listed below are the twelve areas recognised in the profile, followed by a description of the process.

The twelve areas

The twelve areas are grouped in four domains:

- Outcomes
- Process at the classroom level
- Process at the school level
- Relations with the environment.

Each of these areas is presented in turn, first with a definition, then with some questions which may help to illustrate their content. At the end of this chapter there is a list of questions which may be of help to people participating in the SEP process (see Figure 10.3).

Outcomes

1 Academic achievement

The question here is 'What do pupils learn in our school?' and it has two aspects: the content pupils learn and the degree of mastery of the content.

The questions to which a school might seek answers are:

- Have pupils reached a satisfactory standard in most subjects by the time they leave school?
- With reference to pupils' prior attainment, is their rate of progress higher, lower or close to what might be expected?

• Does the school widen or narrow the gap between low and high achievers, and between boys and girls, with respect to academic achievement?

2 Personal and social development

Happiness, moral character, contribution to social life and, increasingly, profes-sional status, depend not on academic knowledge, but on attitudes, values and skills which are acquired through classroom and out-of-school experiences. This is what is called personal and social development.

The questions to which a school might seek answers are:

• How successful is the school in enhancing social qualities such as sociability, sense of co-operation, civic attitudes, consideration for others, sense of soli-darity and of equity?
• How successful is the school in producing autonomous individuals, able to meet the future positively and creatively, with a strong moral sense?
• To what extent does the school improve non-academic skills such as the abil-ity to teamwork, to problem solve, to cope with complexity, to communicate effectively, to exercise initiative, to innovate?
• To what extent do all pupils develop these attitudes or skills equally?
• To what extent are the values and purposes of personal and social develop-ment discussed and agreed among staff?

3 Pupil destinations

The value of a school education is frequently judged by information on where pupils go when they leave – either in the academic world or the world of work – what they do, and whether or not the school has contributed to giving them a suc-cessful career or a fulfilling vocation. The questions to which a school might seek answers are:

• Do pupils find satisfactory work, training or further study on leaving school?
• To what extent are these destinations the most appropriate for their level of academic skill and personal development?
• How successfully has the school prepared pupils for these destinations?
• Do all pupils with the same level of academic skills, regardless of gender, social class, or ethnic background, reach similar destinations?

Process at the classroom level

4 Time as a resource for learning

One of the most valuable of learning resources is time. Time in school is a limited commodity and has to be used well. Examination of timetabled time is, of itself, a partial measure since it is not synonymous with pupil 'time on task', or, as researchers call it, 'opportunity to learn'. Monitoring learning time in school, and also out of school, is a useful activity for pupils themselves, helping them to gauge the effectiveness of their learning time.

The questions to which a school might seek answers are:

• Is enough class time devoted to learning as opposed to administration, discipline, settling in/packing up?
• Are too many class hours lost for any reason? For example, because of truancy?
• How wide are the inequalities of learning time between most and least able pupils?
• How much time do pupils spend on homework? Is it productive time?

5 *Quality of learning and teaching*

It should surprise no one that school effectiveness researchers have identified 'a focus on learning' as a consistent key feature of effective schools worldwide. This is likely to be associated with good teaching, but the two are not synonymous. Good teaching is generally characterised by the existence of clear criteria, formative feedback, effective assessment, teacher responsiveness, pace and variety. Of themselves, however, none of these guarantees that pupils will learn, since some pupils learn well without teaching and others fail to learn despite considerable instruction and individual help. Therefore, in evaluating the quality of teaching and learning, we must treat these as two separate processes.

The questions to which a school might seek answers are:

• Are standards of learning and criteria of achievement clear and understood by pupils and teachers?
• Are teaching and learning effective enough?
• What procedures are used in the school to monitor or enhance the quality of teaching, to ensure good conditions for teaching, to help teachers who may be in difficulty?
• Do all pupils enjoy equal quality of learning?

6 *Support for learning difficulties*

At some time, all pupils experience difficulties with learning. Some experience more acute and more sustained difficulties. All require support, but in different ways, at different times and at different levels of intensity. A school's ability to know and respond to that range of problems is a critical aspect of its quality.

The questions to which a school might seek answers are:

• Are learning difficulties detected quickly and in a valid way?
• How effective is the support for pupils with learning difficulties?
• Are the pupils who receive support those who are most in need or those who take advantage most?

- To what extent are difficulties with learning a consequence of inadequate teaching or ineffective organisation at school level?

Process at the school level

7 School as a learning place

School is a place for learning. This may seem self-evident, but is it a place in which everyone learns? That is a relevant question not only at classroom level, but at school level where values and commitment to learning permeate procedures and relationships. A 'learning place' is one in which there is a shared belief system, a concern with success for all, a commitment to raising standards and to continuous improvement. Even high achievers may learn more with better communication, more consistent monitoring, higher expectations and a commitment by the school to continually explore alternative ways of managing learning.

The questions to which a school might seek answers are:

- Are pupils organised and grouped in ways that maximise their learning opportunities?
- Are teachers committed to reviewing and ensuring the progress of all pupils?
- Are there systems and procedures to ensure quality and to support effective teaching?
- Is the curriculum adapted to meet pupil needs?
- Do pupils see their teachers as helpful?

8 School as a social place

School is a social place; it is an important part of the social life of pupils in their growing years. In school, they meet and make friends, some of which last for a life-time. In school, they test out their social selves and their relationships with the same and opposite sex. They learn about authority and independence and interdependence through the day-to-day routine and informal life of the school. Their opportunities for positive personal development are closely related to the social climate and relationships in and around the school.

The questions to which a school might seek answers are:

- Is there a climate of mutual respect between pupils, rather than bullying and disrespect?
- What is the quality of relationships between pupils and staff?
- Does the school provide opportunities for pupils to exercise decision making and responsibility?
- Are rules clear and accepted by all?
- Are rewards and sanctions applied with equity and justice?
- More generally, does the life of the school contribute to pupils' learning and development?

9 School as a professional place

School is a professional place if it has some system of data-gathering and decision-making procedures which build on this. This is important if schools are to respond in a professional way to changes taking place inside and outside school and to set goals through planned and concerted action. School is a professional place if it enhances competencies of staff and provides for their professional development. The quality of a school as a professional learning organisation may be judged by the extent to which it supports teachers, challenges them, helps them to cope with difficulties and extends their range of skills.

The questions to which a school might seek answers are:

- How does the school respond to changes in its environment?
- Is the school able to move in planned directions?
- What is the quality of discussion and decision-making procedures within the school? Is the optimal range of stakeholders involved in such discussions?
- Does the in-service training provided meet the needs of staff and of the school?
- Is there sufficient and effective help for staff in meeting difficulties?

Relations with the environment

10 School and home

Home and school are the two prime sites for learning and development. Learning is at its most effective when these two work together to the same end and are underpinned by the same values. What takes place in school can be extended and enriched at home, and what is learned at home may built on in the classroom. There are clearly responsibilities for both teachers and parents, but there is a specific onus on schools to inform parents about their children's progress and help them to provide the most encouraging and supportive environment for their children's learning.

The questions to which a school might seek answers are:

- Is the information provided to parents what they want and what meets their needs?
- Do parents feel welcome in the school?
- Are they equally treated, whatever their social status or ethnicity?
- Are there opportunities for teachers to learn from parents about pupils' needs or problems?
- Are parents enabled to support their children's learning? Is school policy well developed in this area?

11 School and community

Schools exist within communities and draw their life from them. They receive support from the community and benefit from its resources and opportunities. They are also deeply affected by its economic and social difficulties and have to cope with the repercussions of poverty, unemployment or violence. Evaluation in this area may consist of examining the extent to which the school is proactive or reactive to community influences and the extent to which it sees itself as a resource for its neighbourhood.

The questions to which a school might seek answers are:

- Do the conditions of life in the community (wealth, employment, cohesiveness, confidence in the future) influence school ethos and climate?
- What expectations does the community have of the school? How do expectations differ among different groups?
- What does the school offer to the community?
- What does the school do to enhance school–community relationships?

12 School and pupil destinations

The quality of work available to a young person depends to a large extent on his or her success at school; that is why parents and employers are interested in what schools do to prepare pupils for working life. This can be greatly enhanced by schools which develop strong links with employers. While this is obviously important for vocational schools or courses, it is now increasingly common for young people in all schools to spend some time in work experience or for employers to spend some time in schools.

What is true of work also holds good for further or higher education. They also have expectations and specific requirements which pupils need to meet and be prepared for. The questions to which a school might seek answers are:

- Is the school helping young people to develop the skills and qualities which fit them for employment and further/higher education?
- Do employers and institutions of further/higher education provide information, support and resources for pupils, staff and parents in respect of their expectations and requirements?
- Does the school ensure that other agencies are fully aware of the knowledge and skills of pupils in its charge?

The SEP as a process: how to use it

The purpose of the SEP is to:

- Provide a picture of school quality and effectiveness as perceived by staff, pupils and parents.
- Assist in selecting the area for further investigation by consideration of the evidence.
- Further a culture of open and serious discussion among all stakeholders, thereby creating a favourable climate for self-evaluation.

The following is the sequence of steps that is most likely to guarantee that the purposes outlined above are achieved:

1   Discuss as widely and openly as possible the purpose and commitments of the initiative, its potential challenges and rewards. Do not underplay the commitment of time and energy required. Invite volunteers and build on their enthusiasm.
2   Appoint or elect a group to manage the project.
3   Form groups of stakeholders. These may be homogeneous groups of pupils, parents and teachers, together with members of the school board or governors, each group consisting of about 5–10 people. Or they may be mixed groups, each small group containing a mix of different stakeholders. It is helpful for the groups to have a facilitator whose job it is to ease the flow of discussion, to prevent domination by any individual or clique and to ensure that all voices are heard. Where an individual (a parent, for example) is at a disadvantage because of language or jargon, the facilitator can help to make the discussion more accessible.
4   Each group completes the SEP independently, taking time to consider evidence, to challenge off-the-cuff judgements, justifying statements with reasoned arguments and in the process trying to reach consensus. It may be helpful to give participants some information or data before they meet – for example, achievement or attendance rates. Care has to be taken, however, not to inhibit the free flow of discussion by an overload of data.

   At the outset, the facilitator indicates the ground rules, distributes the SEP and explains the purpose of any data that may be given to participants to inform the discussion. He or she asks each person to go through the SEP, giving their own rating in each area. When this has been done individually, the group works systematically through the SEP together, discussing each area in turn. Participants should be encouraged to say something about what led them to their judgement – experiences, impressions, information and clues. This is followed by a general discussion with the intention of coming to an agreement on the group's rating.

   Discussion may lead to a group agreement but there may still be differences of opinion and these should be noted. So, for example, three of the group may agree on a plus score while three insist on a minus. This may be entered on the SEP as 3 in the plus column and 3 in the minus column. This will provide more information than a simple X. The mean score on each item may also be calculated by adding individual scores and dividing by the number in the group. Voting and aggregating should, however, be discouraged because the purpose is not to end up with a list of numbers but to listen to argument and evidence and come to a reasoned agreement wherever possible.

   The facilitator should remind the group that the object of the exercise is not to find solutions to all the problems that are touched on, but rather to agree an initial diagnosis of where the strengths and weaknesses lie. Nor is it helpful to try and force a false consensus. If, after discussion, there is still considerable

1. The facilitator describes the purpose of the exercise and sets out the ground rules.

2. The facilitator draws people's attention to the content of each of the twelve areas.

3. Participants go through the SEP on their own, grading each area in turn from positive to negative.

4. The facilitator goes through each area in sequence, spending 5–10 minutes on each, asking participants to give their rating and explain their choice. Some areas will require much more discussion and negotiation than others and time needs to be managed accordingly.

5. Group rating is noted, either as a group consensus or divergence.

6. The facilitator checks that group opinion has been accurately recorded across the twelve areas.

Figure 10.1 Protocol for the session.

divergence of opinion, this is important 'evidence' for future investigation in this area.

5   Each of the separate groups then appoints a representative to attend a larger, school-wide group (the school evaluation group). This group has the job of revisiting the SEP and engaging the debate once again, but at a deeper and more rigorous level. It should try to arrive at agreement through robust discussion, critical challenge and concern for evidence. This 'second-level' group also requires a facilitator, and this may be the critical friend. He or she should not represent any interest group, but should be a neutral chair, trying to ensure that decisions are reached on the basis of evidence and argument and that all voices are heard.

6   Having reached agreement on a group profile for the SEP, with disagreement and divergence noted, a recommendation is made on the specific areas to be the subject of further evaluation or action. The final results and recommendations are then conveyed to the school steering group to translate in to action. Figure 10.1 summarises the protocol for the session, and Figure 10.2 suggests ground rules for the discussion.

Lessons learned

The following lessons may be drawn from the way schools used the SEP in the European Project.

The relevance and reliability of the agreed profile depends on the 'representativeness' of those involved in the discussion. It is important, therefore, to involve all stakeholder groups in the process. Several schools reported that parents and pupils found it hard to advance an argument in some of the twelve areas, either because they had no evidence on which to base their judgement, or no previous experience of that kind of quality work. When approached as a learning opportunity for everyone, however, with everyone's lack of knowledge recognised, it was

1. No trading ('I'll let you have that if you let me have this').

2. No insisting on your own position.

3. Listen to other people's position.

4. Do not force agreement just to keep the peace. Present your case as fully as possible with regard for evidence. Listen equally carefully to the arguments of others. Differences of opinion may not be resolved during the meeting but they can be put on the agenda for further exploration.

5. Don't try to solve problems. That will come later. This first stage is about evaluation only. Take time to weigh up the evidence carefully.

Figure 10.2 Ground rules for discussion.

both an engaging and powerful experience; for instance, some schools reported how enthusiastic and constructive pupils could be and how it had subsequent spin-offs in staff–pupil relationships.

It is important not to choose only pupils or teachers from the 'better class-rooms', or those parents most favourably disposed towards the school. If certain sectors of the school population are neglected, it may reinforce the feeling that the school doesn't want to hear dissenting voices and may lead to even more entrenched divisiveness.

Reliability of data refers to the likelihood of getting the same outcomes if the exercise were repeated at a later point in time. This depends in part on the time devoted to discussion. When schools spent too little time on this exercise, it led to superficial and unreliable findings. By contrast, when there was enough time it led to thorough, systematic and methodical discussions and people had greater confidence that their views were adequately recorded.

In order to save time during the meetings, it is possible to distribute the SEP to participants several days beforehand. In this case, participants are asked to think carefully and decide on their ratings before the meeting. This may, on the other hand, sacrifice some of the spontaneity.

The process of filling in the SEP encouraged different categories of stakeholders to work together, very often for the first time, but it also had more far-reaching consequences on further collaboration. In several cases, the SEP activities became the first stage in involving stakeholders in development planning and school improvement.

Suggested questions which may be of help for schools participating in the SEP process are listed in Figure 10.3. Figure 10.4 provides an example of how one school presented this in graphic form.

OUTCOMEO

Academic achievement

Do the pupils reach a satisfactory standard in most subjects when they leave the school?

With reference to pupils' prior attainment, is their rate of progress higher, lower or close to what might be expected?

Does the school widen or narrow the gap between low and high achievers, boys and girls, in academic achievement?

Personal and social development

How successful is the school in enhancing social qualities such as sociability, sense of co-operation, civic attitudes, consideration for others, sense of solidarity, equity?

How successful is the school in producing autonomous individuals, able to meet the future positively and creatively, with a strong sense of morality?

To what extent does the school improve non-academic skills like the ability to teamwork, to problem solve, to cope with complexity, to communicate effectively, to use initiative, to demonstrate a capacity for invention?

To what extent do all categories of pupils equally develop these attitudes or skills?

To what extent are the value and purposes of personal and social development discussed and agreed among staff?

Pupil destinations

Do pupils reach appropriate destinations on leaving school?

To what extent are these destinations the most appropriate for their level of academic skill and personal development?

To what extent has the school prepared pupils for these destinations?

Do all categories of pupils with the same level of academic skills, regardless of gender, social class, ethnic background, enjoy the same opportunities after school?

CLASSROOM LEVEL

Time as a resource for learning

Is enough class time devoted to learning as opposed to administration, discipline, settling in/packing up?

Are too many class hours lost for any reason? for truancy?

How large are the inequalities of learning time between most and least able?

How much time do pupils spend on homework? Is it productive time?

Quality of learning and teaching

Are standards of learning and criteria of achievement clear and understood by pupils and teachers?

Are teaching and learning effective?

continued ...

Figure 10.3 Content of the areas.

What procedures are used in the school to monitor or enhance the quality of teaching, to ensure good conditions for teaching and to help teachers who may be in difficulty?

Do all pupils enjoy equal quality of learning?

Support for learning difficulties

Are learning difficulties detected quickly and reliably?

How effective is the support to pupils with learning difficulties?

Are pupils who receive support those who need it most? Or those who take advantage most?

To what extent are difficulties with learning a consequence of inadequate teaching or ineffective organisation at the school level?

SCHOOL LEVEL

School as a learning place

Are pupils organised and grouped in ways that maximise their opportunities to learn?

Are teachers committed to reviewing and ensuring progress of all pupils?

Are there systems and procedures to ensure quality and to support effective teaching?

Is the curriculum adapted to meet pupil needs?

Do pupils see their teachers as helpful?

School as a social place

Is there a climate of mutual respect between pupils?

What is the quality of relationships between pupils and staff?

Does the school provide opportunities for pupils to exercise decision making and responsibility?

Are rules clear and accepted?

Are rewards and sanctions applied with equity and justice?

More generally, does the social environment in school help pupils' learning and development?

School as a professional place

How does the school respond to changes in its environment?

Is the school able to move in planned directions?

What is the quality of internal discussions and decision-making procedures within the school?

Is the optimal range of stakeholders involved in such discussions?

Does the in-service training provided to the staff meet their needs and those of the school?

Is there sufficient and effective help for staff experiencing difficulties?

continued ...

ENVIRONMENT

School and home

Is the information provided to parents what they want and what meets their needs?

Do parents feel welcome in the school?

Are they equally treated, whatever their social position or ethnicity?

Do teachers learn enough from parents regarding their children's needs or problems?

Do parents support their children's learning? Is the policy of the school sufficiently developed to support this?

School and community

Do the conditions of life in the community (wealth, employment, cohesiveness, confidence in the future, what it expects from the school) create a supportive environment for the school?

What does the school offer to the community?

What does the school do to enhance school–community relationships?

School and pupil destinations

Is the school helping young people to develop the skills and qualities which employers/further and higher education require?

Do employers/further and higher education institutions provide information, support and resources for schools about their requirements?

Does the school help employers to be fully aware of the knowledge and skills of their pupils?

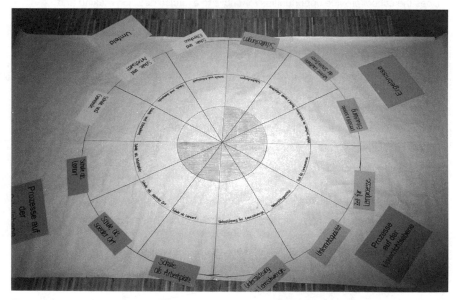

Figure 10.4 How one school represented the SEP in graphic form.

11 Methods of self-evaluation

We have structured the collection of methods and instruments on the basis of the main activities involved in the process. These are presented in Figure 11.1.

In what follows, these evaluation activities are presented in numerical order. Within each category we list methods that are appropriate to that activity, but other approaches may also be included. Each method is presented following a common structure (see Figure 11.2).

In each section, one specific activity is presented as illustrative material. There are, of course, many other possible variants on the theme.

Activity 1   Asking

Evaluation activities are aimed at finding the right answers to given problems and that is why asking for the answers is the most popular way of evaluating activities. Since, traditionally, asking is also the main form of pupil assessment, more formal structured approaches to 'asking' have to be dealt with sensitively as well as systematically. As in the classroom, evaluation by asking can be in oral or written form.

Figure 11.1 The main activities in the process of self-evaluation.

1. What is it? *(Description)*

2. What is it for? *(Purpose)*

3. How to do it? *(Procedure)*

4. How can it work? *(Example/s)*

Figure 11.2 The structure of evaluation.

Asking orally: interviews

What is it?

Interviewing people orally is an evaluation method which uses spoken language as a main source of information and therefore offers a wide range of possible responses.

What is it for?

Interviews are helpful in getting more detailed information about issues on a personal, face-to-face level. Depending on the goal of the self-evaluation exercise, decisions have to be made about whether people are to be interviewed individually or in groups. Regarding the scope of interviews, the terminology ranges from the problem-oriented interview, which focuses on issues which structure the interview process, to the narrative interview, which is minimally structured by the interviewer (see Figure 11.3). The advantage of interviews over questionnaires lies in the possibility of tailoring questions to the immediate social situation and conveying a sense of respect for the interviewee.

How to do it

In self-evaluation, interviews are mostly used to get a quick overview of how people think about situations and which multiple perspectives have to be taken into account. If the purpose of interviews is to solve a problem such as 'How do the teachers handle conflicts in class?', it will be helpful to design a set of questions together, on the one hand open enough to leave space for the individual interview, on the other hand containing a common core of items. Different interview types are presented in Figure 11.3. This provides an overview of the terminology used for different interview forms (from Mayring, 1990: 45).

Open (vs. closed) interview	Relates to the 'degrees of freedom' of the **interviewee**	The interviewees can answer freely without having to give responses in pre-specified categories in advance and can say what they consider relevant with regard to the topic.
Unstructured (vs. structured) or **unstandardised** (vs. standardised) interview	Relates to the 'degrees of freedom' of the **interviewer**	The interviewer does not have a strict set of questions, but can freely set questions and topics according to the interview situation.
Qualitative (vs. quantitative) interview	Relates to the **analysis** of the interview data	The analysis is done by means of interpretative techniques.

Figure 11.3 Interview types.

The interview triangle

The interview triangle is often used to get information on one particular aspect from a number of different angles. It derives its name from the following constellation: an external person (E), usually a teacher who is not familiar with the particular class, is asked by a teacher (T) to gather information from one or more pupils (S) on a particular question or problem which has been identified by (T) (see Figure 11.4).

After the external person (E) has interviewed the teacher (T) on the issue at hand, he or she tries to gain corresponding information from the pupils (S). This will help the teacher to examine the learners' perspective, which may contrast with what the teacher sees or understands. Interview triangles are very helpful when teachers form peer groups for visiting one another's classrooms. Then they are not only sitting in as observers but are also a valuable resource for the class

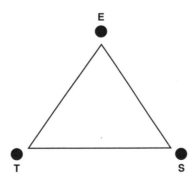

Figure 11.4 The interview triangle.

teacher, because they are able not only to feed back their own observations but those of pupils whom they interview.

As the ownership of the data always plays an integral part, it is important that the person who acts as a 'critical friend' is a person of trust. T, therefore, needs to meet and inform E beforehand of what he or she wants to focus the'research' on in class. It helps if a cassette recorder is used by E to record the initial interview with T. This technical device is also helpful for the analysis of the interviews with the pupils, who are either chosen at random by E or given by T for particular reasons. Enough time should be put aside for the discussion of the data afterwards, particularly in respect of further steps to be taken. Of course, there are various other ways of making use of the three positions in the triangle.

How does it work?

In a Danish school fifty pupils and twenty teachers were selected randomly 'by lot' and fifty parents chosen from class council members to be interviewed on the quality of teaching and learning. The working group met three times for a total of twelve hours to agree criteria of quality and to devise an interview guide. Parents interviewed parents, teachers interviewed teachers and pupils interviewed pupils. The group also had the task of analysing the responses.

An English school used a novel form of interview, a form of on-the-spot reportage in which younger pupils visited classes throughout the school choosing at random someone engaged in an activity (baking a cake, conducting an experiment) and taping a short interview on what was happening, what was being learned and the pupil's attitude to the activity.

Following through on the theme 'school and community', pupils in an Austrian school conducted interviews in the school's external community. Pupils were entrusted with responsibility for carrying out the project, choosing seven categories of people within the community to interview, including public services (the kindergarten, the church, the post office, doctor, chemist); the service sector (travel agency, cleaning services, solarium); political agencies and so on. Before conducting the interviews for real, pupils developed their technique through role play. They then conducted twenty-five interviews in the community.

Asking in written form: the questionnaire

What is it?

The questionnaire is one of the simplest and therefore most often used methods in evaluation because it lends itself to a wide variety of possible audiences. People are usually asked to respond in different ways depending on the purpose of the inquiry and the level of detail required. If certain characteristics (gender, ethnicity, age) are included, questionnaires can be analysed to show how groups differ in their views.

What is it for?

The questionnaire is used to elicit more or less standardised responses which can be compared and contrasted more easily than answers to interviews. Its great advantage is the confidentiality or anonymity it offers, allowing pupils, teachers or parents to respond honestly without fear of recrimination. According to the grade of standardisation we can differentiate between closed and open questions:

QUESTIONS

Closed ◄———————————————————————► Open

The advantage of closed questions lies in their range: in a short space of time it is possible to obtain responses to the same questions from a large number of people and also to process them fairly quickly. The less standardised questionnaires are, the more difficult it is to work out the results. For example, there may be open-ended questions like 'Describe the climate of your school'.

The person filling out the questionnaire then has the freedom to write down whatever she or he wants to. In this case the responses have to be looked at and interpreted individually. People can find these open-ended questions hard to answer and responses take time to process. There are, however, alternatives that lie midway between closed and completely open-ended questions – for example, sentence completion. This offers less freedom but answers may still be individualised. Figure 11.5 provides some examples of sentence completion used to find out how individual staff members evaluate meetings.

The results of such a questionnaire should be discussed soon after the meeting as they can then have an influence on the format and content of future meetings.

How to do it

It is important to try out written questionnaires with a pilot person or group who is/are representative of the target group, as the way in which questions are phrased is a powerful determinant of the answers you will get. This is particularly important

---

Staff meeting of . . . . on . . . . at . . . .

During the meeting I felt. . . . .
. . . .
For me the most important point was that . . . .
. . . .
I found it very helpful that. . . . .
. . . .
I had the greatest problems when . . . .

Figure 11.5 Evaluation by sentence completion.

as the respondent cannot normally enter into dialogue with the author of the questionnaires.

The more open the questions are, the more freedom there is in responding (see Figure 11.3). If closed forms of questions are used, we can differentiate between the following types:

Alternative options   When posing a question, two options are given and the respondent has to choose between the two. The options are generally two alternatives, usually opposites, for example:

yes	no
correct	incorrect
agree	disagree
positive	negative

The advantage of using alternative options is a practical one: even large numbers of questionnaires can be analysed quickly – similar to a voting system where the results are counted shortly after the last vote has been cast. Its disadvantage, of course, lies in the limitation of its range. Only simple and clearly structured questions can be answered in an either/or way. There is no option between 'agreement' and 'disagreement', 'yes' or 'no'.

Multiple choice questions   With multiple choice a range of items is provided and respondents have to choose the one they see as being the most appropriate. It is not necessary to use words or numbers for response categories, as can be seen from the example in Figure 11.6.

Rating scales   This is a special form of multiple choice system. Answers are graded from strong to weak, high to low, positive to negative. This can be done by giving options to choose from, as can be seen in Figure 11.7.

In Figure 11.8, pupils are asked their opinion on certain aspects of learning and teaching in class by means of simple questions, and Figure 11.9 shows how the rating can also be given by providing an answer in between two opposing poles.

The advantage of rating scales is that certain information is given, and respondents have the choice of which grade to select. This is helpful when processing the data because they are, in a sense, standardised. However, this is also a disadavantage, as the meaning of the grading between the two poles is subjective to the individual and there may, therefore, be a difference in interpreting what the scales actually mean. Ratings give the impression that the measuring is very precise, which is, of course, not the case. This apparent precision has, therefore, to be taken into account when interpreting the data. But beware: the more complex or

How do you experience the members of staff as a group?
Which of the following drawings (1–4) depicts it most appropriately?
If none, please draw your own interpretation in 5.
Please tick the appropriate number ✔.

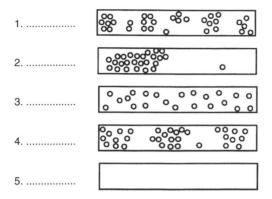

1. ....

2. ....

3. ....

4. ....

5. ....

Figure 11.6   A graphical interpretation of a multiple choice question.

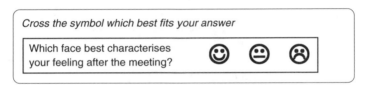

Cross the symbol which best fits your answer

Which face best characterises
your feeling after the meeting?   ☺   ☺   ☹

Figure 11.7   A graphical interpretation of a rating scale.

I can ask my teacher for help when I don't understand things:
,..... all of the time
...... most of the time
...... sometimes
...... never

I understand my teacher's instructions
...... all of the time
...... most of the time
...... sometimes
...... never

The teacher knows when I don't understand my work:
...... all of the time
...... most of the time
...... sometimes
...... never

I can ask my teacher to explain the programme:
...... all of the time
...... most of the time
...... sometimes
...... never

The teacher helps me straight away when (s)he knows that I don't understand my work:
...... all of the time
...... most of the time
...... sometimes
...... never

I know the reason for doing each activity:
...... all of the time
...... most of the time
...... sometimes
...... never

Figure 11.8   Rating using simple questions.

Cross the circle which best fits your answer
At our school the teachers have a common understanding of how
to mark the pupils' work

| completely true | O | O | O | O | O | not true at all |

Figure 11.9   Rating between two opposite poles.

abstract the scale is, the less you can be sure that people mean the same thing by their answers.

Figure 11.10, an example of a questionnaire (from Schratz *et al.*, 2000) which was used to find out about the experiences of former pupils, gives an idea of the variety of questions which can be employed.

Computer-assisted questionnaire design and analysis

Since their first appearance computers have been valuable tools in statistical work. They have made data handling easier, especially where large numbers of questionnaires are involved. More recently, the use of computers in the data-gathering phase has shortened enormously the period between administering the questionnaires and presenting the results. Different forms of software have been developed in different countries. In Scotland, for example, a software program allows pupils, parents and teachers to enter data directly, using keyboard or mouse. Data are automatically processed and different forms of report are produced.

This type of computer program can also be used to store information and compare new developments after certain periods of time. For example, the results from a previous year's enquiry can provide a helpful baseline for comparison in the following year. This can not only help in connecting past with future, but can also enhance discussions on the strengths and weaknesses of the school, and – more importantly – on where to go from there.

How does it work?

The most common target groups for questionnaires are teachers, parents and pupils. Questions put to all three groups can be more or less the same (although perhaps worded slightly differently), allowing the school to compare different perspectives on the same issues.

Questionnaires can help to focus on the area being investigated in greater depth – for example, personal and social development, the school as a learning place and so on. Parent questionnaires tend to focus on the school and its relationship with parents – parental satisfaction, homework, concerns over the progress and behaviour of their own children. Teacher questionnaires tend to deal with school ethos, professional development, teaching and learning. Common issues for focus among pupil questionnaires are classroom environment and quality of teaching or, in some cases, 'teacher behaviour'. The latter has to be handled with

1 *Please cross the appropriate box ⊠:*

(a) How often have you had contact with your school since you left it?

☐ never   ☐ 3x
☐ 1x   ☐ 4x
☐ 2x   ☐ 5x and more

(b) Would you like more contacts?

☐ yes

☐ no

2 If you think back to your own time at school, which feelings do you have (generally)? *Please tick the appropriate box ⊠ between the poles:*

Very positive ☐ ☐ ☐ ☐ ☐ ☐ ☐ Very negative

3 How would you assess the impact of the school in following areas with regard to your present situation? *Please cross the appropriate box ⊠:*

Knowledge	Personal competence	Social competence
☐ very high	☐ very high	☐ very high
☐ high	☐ high	☐ high
☐ low	☐ low	☐ low
☐ very low	☐ very low	☐ very low

4 How has school helped you in coping with both your professional and private life? *On each disk, mark the number which matches your opinion best (centre: highest, outside: lowest)*

professional life   private life

5 How would you rate your time in school according to the following statements? Please cross the box ⊠ which you regard as most appropriate!

Completely true ☐ ☐ ☐ ☐ ☐ ☐ ☐ Not true at all

Figure 11.10 An example of a questionnaire *(continued on next page).*

1	The teachers made the effort to deal with us in an adult way.	□	□	□	□	□
2	As a student I was given enough freedom to become independent.	□	□	□	□	□
3	When I had problems the teachers supported me with professional knowledge.	□	□	□	□	□
4	I felt that teachers treated me justly.	□	□	□	□	□
5	Teaching in class was interesting and versatile.	□	□	□	□	□
6	I often had the chance to work on projects.	□	□	□	□	□
7	The teachers were role models for my later life.	□	□	□	□	□
8	Teaching was just about the right standard for me.	□	□	□	□	□
9	All in all, I liked going to this school.	□	□	□	□	□
10	I have also learnt a lot for my later life in school at large (not only in the classroom, that is).	□	□	□	□	□

6   From your present view, which of the following attitudes, competencies and skills do you find important for both your professional and private life, and how seriously were they taken by your teachers in school?
Please cross the most appropriate symbol between the two poles in each column ⊠:

highly important ++ + O - --   not important at all

NOW   **IN SCHOOL**

++ + O - --	self reliance	++ + O - --
++ + O - --	self-esteem	++ + O - --
++ + O - --	flexibility	++ + O - --
++ + O - --	communication skills	++ + O - --
++ + O - --	conflict skills	++ + O - --
++ + O - --	tolerance towards others	++ + O - --
++ + O - --	innovation capacity	++ + O - --
++ + O - --	openness for new challenges	++ + O - --

7   Other aspects which I think are important for my former school to know
Please add further comments which you think important looking back to your school days from your present perspective! (Please also use the back of this page.)

Figure 11.10 (continued)

care and depends very much on how it is introduced (see the forces in the evaluation cube, Figure 8.1 on page 93), taking account of the existing readiness of the school and taking care to adapt the nature of the exercise to the context and expectations of staff, pupils and parents.

An original idea was a cohort study in a Danish school. Attitudes of school leavers in 1991 and 1996 (for whom the school held data) were compared with school leavers in 1998. Respondents were asked a number of questions about classroom methodology and about the influence of the pupil council. In the view of the school this had given them a good basis for discussion of school quality and future development.

Working on the theme 'pupil destinations', two Portuguese schools gave questionnaires to pupils who had already left school and were currently in higher education or employment. Questionnaires were also sent to employers. The responses generated a wealth of information, not just on what happened to pupils after school, but on how they evaluated their learning experiences in retrospect.

Survey

What is it?

The survey is a variation on the questionnaire. It differs in that it is administered by someone who supervises or plays a direct part in data collection. A survey is an examination of data which exist in or around schools.

What is it for?

This method is used for data gathering in order to survey certain aspects of school life or learning. It may involve a survey of the use of computers, for example, or time taken to move from class to class, the frequency and quality of letters to parents, or parental perceptions of school meetings. It can be a more efficient method than questionnaires because it avoids distribution, collection, collation and analysis, all of which can be very time consuming. It does, however, sacrifice confidentiality.

How to do it

Depending on the purpose of the survey, a relevant question forms the basis for the study of, or investigation into, the issue at hand. A survey protocol, written or in the form of a CD-ROM, is then produced in order to collect and analyse data.

For a staff development survey indicators such as the following might be used:

- Number of teachers taking part in in-service training.
- Time teachers spend in school outside lessons.
- Amount of time devoted to planning tasks.
- Time spent in decision making on whole-school issues.

Day:		Time:	

Computer use for	*girls*	*boys*	*total*
Word processing			
Graphics and art work			
Internet surfing			
Web design			
Hypermedia			
Desktop publishing			
Learning in subject area			
Accounting			

Figure 11.11 Survey sheet.

- Policies on transfer of in-service training activities,
- Time spent with stakeholders.
- Amount of time devoted to external agencies (for example, social services or police).

For a school–home survey indicators such as the following might be used:

- Percentage of parents that (head) teachers see individually in a year. Nature of these meetings.
- Time devoted by (head) teachers to relations with parents.
- Parents' knowledge of decisions taken by the school.
- Information teachers have about the home situation of pupils.
- Percentage of letters home over the course of a month. Percentage of letters positive and negative.
- Percentage of phone calls initiated by school or home. Nature of these phone calls.

How does it work?

Example: a school wants to find out what use pupils make of the computer room during the free access time, differentiating between girls and boys. The sheet shown in Figure 11.11 is prepared for the survey.

In the course of a week a new survey sheet is used every day to find out what pupils' specific preferences are, examining differences among boys and girls.

Time started	Time finished	Time spent	Subject or topic	When was it given out?	When has it to be done by?	Difficulty?	Help given by?	Did you enjoy it?	Was it useful?

Figure 11.12 Time log.

One Spanish school used a format which combined a survey with questionnaires. In this school older pupils, under the guidance of a teacher, administered a form of questionnaire to younger pupils as part of their socio-cultural studies programme. The embedding of this kind of activity within the curriculum is one way of lessening teachers' extra burden and at the same time involving pupils and helping them to see such investigations as part of their mainstream education.

Log

What is it?

The log derives its name from a log book used on journeys to keep track of the course one is following. Similarly, recording events in a log (book) over a predetermined period of time can keep track of the educational journey, recording events and developments over time.

What is it for?

The log (book) is a valuable tool for examining how people use their time. For example, if the school wants to develop better time management among the staff, it is a good idea to find out the patterns and amount of time teachers spend on different tasks. So, teachers keep records of their activities for one week and collate their findings afterwards. The results of this record keeping form the basis for further steps in the development process.

How to do it

Asking a sample of pupils to keep a log for a week can provide a valuable source of information on time spent by pupils on their homework and their patterns of work. The grid shown in Figure 11.12 suggests some ways in which the log might be structured. Pupils are asked to keep a record of each study session, recording *what* they did and *when* (for example: 3.26–3.42 p.m. mathematics; 4.05 – 4.37 p.m. French).

The completed logs are then compared and analysed according to the distribution of work at different stages or by different ability groups.

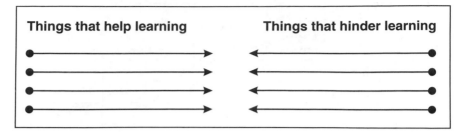

Figure 11.13   Force field.

How does it work?

In one secondary school in Scotland, all third-year pupils were asked to keep a detailed log over the course of one week, including Saturdays and Sundays. These were then handed in and examined by a group of teachers who taught that cohort of pupils. It provided the source for a lively discussion and presented a number of surprises. Teachers had underestimated the amount of time pupils spent on homework in some areas and in particular the concentration of work into Sundays. The logs revealed that some pupils did 5–6 hours' work on a Sunday but little else during the week. The patterning of pupil work was a revelation to teachers, as was the tendency for many pupils to work with the television on or to the accompaniment of music. The telephone was frequently cited as a medium for making homework more social. With the insights gained through the use of the log, teachers were encouraged to discuss and document homework and home study in a more systematic way with their classes.

Force field

What is it?

The force field analysis is used to examine dynamic 'forces' that act in opposite directions, pushing towards or pushing away from the achievement of goals.

What is it for?

Very often evaluation data signal opposing forces in a development process. Since school development has to deal productively with the dynamics of the processes involved in a particular issue, the force field can help in making them visible on both a personal and organisational level.

How to do it

The force field instrument is usually constructed setting opposing forces side by side on a page. The force field in Figure 11.13 asks pupils to identify those things that help and those that hinder their learning.

How does it work?

In a Belgian school the following items were identified by the pupils:

Things that help learning	Things that hinder learning
Teachers who accept me as I am	Teachers who treat me unfairly
Teachers who give me feedback on my achievements	Teachers who give their attention only to the best pupils
Material well prepared and well structured	Teachers who belittle my work
Clear and precise questioning	Disruption to learning
Other pupils explaining things to me	Pupils who don't help you
Other pupils I can talk to freely about anything	An overloaded timetable on certain days
A good classroom atmosphere	Lessons where I don't see the point of what we're doing

The results formed the basis for a thorough discussion of do's and don'ts among teachers.

Activity 2   Observing

Observation is a natural activity, thus making it both easy and difficult when used for evaluation purposes. As we tend to see what we want to see, we have to exercise particular care about bias and preconception and adjust our observation carefully to the criteria specified.

Observation

What is it?

Observing is an activity which is distinctly different from seeing. Observing for professional purposes is a disciplined way of focusing one's view of certain matters. For Jack Sanger (1998: 5) observation is 'a slippery business: the world is exponentially messier than a laboratory.'

What is it for?

Collecting data through observation is a good start to self-evaluation, because it does not require a lot of material. Moreover, most teacher training programmes include some kind of observation practice (cf. Hook, 1981; Stubbs and Delamont, 1976; Walker, 1985). What is important for the purpose of school development is that observation tasks should not be limited to improving practice in a single classroom but should involve as many teachers as possible (cf. Schratz and Walker, 1995). In observation, data are gathered by bringing some issues into the foreground while others move into the background. This method is most powerful where complexity needs to be reduced and a sharper focus brought to bear. While observation is necessarily subjective, through the exchange of observation data findings can be refined to give an inter-subjective view.

How to do it

Observation can be directed towards a particular problem (for example, boys' behaviour v. girls' behaviour) and it can be inside classrooms or outside (or both). There are, of course, different ways of observing, which lie along a spectrum between two poles. Observation activities can be classified according to the visibility of the observer.

OBSERVATION

Visible/open ◄━━━━━━━━━━━━━━━━━━━━━━━━━► Non-visible/covert

The choice between open or covert observation has an effect on the situation, even if the observer is not 'visible' to those being observed. Covert observation has the advantage that one is able to gather 'authentic' data, but there is an ethical aspect involved, which:

> confers upon the researcher the responsibility to act ethically for the other. What this means is that the researcher, given his/her privileged status and knowledge of the consequences of research activitites, must protect, as well as possible, participants who are unaware of the consequences research and evaluation may have for them. (Sanger, 1998: 36)

Observation activities can also be classified according to the focus:

OBSERVATION

Free/unstructured ◄━━━━━━━━━━━━━━━━━━━━► Focused/structured

The advantage of free observation is at the same time its biggest disadvantage: the more one tries to observe, the less one actually sees, because there is no focus. On the other hand, the more one structures observation, the more one loses out on the richness of the social context in which an observation takes place. Therefore, whatever orientation we choose, we should always keep the opposite perspective in mind!

In a focused observation it is helpful jointly to produce a checklist which gives every person involved some guidance as to his/her observation. The example in Figure 11.14 is taken from a school development project where teachers were interested in observing the effects of their decision to allocate certain areas in school to the girls to 'protect' them from boys' interference.

After processing the observation data, it turned out that the protection was not seen in a positive light by the girls; moreover, the boys thought all the other areas could now be occupied by them, which caused further problems. The whole idea was therefore promptly abandoned and new solutions had to be found.

Checklist
• How much use do the girls make of the protected areas? (age of girls? numbers? individuals/groups?) • In what instances do the boys enter the protected areas (fights? individuals/groups?) • What happens when a boy/boys enter the protected area?
Date: Time:

Figure 11.14 Protected area checklist.

How does it work?

PEER OBSERVATION

Paired, or peer, observation by teachers was used in a number of schools. Teachers joined with a colleague of the same status to observe and give feedback on learning, teaching, support for learning difficulties or other aspects of classroom life. The value of conducting this on a collegial, peer basis was that teachers could work together with colleagues in a spirit of trust but also with a willingness to challenge one another. Where this occurred it was seen as important to negotiate beforehand what the focus of the observation would be, the nature of the feedback to be given and the instrument or observation schedule to be used. This protocol tended to be worked out between the teachers themselves or decided on as part of a wider school initiative. In an Icelandic school, eight teachers divided themselves into pairs and visited one another's classrooms. They met beforehand to discuss and plan the visit, making a list of nine different observation points to feed back on. Each made three visits, allowing time to become familiar with the procedure and overcome any initial inhibitions. The keys to the success of this strategy are trust, honesty, planning, agreement on areas of focus, and feedback which is both affirming and challenging.

PUPIL OBSERVATION

Pupil observation was used by schools in a number of countries and took a variety of different forms. In some cases pupils devised their own observation schedules, in some cases they worked together with their teachers and/or the critical friend. In a Finnish school teachers were not aware of the times when observation would take place but had agreed that this would be the procedure, so allowing a more 'typical' sample of classroom interaction.

This method was generally highly rated by pupils and some wrote fulsomely in the newsletter about their experiences. The general tenor of these comments was that the observation had raised their awareness of the teachers' task and role as well as of the tension between teaching (what the teacher is doing) and learning (what the pupil is doing). This was expressed by a Greek pupil: 'For the first time as a pupil I did something I will remember all my life. I attended one of the lessons in our school as a simple observer. During the lessons I filled in a questionnaire based on my observations. I realised that some pupils were interested in the lesson, while others neither paid attention nor took part ... I wondered who is to blame for this situation. To what extent are we pupils responsible, or our teacher? ... That experience made me reconsider my role and attitude as a pupil in the school environment. I felt that I had become aware of many things for the first time. I wish most of my fellow pupils could be given the same chance.' (EVA Newsletter 3)

Shadowing

What is it?

Shadowing is another form of observation. The observer acts as the shadow of a pupil, a teacher or of a headteacher, following that individual over a certain period of time.

What is it for?

Rather than concentrating one's observation on particular issues or processes in the complex world of teaching, learning and schooling at large, shadowing is a method which focuses on an individual or group. Thus, a pupil or other person is accompanied by an observer who follows the observed person like a shadow (for example, over the course of a day). Shadowing of a whole class for a day or more is also an option. Shadowing is particularly valuable in giving a longitudinal view, because it helps to identify a pattern of events over time rather than simply offering a single snapshot at a given moment. In other words, it provides a longitudinal slice of school life.

How to do it

For ethical reasons, it is important to inform the people who are to be shadowed, so that they are aware of what is going to happen and what the purpose of the evaluation activity is. Moreover, the 'shadows' have to be clear about their tasks before, during and after the shadowing.

How does it work?

A school improvement group described in 'The Jarvis Court Files' decided to shadow some pupils in order to find out what learning is like at Jarvis Court. The questions shown in Figure 11.15 (MacBeath *et al.*, 1998) helped them to prepare, undertake and debrief their shadowing sessions.

Similarly, in one of the pilot schools, parents and governors were invited in to

Before embarking on pupil shadowing:

- Is it appropriate to stay with the pupil during break and lunchtime?
- Should the teacher/pupil match be the same sex and ethnicity?
- How do you communicate to all staff concerned that the purpose of the exercise is not to check on them?
- What do you report back to staff (and pupils) on your experience?
- How do you ensure that the exercise is used to improve school practice?

While pupil shadowing:

- What sort of range of teaching styles does your pupil encounter during her day, e.g. whole class/group work?
- Does the content of the curriculum in any way reflect her experiences or heritage?
- Is she encouraged to be an independent and responsible learner?
- Does she have an opportunity to participate in oral work in the classroom? If so, does she do so?
- How many interactions does she have with teachers during the day? Are they generally positive? Is she called by name in the classroom or corridors?
- How does the pupil relate to her peer group?

After pupil shadowing:

- If relevant what was the extent and effectiveness of learning support?
- Were there connections between subject areas? Were they made apparent to the pupil?
- Did the day appear to have coherence?
- Did the pupil receive mixed messages from the different adults she encountered?
- How did she spend her out of classroom time? Was there somewhere appropriate for her to go? Were the corridors safe?
- What did she think of her schooling in general and the day you have observed in particular?

Figure 11.15 The Jarvis Court questions relating to pupil shadowing.

follow one pupil each over the course of a day, taking a few minutes after each of the six periods to debrief the pupil, asking them about their experiences, their learning, the high and low points.

Activity 3 Sorting and prioritising

Q sort: sorting

What is it?

The Q sort is a set of cards with a statement on each card. Individuals or groups of people are given one set and asked to sort them according to specific criteria.

What is it for?

The sorting activity gives an insight into how individuals or groups use certain criteria for the selection of items (that is, statements on a certain issue). It has an advantage over questionnaires or other paper-based forms by allowing respondents to be more interactive in a more user-friendly medium. The result of the individual or group sortings helps in assessing further measures to be taken in the development process.

How to do it

Individuals or groups receive a set of cards and are asked to sort the cards according to the criteria which are most relevant for the purpose. For example, if a school has decided on key issues for development, these issues or priorities can be put on to individual cards and groups (or individuals) can then sort them according to importance or in terms of immediate or long-term priority.

How does it work?

To give one example: teachers may want to find out their pupils' attitudes to school, to learning, to self or to relationships. They use imaginary characters to illustrate a situation, each of which is written on a separate card. For example, 'Tim blamed his friend, Peter, when they had done something wrong'; 'When she saw them fighting she ran away'; 'They tried to get away without anybody knowing after they had taken the purse.' Each pupil is given a set of cards and is asked to sort them into the following four categories:

> Is exactly like me
>
> Is a bit like me
>
> Is not much like me
>
> Is not at all like me

Pupils place each card under the heading or in one of the four boxes which they think is most appropriate. Results can be used to explore further reasons for their choices.

Q sort: prioritising

What is it?

This is a variation of the Q sort in the previous section. Individuals or groups of people are given one set of cards with statements on them and are asked to prioritise these.

What is it for?

This version of the Q sort is useful in finding out quickly about individuals' and groups' priorities if a decision has to be taken. As the results are available to everyone by the end of this activity, decisions about further actions can be taken immediately. The more people are involved in the process, the more they are likely to accept the outcome and participate in the work to follow. Since everybody can argue for his or her priority ranking, the discussion plays an important part in the process and in reaching a decision. In this sense prioritising is, and can be seen to be, a democratically driven procedure.

How to do it

As in the previous section, cards have to be sorted, but the criterion for the ranking is the priority of the individual or the consensus of the group. The cards used should be limited to a fairly small number. This focuses the task and enhances the quality of discussion. Another way of stimulating the discussion process is by including a negative ranking (containing the least liked options). For example, this can be done by giving the following pattern for the final choice of cards.

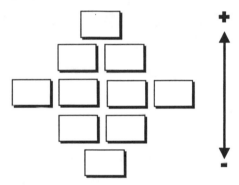

How does it work?

A group has been appointed to prepare the programme for an in-service day which the school wants to dedicate to a discussion about what teachers, parents and pupils regard as a good school. They want to structure the discussions – which could otherwise be endless – by using the Q sort activity. They prepare a set of cards with statements from school effectiveness studies (see the examples in Figure 11.16).

They also include blank cards so that everyone can also add a statement of their own. The same procedure can be used as with the SEP (see page 97). The school can work until a final agreement is reached for the first five priority statements to be dealt with in further school development.

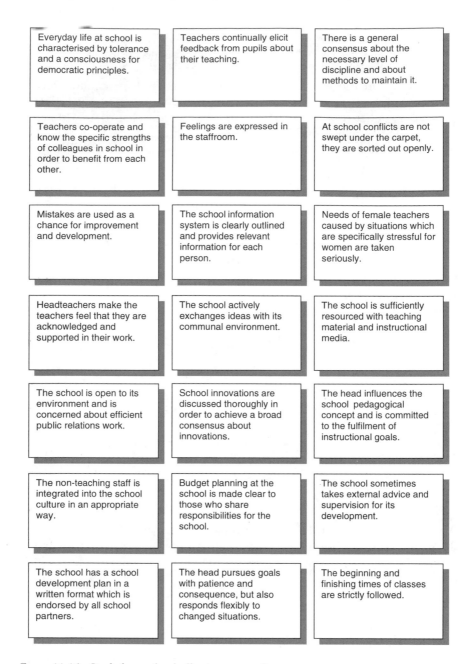

Figure 11.16 Cards from school effectiveness studies.

Activity 4   Collecting

In any organisation there are many documents and artifacts which can be collected and analysed for evaluation purposes. The findings usually offer a particular insight into the issues under scrutiny.

Document analysis

What is it?

In many cases there is sufficient 'evidence' available in documentary form which lends itself to self-evaluation. It is important from the outset to decide on what the school actually wants to find out, because data analysis is usually very time consuming.

What is it for?

Achieving the intended purposes of the evaluation depends on having sources which can provoke useful discussion and provide helpful insights. Here is a list of examples of existing recorded documents which are worth looking into:

- Attendance records
- Reports
- Pupils' work
- Minutes of meetings
- Statistics
- Demographics
- Schedules
- Circulars
- Correspondence
- Appointment diaries
- Local newspapers

How to do it

It is important to formulate the relevant questions together before beginning to search through the documents. Questions might include the following:

- What insight do they give us into our current situation?
- What has changed over a given stretch of time and why?
- What do the documents not tell us?
- What needs to be changed in the school?

When analysing the content of documents, it might be necessary to think of categories which help in interpreting the data. This will assist in classifying the findings in the light of further steps to be taken. For example, it might be interesting for a school to follow up the minutes of a year's meetings and see how decisions have been taken – for example, by individuals or consensus building. When the categories have been decided on, the next step is to find and count sentences or parts of text which fall into each category. They will also need to be analysed qualitatively, in other words, examined from an interpretative perspective. The negotiation which this entails is an important aspect of the whole evaluation, and has consequences for how meetings should be structured in the future.

How does it work?

As an illustration, imagine that a school wants to find out about the civic attitudes of a cohort of pupils. They decide to look at material which pupils have produced during a certain period of the school year. Documents are collected and analysed against agreed criteria of civic attitudes; this may be material produced in school but it may also be the outcome of project work in the community or something similar. Guiding questions for the analysis might be:

- How does the pupil present himself or herself in the material?
- What is his or her attitude towards others?
- Is there a consistent attitude across teachers and subjects?
- What kind of personal profile do the data suggest?

Portfolio

What is it?

A portfolio is a collection of documents which gives an overview of an individual's, or a group's, work or achievements. Like artists, pupils can assemble portfolios of their work to represent their capabilities and achievements. This can be a powerful example of inclusive, pupil-centred communication.

What is it for?

In most educational systems the academic achievement of pupils is usually measured in terms of their success rate in exams. This indicator, however, only mirrors the knowledge and skills pupils show in a particular area at a certain period of time, and does not reflect their academic achievement in general. In order to find out more about the latter, pupils can be asked to compile a portfolio collecting their achievements.

How to do it

Pupils are asked to go through their school work over a certain period of time (for example, half a school year or one year) and put together evidence of learning in specific academic areas. This can be done in different ways: either they collect materials only from those areas in which they feel competent, which gives an insight into their personal strengths; or they can be asked to differentiate between areas of excellence, areas of average performance and problem areas. Portfolios are discussed and used as an indicator of the pupils' self-assessment and of their individual academic achievement.

How does it work?

Since the portfolio is a very personal way of communicating one's capabilities and achievements, it should not be regarded merely as a technical task. It is not just about collecting materials and putting them together, but builds on inclusive, pupil-involved communication. Therefore, as Richard Stiggins argues:

> Of all the dimensions of portfolios, the process of self-reflection is the most important. If we are to keep our pupils in touch with their emerging academic selves, we must share in understandable terms our vision of what it means to succeed, provide our pupils with a vocabulary to use in communicating about it, and keep them in touch with the accumulating evidence of their own proficiency. One way to hold them accountable for achieving a clear sense of themselves as learners is to have them write or talk about that accumulating evidence. (1997: 459)

This self-reflection can be enhanced by asking the pupils to put a summary sheet on top of each document they include in their portfolio, on which they:

- Give a reason why they have chosen this piece of work to be included.
- Write a summary of what the document contains.
- Give some background information which might help the reader to understand what might not be evident in the document.
- Hint at what the reader should pay particular attention to.

This communication should also flow both ways, of course, which means that the pupils should get some feedback on their achievements!

Activity 5   Discussing

Discussion is, of course, a type of communication which can be found in most evaluation activities, because it is intrinsic to the negotiating process. There are some methods, however, which specifically build on the discussion of issues between individuals or groups, and we have therefore grouped them under this heading.

Peer review

What is it?

Teacher development needs professional forms of feedback. Peer review is a

Worksheet for Peer Review

Reviewer _____ Reviewee _____ Class(es) _____ Date _____ Page ___

Agreed topic for peer review: _Self-regulation of the pupils in learning_

Indicator	Review issue	Comments
The pupils are allowed to decide independently in their work.		
The pupils are given time to do their work according to their own speed.		
The pupils ask if they have problems in fulfilling their task.		
The pupils monitor their work progress actively and reflect on their achievement.		

Figure 11.17 Worksheet for peer review.

formalised way of exchanging professional knowledge by mutual feedback on one another's work.

What is it for?

Teachers have a wealth of professional knowledge which, however, often remains restricted to their own classrooms. Self-evaluation taps into these individualised knowledge bases by bringing together different stakeholders. Peer review is a means of comparing and contrasting different procedures, habits and activities with a view to finding agreement or disagreement and thus providing a set of challenges which will drive the school forward.

How to do it

The most popular form of peer review is the mutual classroom visit. This can take place on an individual basis or at whole-school level. It is helpful to focus on a particular issue in peer review so that the discussion can take place around a topic which has been agreed on beforehand. In order to concentrate on the agreed focus, it may be helpful to keep track by means of a worksheet or schedule. The example in Figure 11.17 has been used to review the self-regulation of pupils in the learning process.

How does it work?

Since academic achievement plays a decisive role in pupils' success in school and thereafter, the quality criteria for testing and marking should be the subject of regular evaluation. Quality criteria can best be assessed by comparing and contrasting processes and results of testing and examining. There are several methods which may be used:

Within the school   Teachers exchange their tests and examinations, including results and/or gradings, among teachers of the same subject area (or across subjects), discussing differences and agreeing common standards.

Across schools   Teachers (in a particular subject area) find a school (of the same or a similar type) and arrange a peer review system, exchanging their tests and examinations, including the results.

Across countries   The same procedures can be used with schools in different countries, giving the review process a European perspective. (For setting up a review with another country, the use of email is an efficient way to proceed.)

Focus group

What is it?

Focus groups are put together to get a quick overview of the opinion of a group of people on a particular issue. This opinion is then taken to be representative of a larger part of the same constituency. Thus, focus groups provide a form of sounding board for the school.

What is it for?

Focus groups bring together anywhere from six to twenty people, representing a constituency of opinion. So, for example, a focus group of twenty parents might be selected to represent 'parents' views' as a whole. Questions and discussion then seek to elicit, with as much honesty and detail as possible, the views of that stakeholder group. This strategy, widely used by marketing firms and by governments in policy making, has the advantage of being economic and efficient and allowing for qualitative data and follow-up probing, but may be less reliable than questionnaires which draw on a larger, and possibly more representative, sample.

How to do it

It is important to prepare criteria for the selection of people who are invited to take part in the focus group(s), and these depend on the purpose of the inquiry. If parents are the focus group, they should be a representative group, including those parents who do not usually show up at school as well as those who do, because they are often the silent voices not usually heard. It is important to allow people to discuss things in detail in order to find out as much as possible about assumptions and expectations, so a time has to be found which enables everyone to attend. If there are multiple groups, it is helpful to draw up a list of questions so that in all groups the same questions are being asked. Results from different groups should then be collated. Sometimes it is helpful to use a validation process, in which results are sent out to the focus group(s) in order for them to verify that what is written accurately represents their views.

How does it work?

Schools using this methodology brought together samples of parents or pupils and used brainstorming techniques and discussion to explore issues of concern to the school. There were difficulties for schools in respect of sampling parents, therefore care needed to be exercised so that a fairly representative view was obtained. Management of these sessions also requires considerable skill so that people are not led in any preferred direction and are allowed to air their views openly and without censorship. This is where the critical friend can play an important, neutral, facilitating role.

In an Irish school, focus groups were used to evaluate the functioning of the tutor system (the pastoral role in which a teacher has responsibility for a class which he or she meets daily). Staff were divided into four groups, each group meeting four times to assess the operation of the system in light of pupils' needs. This was complemented by a questionnaire to a sample of 25 per cent of pupils on their experience of the tutoring system.

Another common form of follow-up was group discussions to analyse and interpret the questionnaire results. These sometimes involved pupils, teachers and parents in separate groups, sometimes in large groups, bringing all the stakeholders together. The use of provocative statements to guide people into discussion was a technique used in Finland, but again this is a procedure that demands great care and skill.

Activity 6   Enacting

Acting out a particular scene, experience or vision is a meaningful way of identifying issues and arriving at solutions or highlighting areas for further development.

Role play

What is it?

Role play is an activity which makes use of the human capacity for acting; what is acted can be a 'true' story or something imaginary. Role playing is always a total activity because it brings together thinking, feeling and acting as well as re-acting.

What is it for?

Role play can be used both as a form of evaluation and as a strategy following an evaluation. Its role in evaluation is unusual but potentially powerful. For example, asking pupils to act out how they see their class and their teacher can bring out into the open feelings, expectations, perhaps deeply buried experiences, of classroom life. But teachers can also role play situations – for example in training, by rehearsing or representing issues which are relevant for the development of the school.

How to do it

Role plays can be acted out spontaneously or after preparation, depending on their purpose and function in the evaluation process. Preparation time should be sufficient for the 'actors' to decide on the storyline and the 'plot', encapsulating the main messages to be conveyed. However, preparation should avoid scripting of all the dialogue, because role play has to build on the impromptu experiences of people acting out a known or imaginary event, with all its emotional connotations.

If younger pupils are involved, it may be helpful to prepare some role cards which contain the main aspects they have to think of in preparing the role play. Some rehearsal time gives more confidence before actually acting out the play. Because of its evaluative purpose, debriefing and follow-up play an important part, too. How this is handled will depend on the specific context in which the role play takes place.

How does it work?

In an English school, pupils took turns at being the teacher and role-playing a range of incidents in the classroom; for example:

- Two pupils talking while the teacher was talking.
- A pupil who didn't understand something.
- A pupil who wouldn't do what she was told.

The pupils offered different interpretations of what some of their teachers did, and what they might do differently, to manage the situation. This serves both purposes – being both evaluation and the potential for action.

A role play described by one Greek school also appears to serve both diagnostic and formative purposes. The teacher's group had identified racism as an issue at both school and national level and chose to explore the issue through a role play involving twenty pupils and three teachers. 'We acted out ideas that startled even ourselves' is how one pupil expressed his view of what had been learned through this initiative.

Story telling

What is it?

Another form of enacting is story telling. Story telling has a long tradition of keeping history alive and depends more on the personal interpretation of the story teller rather than on an exact replication of events.

What is it for?

Since stories are framed by deeply rooted experiences and feelings, they bring to the fore valuable data on a personal level. Stories are usually value driven – they have an implicit or explicit moral. Stories used for evaluation purposes are not the 'gossip' kind of stories told at coffee breaks (although this might also be interesting from an analytical perspective), but are structured within a formal framework, which, of course, depends on where and how they are used.

How to do it

Stories can be told in many different ways and by different people – by teachers, parents, pupils or other visitors. They may be true or fictitious but are told for a purpose and with an underlying moral. They are usually followed by discussion, teasing out the issues, suggesting alternative endings, or identifying critical points at which the story might have taken a different turn.

Advance organisers are often used to focus the listeners' attention on key themes or characters. For example: 'There are seven characters in the story. Each plays an important part in affecting the final outcome. As you listen, consider who was most responsible.'

How does it work?

Pupils form groups of three or four. Each group member tells his or her story about learning: 'Tell the others a story about when you really learned something (in class or outside class)!' Finally, the pupils of each group find out what was common in the various learning stories they have heard. Data from groups are collected and form the basis for further investigation and discussion.

Stories are deeply embedded in schools and other organisations, therefore they can become part of an annual calendar of evaluation activities. A good example comes from Minneapolis, where a large community services agency developed a 'Story-telling Day' as part of their annual evaluation cycle. This involved teams telling exemplary case stories of what their work that year had been all about. It took place in a large hall with hundreds of fellow workers present. It was extremely energising, helping to build the agency's sense of collective purpose.

Activity 7 Measuring

This section is devoted to methods that use numbers for evaluation. It begins by explaining what is meant by the term 'indicators' and then looks at the measurement of performance using 'value-added' indicators.

Indicators

What are they?

Teachers complain: 'The roll is always increasing in our school'; the head says: 'The drop-out rate decreased last year, for the first time since I came to this school'; while parents may say: 'I read in the paper that the performance of the school was getting worse. Is this situation going to improve or should I send my daughter elsewhere?' The use of indicators such as these is now very common in schools, but what are indicators? How should a school set about choosing those that are most relevant for its purpose? How can they be used for self-evaluation?

What are they for?

Indicators are statistics that say something about the health of the school and which allow for better decision making. 'Like a speedometer and fuel gauge in a car, educational indicators provide essential information about the school's current functioning, suggest whether good progress is being made, and warn of potential problems' (Oakes, 1986).

Focusing on decisions means that an indicator, taken singly or with others, should in the first instance help to determine whether a situation is satisfactory or not. Secondly, if the situation is found to be unsatisfactory, it should help to pinpoint areas for action.

Not all statistics, however, are useful as indicators. For example, the height of the headteacher is not a useful indicator because there is no evidence that it has any influence on the effectiveness of the school; there is therefore no reason to prefer a tall or a short headteacher. The mean salary of the teachers is a statistic but it is not a useful indicator either, as the school has (generally) no way of changing either these salaries or of changing the job according to the amount of money teachers are paid. Examination performance, on the other hand, provides information which has a direct influence on policy and practice at school and classroom level.

How to use them

The value of indicators depends on technical, conceptual and policy considerations.

The first technical consideration is that indicators must have a 'reference point' against which they can be judged: it may be some standard agreed by stakeholders, an objective that has been given by the governing board, by authorities, or, in a less normative way, the mean value of the indicators for similar schools, or their past value for the school. They should also have the following technical characteristics.

They should measure enduring features of the school, and be calculated on a regular basis – for example, every year – because understanding and identifying trends is of great importance for valid interpretation. Without periodic data, indicators cannot provide an early warning of emerging difficulties.

Indicators should be easily understandable by a broad audience. This does not necessarily mean that they have to be easy to calculate. Sometimes a sophisticated indicator is easier to use than a simple, but ambiguous, one. Sophisticated modern computers, for example, are easier to use than those current ten years ago. 'Repetition rate' (repeating a class for a further year) is an example of a simple, but ambiguous, indicator. Value-added indicators are complex, but are not very difficult to understand intuitively (for example, does the school do better than it should, given its intake?)

Indicators should be reliable and valid. 'Reliability' is a technical term describing the precision of the measuring instrument. A truancy rate is not reliable if some cases of truancy have not been registered. Even a measure of achievement through examination is never completely reliable, since the same pupil might perform better on one day than on another, or given a slightly different test. Happily, in good quantitative measurement, it is possible to measure reliability, to abandon the measure if the reliability is too weak, and to indicate a confidence interval which explains the amount of trust we can place in the data.

Validity is a more conceptual question. A measure is valid if it measures what it is intended to measure. The rate of success in a final examination, for instance, is not a totally valid indicator of a school's effectiveness, because there may be other causes, explanations and considerations. On the other hand, a thermometer is a valid instrument because the height of the mercury column, which is used as an indicator, is determined only by the heat of the air. An indicator may be valid even if it measures only part of a variable, as long as it provides useful information on the indicator as a whole. For instance, a truancy rate may be considered as a valid measure of teachers' time lost, if we accept the idea that the other variables which affect it (time lost during courses, for instance) increase or decrease with the truancy rate.

CONCEPTUAL CONSIDERATIONS

The value of an evaluation depends on the rightness of the global model of interpretation. For instance, a high level of violence may be interpreted as a consequence of laxity, which, in many instances, would not be correct. High rates of repeating classes (*répétition*) may be interpreted as a sign of ineffectiveness, but that will not always be the case. The use of quantitative indicators cannot guarantee that such misinterpretation will not occur.

Generally, an indicator system includes indicators on intake, resources, process and outcomes, but which are the relevant variables for each category is a matter for discussion. Misleading conclusions about the relationship between causes and consequences may lead to the construction or use of indicators which are not appropriate for the purpose or context. Indicators are no more than tools. They do not provide 'scientific' results, but rather offer pointers to areas for improvement or agenda items for discussion.

In order to devise or customise a system of indicators for its own evaluation, a school should :

- Make an inventory of existing indicators (those provided to the schools by educational authorities or other bodies).
- Make an initial evaluation (see the self-evaluation profile, Figure 9.1 on page 97) to determine in which areas they may be most needed.
- Choose the relevant indicators and consider what is still lacking
- Choose a procedure (for example, select a group involving several categories of stakeholders; decide how this group will make its conclusions known to a larger school audience; what kind of discussion will take place; and what action should be taken as a result of this discussion). Once indicators are selected, the real work is not at an end, it is just beginning!

POLICY CONSIDERATIONS

To be effective, a system of indicators has to be understood and agreed by the stakeholders. This means that stakeholders need time, training and experience so that they can take informed decisions about which indicators to ignore or include. Representatives of all stakeholder groups should participate in this. Without understanding and ownership, indicators may appear to have some kind of mysterious 'validity', so actually distancing the process from people rather than bringing it closer to them.

How do they work?

Using indicators of destinations, one school found that pupils from the vocational track were very often unemployed nine months after leaving school, while pupils from the same track who left school later found jobs quite easily. They drew the conclusion that the significance did not lie in the track itself, but in the higher degree of qualification. It provided a powerful argument for asking the authorities to lengthen the course requirements.

Another school investigated positive and negative sanctions given to pupils, using both qualitative and quantitative indicators. Parents, teachers and pupils gave their views on the findings, and a new system of rules was drawn up. The quantitative aspect of the inquiry produced indicators that were then used to monitor and evaluate the workings of the new rules.

From a careful analysis of tests in maths at entry to the school, maths teachers designed remedial courses and devised tests on specific remedial skills, then went on to provide indicators in respect of skills still to be mastered.

Measuring school performance

What is it?

What pupils know and can do on leaving school depends not only on the quality of the school. The creation of value-added indicators allows comparisons of schools with reference only to the part of the pupils' performance which the school itself is accountable for. They therefore provide a more valid representation of the quality of the school than 'raw' measures of these performances.

What is it for?

Most often, school performance is assessed by the rate of success in an examination or a test at the end of the final year – for example, the rate of success in the baccalauréat in France, or the percentage of pupils achieving five or more grades A to C in GCSE, in England and Wales. Alternatively, a school may be judged on an index such as this: 'I know a boy from this school who became a very famous surgeon'. In both cases, judgement of the school's quality is flawed. There are two reasons for this: First, this kind of measure takes no account of pupils' attainment on intake. If very good pupils are enrolled in a school, even a rather ineffective school can achieve good results.

Second, it does not take into account pupils who leave school before the final exam or do not sit it. If all weak pupils drop out or are persuaded to leave school before the final year, the school may have very impressive data while actually being quite ineffective.

This is a powerful argument for using value-added indicators of performance. These indicators compare measured performance (success rate in the baccalauréat, or the mean achievement in a maths test, for instance) with the *expected* performance. If the observed value is inferior to the expected value, that means that pupils have made less progress in this school than would be expected.

The expected value is calculated with reference to initial achievement or some other characteristics of the pupils which may affect their final achievement independently of the effect of the school. (For example, girls generally outperform boys, middle-class children generally outperform working-class children). Schools which have a 'better' intake will have a higher expected value (see Figure 11.18).

As shown in the figure, pupils from a number of schools sat an initial test at the beginning of the year, and a final test at the end of the year. Each pupil is represented by a symbol. Taken together, these show that there is a general relationship between initial and final achievement: the higher the initial achievement, the higher also the final one. This is not a surprising finding for any teacher or pupil. If a pupil performs in the final test exactly as predicted by her initial achievement, her position will be right on the 'regression line' which expresses the relationship between initial and final achievement (vertical axis). If she performs better than expected, she will be above the line; if worse than expected, she will be below the line. Suppose that your school is in the sample. Its pupils are those represented by a black spot rather than a lozenge. Since most of your pupils are above the line, it is

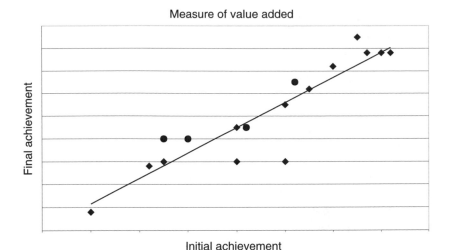

Figure 11.18 Measuring school performance.

an 'effective school' – or at least a school more effective than the mean of all the others in the sample. It has a positive added value in terms of what was tested, expressed by the formula 'In the final test, pupils in this school succeeded in X per cent more items of the test than expected, given the intake'.

Value added may be used to test academic achievement in any subject, as in our example, or for several aggregated subjects, or for some aspects of personal and social development. (For example, pupils' scores on a final test of their civic attitudes is Y per cent higher than expected from their scores on an initial test of these attitudes).

The statistical methods used for these calculations allow the use of more than one predictor. In the example given, the only predictor was initial achievement. But it is possible to add to this predictor some others, such as the social background or the ethnicity of the pupils. This can add to the accuracy of the prediction, bringing the value added nearer to the 'true' effectiveness of the school. It has been shown, however, that initial achievement is the best single predictor of final achievement.

Calculation of value added either requires that several schools engage in the same exercise, or that norms of achievement already exist. Such norms may be provided by local or national authorities, by research centres, or by other agencies which gather and feed back data.

How to do it

Calculation of value added may be done by agencies external to the school, as it is a time-consuming and expert exercise. For schools it is more important to know how to read and interpret the results.

- Data from tests measure achievement with some approximation. Therefore, good systems of indicators provide confidence intervals. For instance, if the value is X, and the confidence interval is ±2, we can be certain that the value of the indicator is somewhere between X–2 and X+2.
- The smaller the number of pupils who sit the test, the less reliable the data and so the bigger the confidence interval.
- Pupil mobility is a problem if initial and final achievement measures are taken more than one year apart. All schools experience 'attrition' through pupils moving on. So value added has to be calculated on a cohort of pupils who are there at both the initial and the final test.
- If a school has a positive value added in one domain, this may not be the case in other domains. While there is generally a positive correlation between overall performance in one academic subject and another, this correlation is not always very strong.
- Value-added indicators are only as good as the tests, examinations or scales with which they are constructed.
- Value-added indicators are powerful tools. However, they are only one part of the evaluation process. They need to be complemented with qualitative data, as they do not explain why performance is low or high. Other methods are needed to shed light on what lies behind rising or falling standards.

While these indicators do not seem too difficult to understand, they do require some explanation, especially for people who are unfamiliar with statistical techniques and representation of data in graphic form.

How does it work?

Value-added indicators give a global picture of a school's effectiveness and rarely point to specific action that needs to be taken. More detailed information is required to understand where the problems lie. For the purposes of school development planning, a combination of quantitative and qualitative data provides the best basis on which to proceed.

For schools and classroom teachers it is more useful to have value-added data at individual pupil level. As the availability and sophistication of technology grows, schools can hold attainment (or attitude) data for every pupil and, plotted against national, local or school norms, can show progression, regression, value added and value subtracted over time. With such data, of course, it is easy to compare the relative value added for individual teachers or departments. Such comparisons have, of course, to be treated with considerable caution and embarked on only where there is an atmosphere of trust.

Activity 8   Imaging

Picture evaluation

What is it?

Pictures can be used as a non-verbal evaluation instrument. These may be produced by participants in the evaluation (for example, children's drawings) or they may be commercially produced images (pictures taken from magazines, for example).

What is it for?

Images are used in evaluation when it is difficult to use language as a means of communication. Visualisation draws on different parts of the brain from the spoken word and taps into additional aspects of the human communicative capacity. When pupils are asked to draw how they see their school, their teachers or their relationships, they are able to express their feelings in a way that other media do not allow. Similarly, adults can use drawing to reflect on particular aspects of their personal or professional lives.

How to do it

If this technique is used to find out about vision or ideals, pupils or teachers can be asked to draw their dream schools. These can then be discussed, extracting and identifying underlying needs and expectations. The findings provide a valuable springboard for further steps in school development.

How does it work?

A Danish school used the 'picture evaluation' method with young children and the drawings they produced formed the starting point for discussion and interview. The picture they started from is shown as Figure 11.19.

The images used can, for example, be pictures of what pupils like and dislike about their schools, or how they see their teachers or headteachers.

Photo and video evaluation

What is it?

A still or video camera can be used to record aspects of school life for evaluation purposes. The visual products then provide the basis for further discussion and development. Now that digital cameras are widely available, photo evaluation can provide quick results.

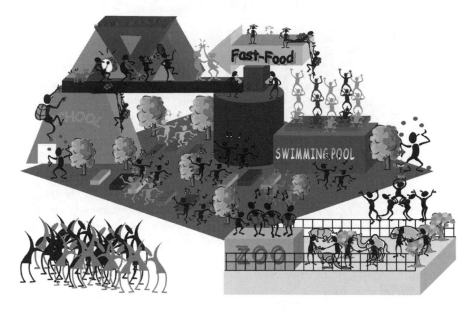

Figure 11.19   Starting picture for a Danish imaging exercise.

What is it for?

Pupils can be given a still or video camera as an evaluation tool to explore the culture of their school as a learning organisation. The pupils' photographic or video images convey a different meaning from the one they might express verbally or in answer to a questionnaire. Moreover, pupils have to collaborate and work towards consensus building in selecting images worth photographing, so they form little communities of action researchers as they explore their daily school settings from a different perspective.

There are several reasons for using a camera for evaluating schools (for example, as a social place):

- Pupils are not confronted with a prefabricated instrument to which they can only respond with agreement or disagreement.
- It breaks through the limitations of language by making use of the visual medium.
- The evaluation deals with different layers of reality inherent in schooling by making use of foreground and background, by using focusing, blurring and other techniques.
- It takes account of the emotional needs of the pupils.
- By presenting photographic evidence, pupils can offer 'hard' facts to support their views which then have to be dealt with by the adult world.

How to do it

As this technique involves pupils moving around the school freely, a clear proce-dure should be suggested, such as the following:

1   Self-selected groups of four or five pupils are formed.
2   Each group discusses the four places in school in which all group members feel happy, and four places where they feel *least* comfortable.
3   Teams decide how to frame their pictures in a way that will most graphically express their views – for example, the place itself or the people in it.
4   Members of the teams take the photographs or video shots according to what has been decided on in 3.
5   After having the photographs processed (if photographs are being used), each group produces a poster on which they arrange the photos and write com-ments to make clear what they like or dislike and why. If video has been used, a short trailer should be edited, containing the essence of the message.
6   Groups then present their posters or videos to the rest of the class and these are discussed with a view to further action.
7   A presentation of the posters or videos to a larger audience (for example, staff and/or parents) is prepared.

How does it work?

Photo evaluation, as described above, was a popular choice among pilot schools. It involved pupils capturing on camera aspects of school life that were significant for them, personally, socially or academically. It is, in a sense, a pictorial version of the force field (see page 128).

   In some countries, video as well as photography was used to complement obser-vation and day-to-day accounts, accompanied by recommendations as to what could be done to improve the school ethos. The Danish national report assessed the benefits of photo evaluation in these terms:

> Photo evaluation gives an opportunity to express some of the underlying so-cial norms in the school, which can be used as a basis for open and construc-tive dialogue naming the parties involved. The method is well suited for the electronic media and the pictures can be presented to an international audi-ence, for example by means of subtitled versions on the Internet.

Activity 9   Diarying

What is it?

A diary is a personal account in written form which combines both professional and personal experiences of the individual teacher or learner (cf. Holly, 1989). As such, it is a valuable instrument for pupils and teachers, who can keep regular notes of observations, experiences, feelings and thoughts. These can be used for mutual reflection from time to time.

What is it for?

Pupils can each be asked to keep a personal journal (diary) for several puposes: it can help them to express their feelings and thoughts; it encourages them to develop the habits of self-reflection and self-expression; they can learn to communicate important issues in their own words; they can focus on specific issues if asked by the teacher to pay particular attention to these aspects. Diaries allow for the recording of information of a more personal kind, written down privately by each pupil (for example, how they experience a day in school, how they are treated outside class, how they deal with conflict situations such as bullying or violence).

Similarly, teachers can use a professional journal to monitor issues over time. Diary entries are private and therefore not written for somebody else. So they can become partners in professional development, keeping track of experiences people may be reluctant to talk about openly with others. Therefore, there is room for anything which is worth recording from the writer's perspective. Entries can range from abstract ideas, or detailed description of observations in the classroom, to interpretations of experiences and feelings in an emotionally charged situation.

How to do it

Pupils can be asked to keep a home–school diary, in which they record information on difficulties they are having in managing a task, a problem with teachers, difficulty with work at school or at home. It is important, however, that the information they provide is as specific as possible, so it is useful to ask them to clarify: When exactly did the problem occur? What was the obstacle to doing the job successfully? What information was missing to complete the task? What have you tried so far in order to solve the problem? Who and what could have helped? And so on.

From time to time pupils can be given the opportunity to get together and talk about certain issues in their diaries and exchange views with their teacher (or another person, such as a social worker or psychologist). While keeping a diary has a strong self-reflective element – its main purpose being as a private record of pupils' experiences – nonetheless it can also have its uses in monitoring personal and social development and as an agenda for more structured sessions.

How does it work?

The following extract from a personal–professional diary gives an idea of the potential of such journal entries if they are used in a developmental way.

> Only today, while I am sitting here, thinking about yesterday's meeting and writing down my impressions, I am grasping the sense of writing a professional diary.

My first surprise appeared when the strict seating arrangement was broken up and we suddenly were sitting across from each other. I found that the atmosphere became more relaxed, although some colleagues felt somehow insecure.

I was not so happy with the result: the discussion reminded me more of coffee house talk than of serious discussion with the topic. I was disappointed by the way the discussion was led.

Activity 10   Profiling

What is it?

A profile helps to make visible the relationships among different factors, people or agencies. It can highlight closeness or distance, importance or relative status. It usually takes the form of a drawing or sketch, reducing complexity into a more graphic, accessible format.

What is it for?

A profile is used to highlight in visual form the views of different groups of stakeholders. The various components of a given situation or set of interrelationships is sketched out on a sheet of paper or flipchart, making clear how they are connected to one another. Symbolic markers are used to flesh out or highlight particular aspects such as closeness and distance, status of relationship or degree of importance. An individual or group profile is a good starting point for discussions about personal and professional development, whether at the individual or the organisational level.

How to do it

School life always reflects other, wider social systems. The school's relationships with these are important to its effective working. A profile of the environment offers a visual overview of how these all interrelate, and can help in developing differentiated developmental strategies.

- Make a list of all the relevant contexts of your school (agencies, groups of people, individuals).
- Differentiate the relevant environments according to:
    their importance for the school (size of circle in the graph)
    distance from the school (nearness or distance in the graph).
- Describe the relationship between the environments and the school from the external perspectives: expectations and fears (+ positive, – negative, ± ambivalent, –* of particular value to the relationship).

See Figure 11.20 for an example of such a diagram.

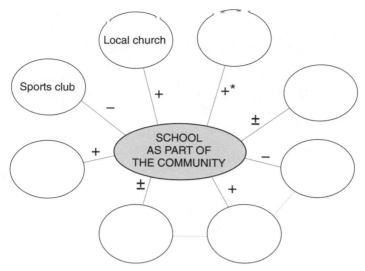

Figure 11.20 Profiling diagram.

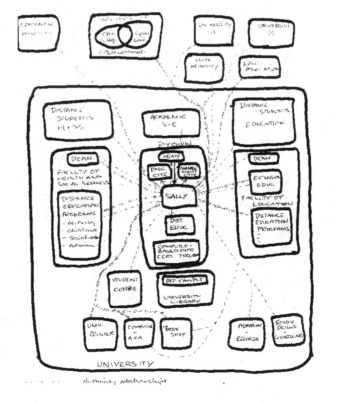

Figure 11.21 Professional map (from Schratz and Walker, 1995: p.152)

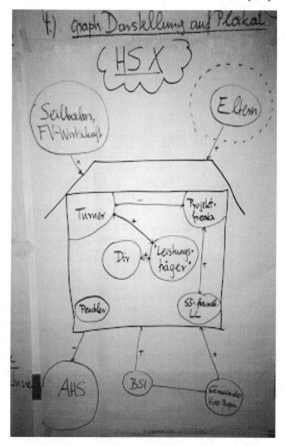

Figure 11.22 Drawing of relationships between system partners (from Schratz and Steiner-Löffler, 1998a: p.103)

How does it work?

Profiles can be used in very different work settings. Figures 11.21 and 11.22 show two examples which have been used to identify particular aspects in the micropolitics of schooling and relationships among people or systems.

Both the professional map, depicting a profile of the work relationships of a head of school, and the drawing, showing the relationships between the different partners the school has to deal with, form the basis for in-depth discussions about possible future steps – on both the individual and the organisational level.

12 The work of the critical friend

The European pilot project on quality evaluation in school education had as one of its central elements a critical friend, working with schools on improvement strategies. The idea of a critical friend has been around for some time and has international currency, although there is little in the way of hard evidence to tell us how effective such a role is, or how it works in different contexts and in different kinds of relationships.

The international character of the project provided a useful framework for examining the workings of this form of support. The critical friend was not neutral, but acted in a support role and as advocate of the school, working alongside management and teachers to help in the work of school improvement with critical input as appropriate. He or she was 'an outsider who was nevertheless familiar with the school' as one school phrased it. According to Costa and Killick a critical friend is:

> A trusted person who asks provocative questions, provides data to be examined through another lens and offers a critique of a person's work as a friend. A critical friend takes time to fully understand the context of the work presented and the outcomes that the person or group is working toward. The friend is an advocate for the success of that work. (1993: p. 22)

The premise is that schools need friends. It is widely agreed that it is difficult for schools to be self-sufficient islands of excellence and that it is not easy to be a self-improving school in a world in which change is accelerating and the growth of knowledge is exponential. The value for schools is in having an outside perspective, a reference point and connection with a wider field of knowledge. External support and networking with an 'enlightened eye' can be challenging and motivating. The critical friend is a powerful idea, perhaps because of its inherent tension: friends bring a high degree of unconditional positive regard, whereas critics are conditional, negative and intolerant of failure. The reconciliation of these Janus faces depends on a successful marrying of unconditional support and unconditional critique. It demands, says Sarason (1986) an 'exquisite sensitivity':

Openness	→ Does the CF have hidden agendas or is s/he open?
Listening	→ Is the CF a good listener so as to be sensitive to the needs of different individuals and groups of stakeholders in the school?
Understanding	→ Does the CF have a good understanding of the context of the school (structure and culture)?
Advice	→ Is the CF able to give helpful advice?
Relationship with teachers	→ How well does the CF get on with the teachers who are the driving force in quality development?
Communication	→ How well can the CF communicate his/her ideas?
Challenge	→ Is the critical friend challenging enough in a way that his/her critique has some impact on the school?
Resource	→ Is the CF a good resource for the school?

Figure 12.1 Checklist of key issues important for the work of the critical friend.

For an outsider to approach school personnel without being exquisitely sensitive to their feelings and attitudes ... is to guarantee that the chances of having the desired effect will be very small. (Sarason, p. 12)

The critical friend, feeling her or his way in the early stages of a relationship with the school, has to try to get inside, and stay close to, what the school 'is' from different perspectives and what change might mean from those differing standpoints.

From a psychological point of view we might say that without friends it is difficult to live with critics. Implicit in the concept of the critical friend is that he or she embeds any challenge to the school within a supportive and friendly approach. It is designed to be a collegial relationship in which people can listen to one another, weigh up ideas openly and critically and speak without fear of censorship.

Accordingly, the concept of the critical friend works on the inherent tension between a critical attitude to the school so as to challenge its practice, and the unconditional support of the people involved so that they feel accepted and listened to. This tension is managed by the critical friend, drawing on a repertoire of competencies such as those described in Figure 12.1.

Of course, not all competencies suggested by the participating schools could be met by those cast in the role of critical friends. They bring with them their personal and professional experience, their history of other schools and their past successes and failures. The relationship they are able to establish in the early days of their entrée to the school is also a critical factor.

The work of critical friends will be significantly affected by the long or short-term nature of their relationship with the school and the formality or informality of their role. This is depicted in Figure 12.2.

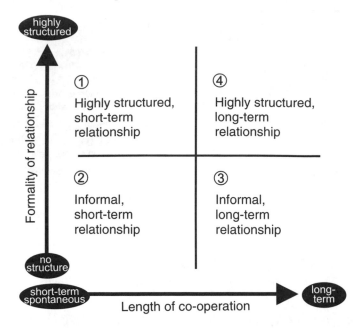

Figure 12.2 Forms of relationship between a critical friend and a school.

The vertical axis refers to the formality and the horizontal axis refers to the length of co-operation with the school. The intersect of these provides four quadrants, each of which describes a different kind of relationship between a critical friend and a school.

A highly structured, short-term relationship is usually established if the school needs support in a critical phase. When a school needs an outside view on a certain issue, the head or somebody else (such as staff or parents) may ask for outside support for a given period. This may be the case where a school is conducting a self-evaluation and wants information on 'blind spots' in their findings. Feedback from a critical friend who is sympathetic and yet critical can help to explore some of the complexities and ambiguities in the findings. 'Recruiting' of the critical friend is usually organised formally by involving the school's decision-making bodies so as to get an agreement on the appropriateness of the critical friend at that juncture and for that task.

Informal, short-term intervention by a critical friend is usually necessary if a school is facing immediate problems which it cannot deal with on its own. For example, if a school is suddenly faced with an allegation from the outside (for example, by the press), the head might get in touch with somebody he or she knows personally who has some experience of media work so that the school can react promptly and professionally, since time constraints often make it difficult to hire somebody through a long selection process; it may only allow an informal, short-term relationship. One school reported that they needed some advice on how to analyse the data obtained from a questionnaire. One member of staff knew

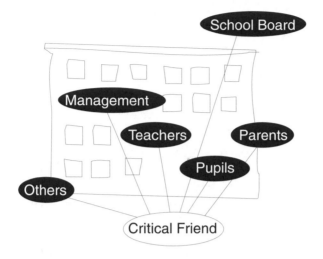

Figure 12.3 Partners of the critical friend in school.

somebody at university whom she asked to help out on that occasion. Only two meetings with the steering group were needed to clarify the task.

An informal, long-term relationship often takes place if there is a loosely coupled co-operation between a school and a university department. An example of this is where student teachers regularly go to one school on teaching practice and their supervisor builds up a relationship with school staff. From time to time they make use of the supervisor on visits to students by asking him or her to stay on for an extra time and discuss recent developments with them. The supervisor is pleased to have this direct contact with school practice and may wish to conduct further studies. Critical friends in such an informal, long-term relationship are usually very knowledgeable about the culture of the school, its history and its micropolitics. With this long-term history, mutual trust among the partners can be built up, making critical friends a valuable source of support for a school.

A highly structured, long-term relationship can be found where schools contact an outside agency such as a consultancy firm. In these circumstances a contract is usually drafted, forming the basis for co-operation and containing working procedures for a formal relationship between the consultants and the school. Where such a contract exists, it is usually difficult to ask for spontaneous intervention because the planning phases are worked out over longer periods. The advantage of this relationship can be in the distance between the critical friend and the various actors, whereas in informal relationships there is often a closer familiarity between individuals or small groups.

Whatever the form of the relationship of the critical friend to the school, as an outsider he or she has only limited time to spend with the school. Therefore the scope for involving people is limited and the critical friend can only communicate with specific individuals or groups. We might describe the nature of the work as 'segmented' by the stakeholders to which the friend has to relate (see Figure 12.3).

Although critical friends are most often involved with management, teachers and other staff, they may also work with pupils and parents, bringing an extra dimension to their involvement with the school.

There are also external factors which influence the work of the critical friend, such as the relationship with the inspectorate and other relevant agencies. External forces, such as pressure from outside, play an important part too.

Key competencies of a critical friend

Because of the complexity of the work involved, a critical friend has to react to the here and now situation found when called to or visiting a school. Therefore they must be competent in whatever the situation asks for. In the pilot project the schools attributed a wide range of competencies to the critical friend. These are illustrated in Figure 12.4.

Of course, not all the competencies mentioned can be met by the people in the role of critical friends. They can only act in terms of their respective backgrounds or day-to-day work situation in the European project. Critical friends came from a range of backgrounds: in-service trainer, researcher, university teacher (with different research backgrounds ranging from education to philosophy), member of town council, parent, consultant, professional evaluator, business manager, psychoanalyst, army officer, headteacher (of another school; retired). It is not surprising therefore to find a school commenting about their critical friend in these terms: 'She was kind and well-meaning, but on issues of methodology and actually getting to grips with the topics her involvement and performance left much to be desired.' Critical friends themselves, however, also remarked on the inherent tension, being critical and yet sympathetic at the same time. Figure 12.4, drawn from people's experiences of their critical friend, illustrates six distinct roles and relevant behaviour within each of these.

Do's and don'ts for a critical friend

Figure 12.5 is an example of what one group of teachers suggested when asked to advise the critical friend on what to do and what to avoid.

How to be successful as a critical friend

From the experiences of the project schools a broad range of success criteria for the work of a critical friend were derived. These are noted in Figure 12.6.

Within this broad spectrum of roles and skills, critical friends have to find the best fit between what they bring (competencies) and what the task and context require (competences). Finding this mix, or match, and making it work to the satisfaction of stakeholders is the challenge to be met.

Scientific adviser	• Provides useful advice • Offers a clear picture of the school's strong and weak points • Gives information and materials about self-evaluation and school development • Provides methods and other support • Gives clear guidelines on how to implement proposals • Shares knowledge • Creates quality through reflection, assists in methodology • Makes work more 'professional' • Helps prepare seminars
Organiser	• Moderates meetings • Keeps time • Structures the process • Helps in organising the SEP work • Provides guidelines for actions • Prepares meetings or whole-school activities • Comments on strategic discussions • Sets out clear objectives • Directs working parties effectively
Motivator	• Gives reassurance and encouragement • Is a good listener • Creates a sense of importance of the project in the school • Demands more from the school • Is inspiring and encouraging • Stops participants from becoming too ambitious • Makes self-evaluation understandable • Helps in finding new ideas • Keeps the work going • Proceeds by small steps • Gives an idea of where things lead to • Promotes ongoing activities • Helps to bridge gaps • Helps in focusing • Encourages a positive approach to collaborative work • Helps pupil motivation and parental co-operation in the project • Prompts the action groups to recast the working tools
Facilitator	• Handles emotions • Keeps the balance between personal and professional matters • Lays fresh emphasis on the context-related aspects of the learning process at school • Asks questions about interpersonal relations <div align="right">*continued ...*</div>

Figure 12.4 Range of competencies of the critical friend.

Networker	• Builds networks
	• Suggests possible partners outside/from other schools
	• Helps in team building, strengthens the co-operation between school and work
	• Acts as a contact person with students of the teacher training college and the university
Outsider	• Brings in an outside view, is critical of the 'ordinary'
	• Occasionally brings in counter arguments
	• Creates multiple perspectives, mirrors one's own perceptions
	• Enhances coherence among diverse viewpoints
	• Calls the school into question in terms of its organisational aspects
	• Analyses the school from the perspective of another enterprise

Figure 12.4 continued

Do	Don't
• Be aware of his/her role	• Rush to a judgement
• Show a positive attitude towards the school	• Assume a directive role
	• Provide instant solution or quick fixes
• Listen and negotiate	• Collude or take sides
• Encourage and support participative decision making	
• Encourage the sharing of ideas	

Figure 12.5 Do's and don'ts for a critical friend.

The clearer the definition of the relationship between the school's representatives and the critical friend the easier collaboration will be in the long run.

If the critical friend is supportive rather than dominating (steering), the school has more opportunity for self-directed development.

Although schools appreciated the expertise of the critical friend, in certain areas she or he was more successful as a generalist rather than a specialist. There were cases, however, when the critical friend (CF) was requested to adopt a more specialist role.

It is important who the critical friend works with. If the CF works with the parents and students (rather than just with the head or the steering group) this is likely to lead to increased involvement in self-evaluation activities.

The impact of the critical friend is likely to be less fruitful if the CF does not identify enough with the work at the school or is not available when the school needs support.

The critical friend seems not to be as influential in a case where the school inspector works intensively with the school. It is important therefore to establish a healthy relationship between a critical friend and the inspectorate.

If there is a culture of positive critique within the school the critical friend has more opportunity to play a critical role. In these circumstances good advice is 'Be careful, criticism can lead to offence'.

Figure 12.6 How to be successful as a critical friend.

13 The schools

We may measure the success of the European project in a number of ways. We may ask:

- What has it added to the common stock of knowledge about self-evaluation?
- What strategies and tools has it contributed to what already exists?
- How has it affected thinking at high policy level Europe-wide?
- How has it contributed to shaping of policy at national level?
- What difference has it made at individual school level?
- What positive impact has it had on the lives of teachers or students?

In the final chapter we suggest some answers to these larger questions, but in this penultimate chapter we consider the impact at the level of individual schools, their teachers and students. The brief accounts which follow illustrate what schools in different countries did, the issues they faced and the changes it made to their policies and practice.

The first two examples are from schools in Belgium and Scotland. Both faithfully followed the suggested protocol, filling out the self-evaluation profile and selecting five areas for further investigation and improvement. In both cases, areas for further inquiry were related closely to the school development plan and fed in helpfully to future priorities for action. Both schools expressed surprise at the maturity and insights of the students and both testified to the impact of the process. In the Belgian school the head chose to be present at virtually all meetings and gained many insights from that experience. In the Scottish school the head chose not to participate in order not to influence the outcome or process of discussion. These are matters for individual balance of judgement, with the optimum scenario probably being a judicious choice of when to be present and when to withdraw. Both schools drew some similar conclusions from their involvement and offer good advice for others.

- To follow through on the evaluation to tangible application.
- To choose carefully the areas to evaluate in greater depth and be clear about grounds for doing so.
- To be clear from the start how data will be gathered, analysed and used.

- To stick with and integrate procedures into the ongoing life of the school.

The Scottish school chose to be described under its real name. The Belgian school has been anonymised by the new head in respect for her predecessor.

The third case study comes from Austria and illustrates an evaluation process that was used across a number of schools. Photo evaluation was new to virtually all schools in the project but it was one that became very popular. At the first project conference in Luxembourg, photo evaluation was introduced in a participative way, with delegates evaluating the conference through pictorial representation of key issues and themes. At the second conference in Vienna a year later, schools came with the products of their photo evaluation, to share, discuss and build on next time round.

Finally there is a short graphic contribution from a group of students in a Swedish school. It illustrates very simply and helpfully the process they went through in their school, from the student-eye vantage point.

All of these case studies attest to the vitality and inclusivity of the process.

Case study: St Fiacre's School

St Fiacre's School – let us call it that – had no culture of self-assessment before it took part in the pilot project. This did not hinder it from carrying out an impressive and coherent series of investigations. As the assessment took place at a time when the school had to draw up its mission statement, it was possible to use the results to plan for the future, and the school grasped this opportunity.

From a technical point of view the evaluation was not particularly innovative: it was based mainly on the use of questionnaires and focused on those areas calling for decisions at school level rather than class level. While the various groups of stakeholders expressed a need for technical support in the development of evaluation tools, they did not really succeed in finding one that closely matched their needs. Even though an external expert paid two visits to the school, it was not seen as helpful in this technical respect. In a nutshell, the evaluation was not altogether plain sailing, but it is in dealing with the imponderables that we get a true insight into how evaluation works.

The background

The school teaches about 500 pupils aged between twelve and eighteen from a rural catchment area in Belgium. It is a Catholic school, but almost all the pupils come from the surrounding villages and choose the school because of its proximity, as a survey of parents undertaken during the pilot project confirmed. In Belgium, independent education is subsidised by the state, so parents pay virtually nothing.

When the self-evaluation project started in September 1997, St Fiacre's School had existed in its current form for only a year. It was created by the merger of two schools, a process accompanied by considerable changes in the school's culture, under the leadership of the new head.

The school started the pilot project late and in a rather unorthodox way. Instead of taking time to study the project and then deciding to apply – which is how things were supposed to happen in theory – the head was asked to take part by the Catholic Education Federation, which had recently been invited to choose a rural school to participate in the project. The head tells the story like this:

> I went down to the cafeteria and talked about it with some of the teachers. I got the feeling that they appreciated being chosen by the Federation, that it was a form of recognition after the difficult times we had been through. So I said yes. But we were entering unknown territory – we hadn't seen the document presenting the project and we didn't really know what we were letting ourselves in for.

The result of this late start was that the school only had a week or two to put together a steering group and complete the self-evaluation profile. The steering group overseeing the project consisted of the head, two teachers, a pupil and a parent. It met once a month during the year over which the project ran.

The completion of the SEP took place in two stages. First, six groups of six people met twice each for one hour to go through and score the self-evaluation profile. Each group then elected a delegate to be part of an umbrella group, and this group then selected areas to be evaluated in greater depth. The thirty-six people were all volunteers but it was not difficult to find them. As one of the two previous headteachers had been highly authoritarian, the opportunity for individuals to air their opinions was welcomed. Indeed, this was the very first time that the pupils, and even the teachers, had been asked for their views on how the school was run.

Almost two years on, the head recalls clearly what happened in these groups (which she attended regularly). She was surprised by the maturity of the pupils and their considerable interest in the exercise. She found she had overestimated what parents really knew about the school and she was surprised at the difficulty they experienced in finding common grounds of agreement.

'As the school had changed a lot in just one year,' she remarked, 'some people's comments related more to the old situation before the merger, whilst other people described the new school. Some discrepancies can be explained in that way.'

Today, with the benefit of hindsight, she still believes that the process they went through really did help to improve relations within the school. The SEP process was challenging and useful although, when it came to the selection of the five areas to evaluate in greater depth, the choice was, in a sense, already predetermined: 'We went for those areas in which changes had already begun to take place. Basically, we used the project to continue what we had already started.'

Those familiar with the Commission guidelines might well have seen this as a lost opportunity, but such a judgement would be mistaken. What the school did was to build on their experience rather than venture into entirely new territory. The five areas chosen for further evaluation were not necessarily the most problematic but rather those where there was the greatest promise of success and growth. These were:

- Pupil destinations
- Time as a resource for learning
- Support for learning difficulties
- School as a social place
- Home and school.

Not just one but several evaluations were carried out in each of these areas. These are described in a detailed and comprehensive 180-page report which was distributed to the school governors. Results were discussed with teachers at a two-hour staff meeting attended by 70 per cent of the staff, and a copy of the report was placed in the staffroom.

Pupil destinations

At St Fiacre's, final-year pupils have a special project to do (*travail de fin d'études* or TFE) which, despite its name, is not a piece of schoolwork. The aim is for pupils to trace, in their own judgement, their development during their school career in two areas: 'Self-knowledge' and 'Personal and professional development'.

A questionnaire on the usefulness and quality of the work performed in the context of the TFE was sent to pupils who had just left the school. The report notes that very few pupils in the technical and vocational streams responded, probably because answering the questions called for a high level of self-awareness plus analytical and writing skills, which made it difficult for them. Their response rate was too low for their results to be used, which is unfortunate for the few who made the effort to respond.

On the other hand, the survey of pupils in the general education stream was more productive. Teachers responsible for the TFE had done their own evaluation in September 1997. Pupils and teachers had agreed on several operational principles, for example that from the outset they should be aware of the criteria by which it would be assessed.

In addition to this, a survey of pupils who had left the school in 1991 and 1994 was carried out to ascertain what had happened to them since leaving and what they thought about how the school had prepared them for life after school. Although respondents thought that the various subjects had been well taught on the whole, they cast doubt on the efficacy of organising secondary education on the basis of rigid subjects. Some believed that the curriculum should be oriented more towards personal development and culture, while others wanted more emphasis on the technical skills needed for higher education, such as note-taking or learning to manage one's own work.

Time as a resource for learning

A two-part questionnaire on time management was distributed to pupils. First, they had to account for the time spent on various activities during a week and second, they had to say whether they were satisfied with the time spent on each activity, taking into account the usefulness and 'quality' of this time. As the survey focused on the division of time between schoolwork and other activities and did not differentiate between different school activities, the usefulness of the data was limited and a more detailed survey is planned for the future. The school also learned that planning and piloting of the qualitative part of the survey would need to be thought through more carefully in the future, with more emphasis being given to the question of precisely why the survey was being conducted.

Teachers were also surveyed, not on their periods of absence as such but on the lessons which were not taught because of absence. While the response rate was only 52 per cent, the survey showed nonetheless that many lessons were still being lost to in-service training. This raised the question: Would it be a good idea to cut the amount of in-service training? To sacrifice that many hours? To ask teachers to do more training in their own time? As a result of the survey, the issue was debated in the staff council, a body comprising members of management and teaching staff. It was decided that the number of in-service training days which could be taken out of normal teaching days should be cut from six to four.

Support for learning difficulties

Under this heading, the report assesses the school's remedial lessons and the tests taken at the beginning and end of the academic year by all first-year pupils.

First- and second-year pupils who are having difficulties receive a 'remedial' lesson every week. This is taken by teachers from the school, but not necessarily the pupils' normal class teachers. The system was initially evaluated in 1996–97, leading to a considerable improvement. However, the 1997–98 assessment yielded similar results to the previous evaluation – that is, pupils were satisfied and teachers felt that while remedial lessons had improved pupils' behaviour they had not raised academic attainment by any significant degree.

This finding left the teaching staff divided as to what conclusions to draw. Some believed that the remedial lessons should concentrate more on working methods, learning techniques and so on, while others believed that they should concentrate more on the subjects themselves.

All first-year pupils, not only those having difficulties, are tested in French and mathematics. In fact, this test is given to all Belgian pupils at the start of the year in order to test the key skills which they ought to have acquired at primary school. The report gives the results for each of the six classes at this level, but it does not give an overall figure for the whole school or provide information about the gap between the weakest and the ablest pupils, between boys and girls, or the proportion of pupils with problems in both French and mathematics. In other words, the results of this test still have to be exploited to their full potential.

Nevertheless, two very important pieces of information came out of the survey.

First, it was noted that pupils having difficulties at the beginning of the year were usually still having them at the end of the year. It was concluded that the tests were effective at identifying difficulties, and so it was decided to use them, in addition to teachers' judgements, as a basis for deciding which pupils should be given remedial support.

Second, hardly any classes showed end-of-year results representing a real improvement on the results at the beginning of the year. (As no significance test was performed on the discrepancy between the tests at the beginning and end of the year, it is difficult to say whether results are real or purely accidental.) In three cases (two mathematics classes and a French class) results were clearly lower. In other words, between primary and secondary many pupils had lost important skills, such as the ability to manipulate fractions, for example. This is perhaps because it was assumed that these skills had already been mastered. As for those pupils with the greatest difficulties, who did not have these skills when they arrived, the report shows that they evidently did not pick them up during the year. The school's development plan for 1999–2002 mentions a new activity based explicitly on the results of these tests: 'Exchange of documents and practices between primary school teachers and those teaching the first year of secondary school'.

School as a social place

All pupils were surveyed on school life, asking them what they thought of their physical environment, the school's resources, school rules, relationships with teachers and extra-curricular activities. The pupils helped to draw up the questionnaire and analyse responses. The experience has shown what could be done differently and better in the future. For example, as the questionnaire asked respondents only about their level of schooling, information about age, gender or previous school career were not available, so preventing what might have been useful comparisons among different categories of pupils. Categories chosen for multiple choice responses proved to be insufficiently discriminating with, for example, only three categories of response ('all of them', 'some of them' or 'none of them') on questions such as 'Were your courses interesting?'

Of course, pupils judge their school in terms of their own experience, and are limited by their breadth of experience and terms of reference. This does not make the questionnaire any less useful but has implications for the design and framing of questions.

The pupil responses did serve to alert the school to those areas about which pupils are very unhappy: the toilets, school rules, teachers 'whose only response is to punish'. There were complaints and suggestions from pupils in an open-ended section which merited closer attention. They alerted staff to things to which they had become so accustomed that they no longer noticed them. For example, that 'the flowers painted on the walls at the end of the playground would be more appropriate at a nursery school', or the request to place benches in the playground.

This evaluation was also followed by action. The management of the school 'tried to introduce a new way for pupils to relate to their teachers', but confessed, 'it's not easy'.

The development plan provides for benches to be installed in the playground and, according to the head, this will happen in 1999–2000. School rules are not going to be changed in the near future. According to the head 'even if we were to get all the parties around a table it would be difficult to achieve anything without first teaching democracy'. Indeed, a new activity included in the development plan – 'Setting up of a school council: learning how to be a class delegate and conduct meetings' – shows that real efforts are being made to teach pupils about democracy.

Home–school links

As an independent school which has recently experienced considerable change, St Fiacre's was concerned about its image with parents. In fact, as we have seen, the links between parents and the school were rather weak, and the school had few informal ways of finding out about its image. A parents' association was created only recently and, even now, teachers are heard to say to pupils whose parents are members, 'You shouldn't think that you can get away with murder just because your parents are in the association'!

A survey focusing on parents' reasons for choosing the school, their perception of the quality of life enjoyed by their child(ren) at the school and their opinion on certain activities, was sent to 450 families. The response rate was about 50 per cent. One significant result of this survey was that the parents of pupils in the vocational and technical streams were far more inclined than parents of children in the general education stream to believe that the quality of life enjoyed by their child(ren) at school was low.

The conclusion to the evaluation focused on three aspects – the school environment, remedial lessons and pupil participation in the life of the school. In fact, these concerns are set out clearly in the development plan. The self-evaluation proved to be very useful in deciding on the future direction of the school, not only because it improved relationships between the various stakeholders, but also because it helped them to become better acquainted with the school and better able to plan ahead.

To conclude this case study, it will be useful to summarise some of the lessons that can be drawn from it:

- Members of a school community are generally willing to take part in an evaluation of this kind but it does creates a moral obligation to use the findings to make real decisions and, to a certain extent, to involve those stakeholders in the decision-making process. It is therefore important to link evaluation and planning, as was done here.
- It is important to choose carefully a small number of areas to assess, taking the

time to think properly about the objectives of the investigation and the best tools to use.

- It should be decided right from the start how to analyse the data and how decisions will be taken on the basis of these data. The evaluation is, in fact, a decision-making process for everyone: the headteacher, teachers and other stakeholders.
- This approach is only worthwhile if you stick with it over the long term. It can sometimes be a good idea to evaluate at several points in time, as demonstrated at St Fiacre's by the gradual improvement in the remedial courses following several separate evaluations. More often than not, however, an individual area will not need to be evaluated in depth every year, so that, over time, it will be possible to assess all the relevant areas one by one.

Case study: St Kentigern's

St Kentigern's Academy was one of the two Scottish schools involved in the project. It had previous experience of self-evaluation, as this is part of the Scottish Executive Education Department's (SEED's) policy for all schools. However, the school saw the Socrates project as an opportunity to broaden and strengthen its approach to self-evaluation and to move to a greater inclusiveness among stakeholder groups – staff, pupils and parents. The project provided the opportunity to test with more rigour and invention the question 'How good is our school?' which, in Scotland, is where the interrogation of school quality and effectiveness begins.

St Kentigern's Academy is situated more or less halfway between Glasgow and Edinburgh. It draws in pupils from the immediate village of Blackburn and a large surrounding rural area, traditionally very dependent on coal mining and heavy engineering but now facing major social change. Shifts in working patterns have created high levels of unemployment and extensive deprivation. West Lothian, the education authority in which the school is located, has the lowest rate of uptake for further and higher education of anywhere in Scotland. In this context, the school sees itself as having two key tasks:

1   How do we help our students become independent learners/thinkers to equip them to play a valuable role in society?
2   How do we prepare our students to be enterprising, confident and self-reliant?

Each year St. Kentigern's admits 200 students into its first year of secondary education. These students come from ten primary schools varying widely in socio-economic background. On leaving school, the majority will settle for work in the local area. In their report on the project, the school adds this:

> The opportunity to take part in the Socrates pilot project afforded an exciting extra dimension to the school's work in the quality assurance field, since it provided our colleagues with ideas from all over Europe and we welcomed the opportunity to learn from others during the project. Moreover, the possibility

of building an active network with European colleagues, particularly those who had identified the same development priorities as ourselves, was a very important feature of the project.

With this in mind, the school chose to pursue learning issues in its follow-up to the SEP process. This is what it did.

The SEP and after

Three discrete groups were formed to go through the self-evaluation profile – parents, staff and students. The headteacher did not have any input to this process in order not to influence the judgements of the groups. The three groups then came together to agree on a common judgement of their school and were surprised to find a very high level of agreement on their ratings. Decisions about which areas to focus on fell out quite easily from this process. These were not only identified as significant areas for all of the three groups, but closely reflected priorities incorporated in the school development plan. Three were closely interrelated and focused specifically on learning. These were:

- Academic achievement
- Quality of learning and teaching
- Support for learning difficulties.

The two other chosen areas were:

- School as a professional place
- School and home.

In the words of the headteacher, Kath Gibbons:

> It was an excellent way to begin. The self-evaluation profile provided the opportunity from the start to involve students and to create a sense of ownership among teachers and parents too.

Identifying areas for evaluation

In their report compiled for the Vienna conference, the school describes the rationale for this choice of areas in the following terms:

> Three years ago, the most distinctive feature of the school approach to learning and teaching was passive, a culture borne out of low expectations of students and staff. In terms of attainment, ceilings had been reached. The socioeconomic background of the school did not encourage the concept of 'challenge'.

With a more consistent challenge to complacency and low expectations, staff believed that levels of academic achievement could be raised significantly across the school. This, it was felt, depended not simply on good or better teaching. The school culture already encouraged an emphasis on good teaching. What it needed was a closer focus on effective learning and an examination of the different contexts in which this took place. So, the focus could encompass classroom learning, learning through whole-school activities (clubs, games, projects), homework, student mentoring and study support (lunchtime and after-school sessions with a learning skills focus).

Choice of 'Quality of learning and teaching' from the twelve areas brought these disparate activities together into a common focus. Involving students and parents in this was, for the school, a new departure. While the school development plan had previously centred on the evaluation of learning and teaching, that process had not, up until this point, taken the step of involving those key players. In the words of the head:

> The ground-breaking aspect of the whole process was the bringing together of these different groups to exchange their perspectives on the key issues. In particular, the joint discussion and investigations between students and staff was revolutionary for us in St Kentigern's.

Examining the extent to which progress had been made in the five chosen areas, the school commented after the first year:

> Progress in the five areas chosen has been steady. It must be remembered that progress must be evaluated in the light of the context of the school – the predominant culture and the vision of what can be achieved by the organisation. Subsequent evaluation which records improvement must stand up to the rigorous test of evidence of improvement in the classroom.

The following are some of the initiatives that were taken within each of the five areas:

1 Academic achievement

The first-year curriculum was restructured to increase time for literacy and numeracy and the teaching of ICT (information and communication technology) through these subjects. A base tutor was given the responsibility for teaching these subjects as well as being the primary pastoral care tutor for that group of pupils. This 'base tutor' also has responsibility for study support, which is the help given to young people out of school hours – at lunchtimes and after school.

2 Peer tutoring

To support the development of reading skills, all first-year pupils with reading difficulties have a senior student to help them in the reading club which operates at lunchtimes. Parents are also involved in helping to improve reading skills and work with the learning support department. Able readers also have access to the reading club in order to encourage their private reading.

3 Homework study review

Another strand was the evaluation of homework and study undertaken out of school hours. Questionnaires were issued to pupils, parents and teachers to gather their views on homework – the time spent on it, parents' expectations and the design and use of the home/study planner. The planner was produced by parents and the cover designed by pupils and it was put into use from September 1998.

4 Examination analysis

A review of examination performance was carried out with each department of the school showing the relative performance at Standard Grade (the external examination at the end of the fourth year of secondary school), illustrating patterns of development over the last three years – 1995, 1996 and 1997. Areas of weakness were then targeted by providing further resources and improved teaching materials and strategies, as well as focused staff development. While this was not a new initiative under the Socrates programme, the introduction of self-evaluation was seen as very important in giving this further impetus.

5 Professional development

As part of the Socrates project, a staff development group was set up involving a wide range of teachers from different disciplines, focusing specifically on quality assurance issues. Performance indicators used by Her Majesty's Inspectorate of Schools were discussed by staff and the staff development group drew up a 'quality features list' as a basis for determining strengths and weaknesses in classroom teaching. In addition to this, forums were set up to allow joint discussion between teachers and senior students, focusing the discussion on 'time as a resource for learning' and examining that from different perspectives.

One year beyond the end of the project, St Kentigern's has assessed its benefits in these terms:

- The quality of student–teacher dialogue has improved.
- Students have an input into school reports.
- Students are routinely asked to evaluate courses and units of learning.
- Study support is based heavily on student feedback and choice.
- Students work creatively in teams.
- Students lead parent workshops.
- Students now have a clearer focus on target setting to improve performance.
- The school now has a student council.

Summarising progress, the headteacher writes: 'One year on we haven't looked back. Having involved students in self-evaluation, we now take it for granted that they will play an active part in the planning and evaluation of our programme for teaching and learning in St Kentigern's.'

Case study: Pupils speak through the lens of a camera

How pupils come to play an active part in their learning is illustrated in the third case study. Photo evaluation puts the tools of evaluation in the hands of pupils in a very literal sense. It captures in an objective medium their subjective impressions. It is a tangible signal that the school wants to hear from them and that they are active players in their own learning.

Finding a silent voice

A group of pupils wanders through the school building looking at different objects, discussing various positions, arguing, changing positions, moving back and forth as if guided by a hidden conductor until they find a satisfactory spot: Silke puts a camera up to her eyes, takes it away again, shakes back her hair and refocuses; then she says 'cheese' and takes a picture of her mates in front of the toilets – doors open. Then they move off and go through the same procedure again: looking for places, finding appropriate positions, discussing the right postures and pressing the button ... (Figure 13.1)

All in all, fourteen groups consisting of three pupils each from years 5 to 11 moved through the buildings of a Viennese secondary school looking in every corner, trying to find suitable motifs for their pictures. Sometimes they even knocked on classroom doors, asked the teacher present if they could quickly take a picture – and left behind a puzzled teacher whom they could sometimes hear complaining about the unexpected interruption.

The activities described here are part of a self-evaluation process which several schools put into practice when they tried to find a method which would help to give pupils ownership in the process of evaluating school as a social place. They chose the method of photo evaluation (cf. Activity 8 in Chapter 11 and Schratz and Steiner-Löffler, 1998b) for this purpose because pupils, especially younger ones, find it very difficult to deal with more conventional or standardised forms of feedback, nor do they take easily to elaborate written reports. Also, the power relationship can be too heavily weighted in favour of the adults when pupils are required to make their case verbally. The use of photographs 'touches on the limitations of language, especially language used for descriptive purposes. In using photographs the potential exists, however elusive the achievement, to find ways of thinking about social life that escape the traps set by language' (Walker, 1993: p. 72). Therefore, for many pupils, finding a 'silent voice' by using photographs was a welcome way of evaluating their schools.

Taking pictures builds a bridge to the pupils' everyday lives, especially to the feelings of young people, because they usually perceive that there is a gulf between

Figure 13.1 Finding a silent voice.

their own priorities and those of adults. They often experience a discrepancy between what they themselves value and what the school sees as important. Photo evaluation has proved to be a valuable way of bridging this gulf, because by taking pictures of significant 'hotspots' in the school, many areas take on a new meaning when seen, and captured on camera, from a pupil's-eye viewpoint.

Teachers learning

Teachers often teach the way they have been taught rather than how they have been taught to teach. In order to widen their repertoire and offer new insights, photo evaluation was introduced in a training workshop at the Luxembourg Conference. Participants from eighteen countries familiarised themselves with this unusual evaluation method by actually photo evaluating the conference. After a short introduction they were given a Polaroid camera and asked to use this approach in a learning-by-doing situation. Most of what pupils experience using this method was reflected in the way adults went about it as well. They described it as a total human experience, making use of all the senses, exploiting their imaginative power, negotiating meaning and, last but not least, having fun (see Figures 13.2 and 13.3).

Figure 13.2 A major theme: reaching out for time.

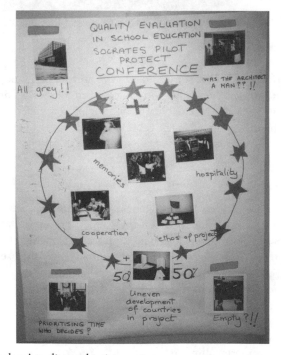

Figure 13.3 Teachers' quality evaluation poster.

Photo evaluation at work

In photo evaluation, students typically portray the school as a place of learning and communal living. They take photos of places where they feel happy and at ease and places where they feel decidedly uncomfortable. The photos are then displayed on posters with short descriptive texts. The students say why they feel particularly at ease in certain places and what could be improved in the 'unpleasant' places at school. (For the procedure, see Chapter 11.)

The way in which schools put their experiences into practice depended to a large extent on the imagination of the people involved and on the situation in which they found themselves. The following example (from the Hauptschule Pabneukirchen in Upper Austria) is a straightforward way of making use of the potential of this approach.

When planning the project, great care was taken to ensure that at least one group from each school year was included in the activity, since it is likely that students of different ages will have different opinions about what makes them feel happy or less happy at school. Each group, containing about five students, chose four locations where they felt comfortable and a further four locations where they felt decidedly uncomfortable. The students then considered what they wanted to emphasise in their picture and how this could best be captured on film (for example, by sitting very close together in a 'cold' room). Finally, the chosen subjects were photographed using an instant camera. Photos were then mounted on a poster, supported with graphics and/or text (for example, a 'happy' place – sunshine; an 'unpleasant' place – rain clouds). When the posters had been completed, they were presented – with a short explanation – to the other students participating in the project, and the posters were then discussed.

In the course of the project, twelve posters were produced. They were hung in the main hall of the school for eight weeks so that other students, who had not been able to participate, had an opportunity to see what others had come up with in their photo evaluation. The students were extremely industrious, even working through their breaks without the slightest complaint. They enjoyed being allowed to express their feelings through photos and the least articulate of the students were particularly active. Using this method of evaluation, they were able to express their opinions in a visual way. Compared to more conventional methods of self-evaluation which advantage students who have a fluent command of language, photo evaluation allows a more inclusive observation of the school.

The discussion process at student level was summed up at the end of the school year. The head girl of the school invited the representatives of each form to name their three most important priorities for improvement to the school building. This provided a student 'Catalogue of Requests' – twenty-four in all, which the head girl then handed over to the school management. Students also had the opportunity to present their suggestions to a teachers' conference. A joint discussion between students' and teachers' representatives then discussed which requests could be met within a given time, as some involved building and structural issues requiring consultation with authorities.

The school management and the teachers involved were naturally fully aware of the fact that, by allowing the photo evaluation project, they had expressed their willingness to carry out alterations to the school building. They had also stirred expectation among the students that teachers would play their part in making the school more attractive. A few of the requests expressed through the photo evaluation could be met with little cost and effort and have already been undertaken in a joint effort of teachers and students (for example, rearranging and decorating classrooms). If a request is rejected, it is important to explain to the students why this was the case. How staff respond to decisions taken and collaborative improvement efforts can, if managed wisely, be a positive step in the development process in the school.

Places chosen by the pupils

The pictures in Figure 13.4 give a glimpse of what pupils can come up with in the process of producing posters with their photographs.

Turning photos into action

A Viennese school collected all the information from the photos taken by the thirteen photo teams of different age groups and produced a table to show the balance between positive and negative features (see Figure 13.5).

In staff meetings findings were discussed and, in consultation with pupils, solutions proposed. For example, because of the negative rating of the corridors, the school arranged with the City of Vienna to keep the plants which were used only for special festivities in the school, making the corridors a more homely place.

Teachers reflecting

At the final Conference in Vienna a follow-up workshop was conducted to find out how schools had put photo evaluation into practice in their respective countries. Presentations from different countries showed the variety of different experiences using this approach. The workshop also served the purpose of reaching a new understanding of the methodology and suggesting innovative ways of approaching it in the future. Thus new ideas were presented for the use of photo evaluation such as:

- Indicators of pupil wellbeing.
- The quality of communication between pupils, between pupils and teachers and between school and community.
- Indicators on the state of school democracy.
- Teaching styles which support or inhibit the pupils' learning processes.
- The acceptance of a 'new culture of curiosity and learning' among the teaching staff.
- The condition of the school buildings.
- The surroundings of the school.

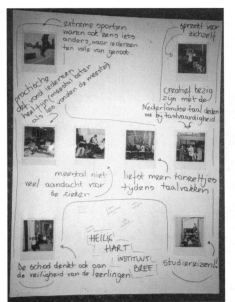

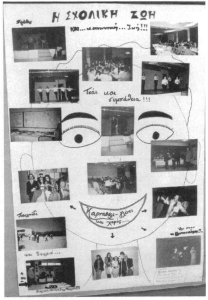

Figure 13.4 Pupils' photomontages.

NENNUNGEN GESAMT		1	2	3	4	5	6	7	8	9	10	11	12	13	14
Bibliothek	13	+	+	+	+	+	+	+	+	+	+	-	~	~	
Hof/Sportplatz	12	+	+	+	+	+	+	+	+	+	+	-	~		
Buffet	11	+	+	+	+	+	+	+	+	-	-	~			
Turnsaal	8	+	+	+	+	+	+	+	+						
Toiletten	7	-	-	-	-	-	-	-							
Musiksaal (gr.)	6	+	-	-	-	-	-								
Physiksaal	5	-	-	-	-	-									
Gänge	4	+	-	-	-										
Klassenzimmer	4	+	+	+	-										
Lift	4	+	-	-	~										
Biologiesaal	3	+	+	-											
EDV Saal	3	+	+	-											
Arztraum	2	-	-												
Chemiesaal	2	+	-												
Musiksaal (kl.)	2	-	-												
Kopierer (-standort)	2	-	-												
Raucherhof	2	-	-												
Spint	2	+	+												
Telefon	2	-	-												

Figure 13.5 Evaluation of a photo survey.

A graphic account

The sequence of graphics from a Swedish school shown in Figure 13.7 not only describes the process in simple, accessible form but also illustrates that the medium is the message – that is, a visual medium can often express ideas and concepts with far more feeling than words alone.

Figure 13.6 A photo evaluation exercise in a Swedish school.

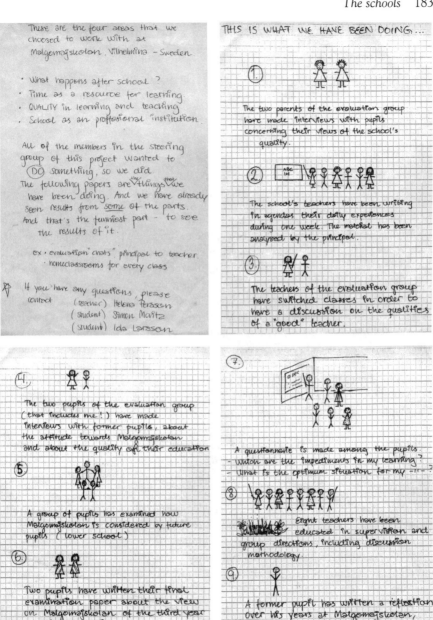

Figure 13.7 Graphics from a Swedish school.

14 What have we learned?

'Evaluating Quality in School Education' deserved to be described as 'the beautiful project'. Its design was simple but its scope unlimited. The launch pad, the self-evaluation profile, met the twin criteria of economy and power. The economy of the single page, immediately accessible by all stakeholders, concealed a powerful force for change. The SEP has been described as a 'door opener' because it led into many interconnecting pathways to school improvement.

Within this common framework, schools enjoyed a large measure of freedom; to exercise initiative, to pilot new approaches, to test ideas, to experiment, to take risks and in some cases to go where they had never gone before. They discovered that involving students in open dialogue, in discussion of technical issues, and in classroom observation, was not threatening but liberating, not only for the students but for their teachers as well. If the benefits of the project were to be described in a word (or two) these would include 'very beneficial', 'highly successful', 'excellent initiative', 'enormous benefits' and a 'rich process'. While there were very typically caveats about time, resources, support and opportunities for networking, involvement in the project had had an impact on virtually all schools. Ninety-eight of the 101 said they would be keen to continue beyond the end of the project.

Among the specific benefits described by schools was heightened self-knowledge. The statement 'We now understand the school better' was a recurrent theme. The project had affirmed the good things the schools were doing, recognising and celebrating aspects of school life which had previously gone unnoticed, 'giving positive value to a wide range of achievements', as one school expressed it. In addition to confirmation of existing strengths, it had also extended knowledge, giving the school confidence to face problems head on, to be more adventurous: 'It has given us added incentive for schools to go and try new things, to take more risks'.

For one English school it has given teachers 'greater confidence in facing external judgements'. This referred specifically to external inspection and the increased pressures on the school for accountability. Self-evaluation had helped the school to recognise how much it knew and that it had a good story to tell on its own account. The accountability theme was also mentioned as a demand of professionalism – in the words of one Irish school: 'We need to examine critically our own performance as a part of what is understood as professionalism today'.

The single most common theme running through accounts from all countries was, however, the benefit of listening to other voices, seeing new perspectives. Many schools expressed surprise and delight at the valuable contribution students made when given the opportunity to participate. In the words of one Italian school: 'We were very pleased with the openness and integrity of students'.

It was not only the student voice but the juxtaposition of different perspectives that was most challenging and opened up new ways of seeing and understanding. As one school described it, it was 'not a tool to attack or defend but to open dialogue', a process which served to strengthen relationships and forge new alliances. The following are typical of the many positive comments from participating schools.

'It has helped us in seeing different points of view.'

'It is rich in possibilities for different groups in the community to express a range of views.'

'The project was a milestone. It was the first occasion in which all partners, including past pupils, examined our performance as a school.'

These words from a Madrid school spoke for many others:

The project has awakened an awareness of evaluation. Now teachers and students take into account the wide positive impact of the rest of the school collective. They realise that evaluating work makes it more effective and better for all.

There was visible evidence of growth in the calendar year which separated the Luxembourg conference and the final conference in Vienna. Students had grown in maturity and self-confidence. Their teachers had shed many of the doubts or apprehension they might have harboured earlier. Headteachers spoke of the benefits it had brought to them personally and professionally. They too had grown.

Analysing conditions for success

We are able to probe deeper into these issues by comparing schools in which the project was most successful with those which reported less success. We found that schools with the highest level of stakeholder satisfaction were characterised by:

- Impact of the critical friend on the work of staff
- Careful choice of area in the self-evaluation profile
- High level of participation by stakeholders
- Positive changes at pupil level.

These features were also found in schools which reported improvement in the school's capacity and effectiveness. A number of other features were also present in relation to the effectiveness criterion. These were:

- Availability of adequate data
- Choice of small number of areas to focus on for evaluation
- Adequate time
- Positive attitudes to self-evaluation.

The analysis of conditions for success led to a number of useful pointers for practice:

- A satisfactory level of participation in the self-evaluation process is more likely to be reached if stakeholders are involved not only with the operational phase but also in conception, monitoring and evaluation.
- A high level of participation is not of itself a sufficient condition to produce a strong impact on the school, nor to guarantee high satisfaction, but it is a necessary condition for that.
- For the participative process to bring about satisfaction there needs to be an impact at school level as well.
- A high level of involvement and commitment of both teachers and pupils is a further condition for a participative process to result in school improvement.
- Satisfaction with the process is not in itself enough to engender positive attitudes to self-evaluation. It requires in addition that the school believes that there will be an impact on effectiveness and improvement and that it will produce a higher level of pupils' commitment to their learning. This is consistent with the finding that teacher satisfaction is related to a perception of greater school effectiveness and capacity for improvement.
- The process that leads to the choice of areas to evaluate or actions to be taken is of crucial importance. This process has to involve an optimum number of stakeholders, to rely on adequate data, to result in evaluations (or actions) of a small number of areas, carefully chosen.

The wider benefits

Learning was not confined to the immediate participants, however. There were valuable lessons for critical friends and for policy advisers at government level. Meetings in Brussels which brought together representatives from the eighteen countries became progressively more positive, even exuberant, as people testified to the impact of the project in their schools.

A number of countries published impressive national reports, in some instances using these to frame national policies on self-evaluation or to drive existing ones. The following is an excerpt from the German report:

In many schools the project served to strengthen the quality discourse, raised self-reflection among teachers to a new level, and with it promoted a greater sensibility to change, promoting a general climate friendly to innovation. In all it improved the capacity of the teaching staff to improve the school.

Many of the countries sustained and increased the impetus of the project. In Portugal, for example, the four project schools provided the core for a much larger initiative. In 1998–99 the four grew to twenty-two and a year later more than doubled to include fifty schools. A national conference in Lisbon in September 1999 brought together the Portuguese schools along with teachers from Belgium, France and Germany.

And what of the Commission and its 'experts', as the project team were known? We did not come new to self-evaluation but the pilot project was a first for all of us and taught us a lot.

As the project was a European initiative, there was a strong focus on networking activities at the European level. Participating schools not only met together for conferences and exchange visits, but were part of something larger. All schools expressed their appreciation of the European dimension and its influence on their participation and commitment. They said that it had 'put them on the map', had given them a 'kick' from their involvement, had raised morale or had been an important endorsement for the school as a whole. The interest of schools in the European dimension was most clearly articulated during the two conferences organised by the European Commission together with the Luxembourg and Austrian presidencies. The fact that ninety-eight out of 101 schools said that they wanted to continue working on these issues at European level suggests that this dimension adds an incisive and creative element to the process of evaluation.

There are few schools who feel self-sufficient enough to go it alone. They need support and encouragement not only at European level but at national and local level, too. While the success of the pilot project can be attributed to a number of different factors, one factor of major importance was the close interest taken in the participating schools by national bodies. Most National Committees held regular meetings and involved all participating schools. This gave schools the opportunity to exchange information and experiences. They were encouraged to network with one another and further support was given on the technical and logistical issues. For the successful implementation of school self-evaluation, such support and encouragement appears to be of major importance.

The concept of the critical friend as a source of support (outside the direct hierarchy of the school) proved to be one of the aspects of the project which was most appreciated. Critical friends can, as we discovered, come from a range of different professional backgrounds, each of which brings its own unique strengths and opportunities. While this person is first and foremost a friend and ally of the school, he or she should also be prepared to critique and to challenge what the school is doing. The ability to make that challenge effectively, however, was shown to be one of the most precious skills in a critical friend's repertoire and the 'exquisite sensitivity' of the role cannot be underestimated. Further work, nationally and internationally, on the role of the critical friend in school self-evaluation, will enhance the potential of this external perspective to support the work and improve the organisation of schools.

The self-evaluation profile provided a highly stimulating starting activity, giving schools the opportunity to bring together a range of stakeholders from the outset. It allowed schools to review their current state of 'organisational health' on the twelve criteria which schools found apposite and challenging. The SEP has proved itself to be an excellent starter for schools with no previous experience of self-evaluation. Two aspects appear to be of special importance. Use of the SEP has been shown to improve relationships among all groups of stakeholders and, moreover, unites their focus of interest in specific areas of school life which need to be more closely evaluated. It does not have to be cumbersome or demanding in time. It can be approached from several directions and used in different ways. It can be adapted to the different contexts and cultures of schools, apparently without difficulty.

The involvement of all stakeholders inside and outside schools was one of the main principles of the pilot project. The improvement of school quality is a process, enriched through opening up the school in a non-defensive way to different perspectives and new insights. Much of the learning and richness of the project arose from that process of examining differences of perspective. The dialogue has its own intrinsic value, but also has longer term consequences because it places the quality issue irrevocably on the agenda. It is the take-off point for a nuanced and balanced approach to improving quality. Involvement of all stakeholders also implies ownership and a shared responsibility for the direction and development of quality in the school.

A first step to effective self-evaluation is the preparation of the ground and a climate conducive to honest reflection. The process of self-evaluation, however, is not an end in itself. Self-evaluation is a tool, and it is judged by schools according to its impact on the effectiveness and improvement of their school. When self-evaluation was followed by an action, schools were apparently more appreciative of the process. Therefore, the process of self-evaluation should be seen in an action perspective and driven in accordance with expected outcomes.

While there will be schools confident and skilled enough to be autonomous in their self-evaluation, there will always be a need for some form of external review or quality assurance. Its primary role will be in encouraging self-evaluation to become progressively more rigorous and self-critical. So, as schools move along the spectrum towards becoming truly learning organisations, there is a commensurate change in the role and function of external bodies such as school inspectors. The challenge at national and at European level is to create the kind of balanced framework which will enhance both school self-evaluation and external monitoring and accountability.

These issues are captured and highlighted in the Declaration from the Vienna Conference, agreed and signed by all participants from the schools in the eighteen countries represented.

Declaration from the Conference in Vienna
20–21 November 1998

Quality evaluation in school education: European pilot project

The pilot project on quality evaluation was launched in the beginning of the school year 1997 with the approval and support of the Council of Ministers of Education. The project involved 101 secondary schools in eighteen countries taking part in the Socrates programme. Decision makers from national administration, researchers, and school stakeholders (headteachers, teachers, pupils, parents, school boards, etc.) have all played an active role in the implementation and monitoring of the project.

We, the participants at the final conference in Vienna, have taken part in the European pilot project on Quality Evaluation in School Education.

The pilot project has raised the awareness of quality issues in our schools and in almost all our schools, the project has helped to improve the quality of education during the project period.

On the basis of our experiences in the project we strongly invite schools to:

- Use self-evaluation in the planning and the strategic development of the school.
- Clarify the purpose and create the conditions for self-evaluation.
- Ensure that all stakeholders have access to essential training and support to enable them to participate in the process of self-evaluation.
- Use self-evaluation to get an informed and critical approach to school and classroom practice.
- Involve and draw on the experiences and insights of all relevant stakeholders inside and outside schools when evaluating the school.
- Actively pursue possibilities of networking of all school stakeholders nationally and at European level in order to exchange information and experiences and learn from one another.
- Make study visits to other self-evaluating schools on national and EU level.
- Acknowledge that schools need to provide transparent information on the quality of their provisions.
- Disseminate results of evaluations to everyone concerned.

We strongly invite stakeholders outside schools to:

- Get actively involved in the process of evaluating the school to add an incisive and creative element to the process of improvement.
- Focus on teaching, learning and achievement.
- Support schools in the process and conditions for improvement and provide advice.
- Ask questions so schools are stimulated to re-examine what they are doing.
- Help schools improve their relations with the local communities.

We strongly invite national governments to:

- Promote self-evaluation as a strategy for school improvement.
- Promote the involvement of all stakeholders in self-evaluation.
- Support the networking and exchange of experiences between stakeholders in different schools and ensure that schools have the competencies and the budgets to participate.
- Ensure that approaches to self-evaluation take place within a framework that is coherent and consistent with other forms of national statutory regulations
- Clarify the purpose and create the conditions for self-evaluation in schools, and ensure the establishment of a balanced approach between internal evaluations and any external evaluation in order to support school development.
- Allow schools to choose for themselves their own approach to self-evaluation, within a clear and robust framework.
- Provide training in the management and the use of methods of self-evaluation to make it function effectively as an instrument strengthening schools' capacity to improve
- Support schools by providing tools for self-evaluation.
- Disseminate to other schools the results and the methodologies of the pilot project.

We strongly invite the European Commission to:

- Support the member states in promoting self-evaluation as a strategy for school improvement at European level.
- Make evaluation and schools improvement a priority theme within the future Socrates programme, to give schools the opportunity to learn from one another at European level.
- Promote the dissemination of examples of good practice between countries, for example by creating a database on good practices, and operating an Internet site where such exchanges can take place.
- Regularly inform on the 'state of the art' and progress of self-evaluation in member states.
- Promote visits and exchange of stakeholders between the member states in the field of quality evaluation.
- Exchange information in the field of training of stakeholders.
- Organise European events like conferences and workshops on evaluation and school improvement.
- Follow-up on the pilot project and ensure that this conference in Vienna will not be a fullstop.

Notes

3   Tom Ericson: the history teacher

The tape Tom listens to in his car is *Leadership and the New Science* by Margaret Wheatley from her book of the same name which is indexed in the bibliography. Full details of books referred to in this chapter (Cornog, Coleman, Joyce and Perkins) may also be found in the bibliography.

4   Mrs Barre: the headteacher

References for Csikszentmihalyi's book *Flow* and Tom's jottings from Margaret Wheatley are in the bibliography.

5   Ursula: the critical friend

The critical friend makes reference to Covey's *Seven Habits of Highly Effective People* and to a critique of objectivity which comes from Hampden-Turner and Trompennars' book *The Seven Cultures of Capitalism* (see bibliography).

6   Coffee with the professor

Reference is made to OBESSU, the European Association of School Students and their publication *Q* which can be obtained from their website.

The reference to students evaluating their teachers and school can be found in MacBeath, *Schools Must Speak for Themselves*, in the bibliography.

For a history of the school effectiveness movement, see Lezotte (1989); Knuver and Brandsma (1989); Meuret and Marivain (1997). References in the bibliography are, of course, not exhaustive, but we have tried to give accessible references and, where possible, to quote research from various countries. However, school effectiveness research in Europe is especially strong in Britain, The Netherlands, and, to a lesser degree, in Belgium and France.

Useful school improvement texts are Fullan (1993), Stoll and Fink (1995) and MacBeath and Mortimore (2000).

Reference to the Cambridge professor is to John Gray, who has carried out numerous studies on effectiveness and improvement and specifically to his latest book (1996; see bibliography). See also Scheerens (1992), who reported a 0.8 correlation for schools, two years in succession.

References to students' judgements in the French study are to Grisay (1993). This result was obtained in French middle schools.

For further information on learning organisations and intelligent schools, see Argyris and Schön (1978) and MacGilchrist, Myers and Reid (1998; bibliography).

7   The professor revisited

References to different models of school improvement can be found in the bibliography under Fullan, Gray, Stoll and Fink.

A source for the reference to learning organisations is Argyris and Schön (see bibliography).

With regard to the discussion on different subjects, Grisay (1993) finds a correlation of 0.3 between effectiveness in French and maths in French middle schools. In Britain, Thomas and colleagues found substantial departmental differences in terms of effectiveness in about 32 per cent of the schools. Grisay also found significant correlations of about 0.25 to 0.3 between maths, sociability and civic attitudes, and between French and sociability. In 100 French middle schools, Grisay found only one which was effective in the three domains of cognitive achievement, social attitudes and attitude towards schooling, and five which were ineffective across the three domains.

The discussion of thermal imaging can be followed up in a large body of literature. Good sources are Sylwester, Kotulak and Ornstein (see bibliography).

The discussion on prior attainment draws on a large body of work. The French professor makes specific reference here to Duru-Bellat and Mingat (1999), who observe in France that, on starting at middle school, the higher the initial mean level of their class, the more the pupils progress. They also observe that what high achievers lose by being in heterogeneous classes is smaller that what the low achievers gain.

The discussion on teacher and school effects draws on a considerable body of research evidence from Thomas and Sammons (see bibliography for exact references). The conversation with Zoe on improving your place by moving school refers specifically to Grisay's work in French middle schools. The PHOG index is the invention of Neville Highett, School Principal at Immanuel College in Adelaide, Australia.

The reference to asking students what makes an effective school is found in MacBeath, 1999; *Schools Must Speak for Themselves* (see bibliography).

The research into wellbeing is a reference to a study of French middle schools by Grisay (1993).

In a meta analysis of several pieces of research in England and The Netherlands, Bosker and Witziers (1996) estimate that, when controlling for both prior achievement and background characteristics, 8 per cent of the variance in student achievement is the result of differences between schools. Note that Grisay (1999) argues that controlling for prior achievement and for background characteristics assumes that better and higher SES students perform better only because of background factors and not because their learning conditions are better. In fact, they do benefit from better conditions in schools. This is problematic in respect of equity but also suggests that school effects are no smaller than those found by school effectiveness research, and are very likely to be greater.

Bibliography

Argyris, C and Schön, D (1978) *Organizational Learning: a Theory of Action Perspective*. Reading, MA: Addison Wesley.

Ball, C (1985) Fitness for purpose. Guilford: SRHE and NFER-Nelson, quoted in *Gestion de la qualité et assurance qualité dans l'enseignement supérieur européenne*. A Report for the European Commission, 1993.

Battistich, V *et al.* (1995) School communities, poverty levels of student populations and student attitudes, motives and performances : a multilevel analysis. *American Educational Research Journal, 32 (3)*.

Bosker, R and Witziers, B (1996) The magnitude of school effects, or: does it really matter which school a student attends? Paper presented at AERA Annual Conference, New York, April.

Caldwell, B J (1993) *Decentralising the Management of Australia's Schools*. Melbourne: National Industry Education Forum.

Caldwell, B J and Spinks, J M (1992) *Leading the Self-Managing School*. London: The Falmer Press.

Coleman, P (1998) *Parent, Student and Teacher Collaboration: The Power of Three*. London: Paul Chapman.

Cornog, G (1970) To care and not to care. In Ryan, K *Don't Smile until Christmas*. Chicago: University of Chicago Press, pp. 1–24.

Costa, A I and Killick, B (1993) Through the lens of the critical friend. *Educational Leadership*, 51(2): 49–51.

Cousin, O and Guillemet, J P (1992) Variations des performances scolaires et effet. *Etablissement, Education et Formations*, 31.

Covey, S (1989) *The Seven Habits of Highly Effective People*. New York: Simon and Schuster.

Csikszentmihalyi, M (1990) *Flow: The Psychology of Optimal Experience*. New York: Harper Perennial.

Dubet, F (1999) Sentiments et jugements de justice dans l'expérience scolaire. In Meuret, D (ed.) *La justice du système éducatif*. Louvain: De Boeck Université.

Duru-Bellat M and Mingat, A (1997) La gestion de l'hétérogénéité des publics d'élèves au collège, *Cahiers de l'Iredu*, 59.

Eisner, E (1991) *The Enlightened Eye*. New York: Macmillan.

Emin, J C (1996) Les indicateurs pour le pilotage des établissements du second degré. In Vogler, J (ed.) *L'évaluation*. Paris: Hachette Éducation, pp. 237–51.

Fullan, M G (1991) *The New Meaning of Educational Change*. New York: Teachers College Press.

Fullan, M (1993) *Change Forces*, London: The Falmer Press.

Gardner, H (1983) *Frames of Mind*, New York: Basic Books.

Gillborn, D and Gipps, C (1996) *Recent Research on the Achievements of Ethnic Minority Pupils*, London University Institute of Education, London: OFSTED.

Glatter, R et al (1997) *Choice and diversity in schooling*, London: Routledge.

Goldstein, H & Myers, K (1996) Freedom of information: towards a code of ethics for performance indicators, *Cambridge Journal of Education*, 26.

Goldstein, H and Thomas, S (1995) School effectiveness and value added analysis, *Forum*, 37(2) pp 36-8.

Gray, J, Goldstein, H and Jesson, D (1996) Changes and Improvements in Schools' Effectiveness: Trends over five years, *Research Papers in Education*, 11 (1): 35–51.

Grisay, A (1993) Le fonctionnement des collèges et ses effets sur les élèves de sixième et cinquième, *Dossiers Education et Formations*, 32, Ministère de l'éducation nationale.

Grisay, A (1997) Evolution des acquis cognitifs et socio affectifs au collège. *Dossiers Education et Formations*, 88, Ministère de l'éducation nationale.

Grisay, A (1999) Comment mesurer l'efficacité du système scolaire sur les inégalités entre élèves? In Meuret, D (ed.) *La justice du système éducatif*. Louvain: De Boeck Université.

Hampden-Turner, C and Trompenaars, L (1993) *The Seven Cultures of Capitalism*. New York: Doubleday.

Haq, K and Kirdar, M (1986) (eds.) *Human Development: The Neglected Dimension*. Islamabad: North South Roundtable.

Hill, P W, Rowe, K J and Holmes-Smith, P (1995) Factors affecting students' educational progress. Paper delivered at the 8th International Congress of School Effectiveness and School Improvement, Leeuwarden.

Holly, M L (1989) *Writing to Grow: Keeping a Personal-Professional Journal*. Portsmouth, NH: Heinemann.

Hook, C (1981) *Studying Classrooms*. Geelong: Deakin University Press.

House, E R (1995) Putting things together coherently: logic and justice. *New Directions for Evaluation*, Winter, 68: 33–48.

Jakobsen, L, MacBeath, J, Meuret, D, Schratz, M (1998) Evaluating quality in 101 schools. Paper presented at the American Educational Research Association, San Diego, April.

Joyce, B R (1991) The doors to school improvement. *Educational Leadership*, 48 (8): 59–62.

Knuver, A W and Brandsma, H P (1989) Pupils' sense of well being and classroom educational factors. In *School Effectiveness and School Improvement*. Swets and Zeitlinger.

Kotulak, R (1996) *Inside the Brain*. Kansas City, MO: Andrews McMeel.

Lee, V and Smith, J B (1995) Effects of high school restructuring and size on early gains in achievement and engagement. *Sociology of Education*, 68.

Lezotte, L W (1989) School improvement based on the effective schools research. In Creemers, B and Scheerens, J (eds.) Developments in school effectiveness research. *International Journal of Educational Research*, 13 (7).

Luyten, H and de Jong, R (1998) Parallel classes: differences and similarities. Teacher effects and school effects in secondary schools. *School Effectiveness and School Improvement*, 9 (4).

MacBeath, J (1999) *Schools Must Speak for Themselves: The Case for School Self-evaluation*. London: Routledge.

MacBeath, J and Mortimore, P (1994) Improving school effectiveness: a Scottish approach. Paper presented at British Educational Research Association, Oxford, September.

MacBeath, J and Mortimore, P (2000) *Improving School Effectiveness*. Buckingham: Open University Press.

MacBeath, J, O'Brien, J and Myers, K (1998) The Jarvis Court Files. *Managing Schools Today*, 8 (6).

Macdonald, J P (1989) When outsiders try to change schools from the inside. *Phi Delta Kappan*, 71 (3): 209.

MacGilchrist, B, Myers, K and Reid, J (1998) *The Intelligent School*. London: Paul Chapman.

Mayring, P (1990) *Einführung in die qualitative Sozialforschung*. München: Psychologie Verlags Union.

Meuret, D and Marivain, T (1997) Inégalités de bien être au collège. *Dossiers Education et Formations*, 89, Ministère de l'éducation nationale.

Myers, K and Goldstein, H (1996) Get it in context. *Education*, 16 February: 30-51.

Oakes, J (1986) *Educational Indicators: A Guide for Policy Makers*. Center for Policy Research in Education, University of Wisconsin-Madison.

OECD/CERI (1995) *Education at a Glance*, vol. 3. Organisation for Economic Co-operation and Development, Paris.

Ornstein, R (1992) *The Evolution of Consciousness*. New York: Touchstone.

Perkins, D (1996) *Smart Schools*. New York: The Free Press.

Porter, A C (1991) Creating a system of school process indicators. *Educational Evaluation and Policy Analysis*, 13 (1).

Reich, R B (1991) *The Work of Nations*. New York: Vintage Books.

Robertson, P J and Briggs, K L (1998) Improving schools through school based management: an examination of the process of change. *School Effectiveness and School Improvement*, 9 (1).

Sammons, P *et al.* (1998) Understanding differences in school effectiveness: practitioners' views. *School Effectiveness and School Improvement*, 9 (3).

Sammons, P, Hillman, J and Mortimore, P (1995) *Key Characteristics of Effective Schools: A Review of School Effectiveness Research*. London: Office for Standards in Education.

Sanger, J (1988) *The Compleat Observer? A Field Research Guide to Observation*. London: Routledge.

Sarason, S B (1986) *The Culture of the School and the Problem of Change*. Boston: Allyn and Bacon, p. 119.

Scheerens, J (1992) *Effective Schooling*. London. Cassell.

Scheerens, J (1997) Theories on effective schooling. *School Effectiveness and School Improvement*, 8 (3).

Scheerens, J and Bosker, R (1997) *The Foundations of Educational Effectiveness*. London: Pergamon.

Schratz, M (1997) *Initiating Change Through Self-evaluation: Methodological Implications for School Development*. Dundee: CIDREE-SCCC.

Schratz, M and Steiner-Löffler, U (1998a) *Die Lernende Schule: Arbeitsbuch pädagogische Schulentwicklung*. Weinheim: Beltz.

Schratz, M and Steiner-Löffler, U (1998b) Pupils using photographs in school self-evaluation. In Prosser, J (ed.) *Image-based Research – A Sourcebook for Qualitative Researchers*. London: The Falmer Press, pp. 235–51.

Schratz, M and Walker, R (1995) *Research as Social Change*. London: Routledge.

Schratz, M, Iby, M and Radnitzky, E (2000) *Qualitätsentwicklung: Verfahren, Methoden, Instrumente*. Weinheim: Beltz.

Stark, M (1998) No slow fixes either: How failing schools in England are restored to health. In Stoll, L and Myers, K (eds) *No Quick Fixes: Perspectives on Schools with Difficulties*. London: The Falmer Press.

Stiggins, R J (1997) *Pupil-Centered Classroom Assessment*. Upper Saddle River, NJ: Merrill.

Stoll, L and Fink, D (1995) *Changing our Schools*. Buckingham: Open University Press.

Stubbs, M and Delamont, S (eds.) (1976) *Explorations in Classroom Observations*. Chichester: John Wiley.

Sylwester, R (1996) *A Celebration of Neurons*. New York: Prentice-Hall.

Thomas, S et al. (1995) Differential secondary school effectiveness. Paper presented at the Annual Conference of the British Educational Research Association, Bath, September.

Thomas, S et al. (1997) Stability and consistency in secondary school effects on students' GCSE outcomes over three years. *School Effectiveness and School Improvement*, 8 (2).

Tymms, P (1997) Paper at the Evidence-based Politics and Indicators Systems Conference, Durham, July.

Voelkl, K E (1994) School warmth, student participation and achievement. *Journal of Experimental Achievement*, 63 (2).

Walker, R (1993) Finding a silent voice for the researcher: using photographs in evaluation and research. In Schratz, M (ed.) *Qualitative Voices in Educational Research*. London: The Falmer Press, pp.72–92.

Webb, N M (1998) Equity issues in collaborative group assessment: group composition and performance. *American Educational Research Journal*, 35 (4).

Wheatley, M (1994) *Leadership and the New Science*. New York: Berrett Koehler.

Index

absenteeism 84
academic achievement 12, 13, 47–8, 103–4, 174
alternative options 120
art 2
asking activity 115–29; force field analysis 38, 49, 50, 128–9; interviews 116–18; logs 127–8; questionnaires 21–2, 30–4, 56, 118–25; surveys 125–7
Austria 89, 118; school case study 176–82

basic skills education 88
Belgium 89, 129; school case study 166–72
biology 5, 14
Bosker, R. 192
brainstorming 4

Caldwell, B. J. 89
capacity 78
Catholic Education Federation 167
cat's cradle 76–7
change: process of 55
A Change of Story 81, 82–93
chaos theory 37
checklists: book/tv review 4–5
classroom level processes in self-evaluation profile 104–6
closed interviews 117
closed questions 119
Coleman, Peter 33
collecting activity 137–9; document analysis 137–8; portfolios 138–9
community: schools and 107–8
computers: questionnaire design and analysis 122
context: local context 83–5; policy making context 85–7, 89–93
co-operation 28, 87–8

Costa, A. L. 158
covert observation 130
Covey, Steven: The Seven Habits of Effective People 54, 76, 191
crises 50, 54
critical friend: do's and don'ts 162, 164; in European schools self-evaluation project 42, 47, 53, 54–5, 58, 158, 187–8; key competencies 162, 163–4; role of 101–2, 158–64; success as 162, 164
Csikszentmihalyi, Mihaly 45
culture 78; cultural background 65–6; drug culture 82–3
curriculum 73–4

decentralisation 89–90
Delamont, S. 129
Denmark 89, 118, 125, 152, 153
Department for Education and Employment (DfEE) 59
diarying activity 153–5
discussing activity 139–42; focus groups 49, 50, 141–2; peer review 139–41
distributed intelligence 92
document analysis 137–8
Don't Smile Until Christmas 27
drug dealing 82–3
Duru-Bellat, M. 192

economic development: education and 86–7
education: achievement of objectives of 89–93; economic development and 86–7; employment and 12, 87–8, 104, 108; for life 87, 89; pupil destinations after 12, 87–8, 104, 108, 168, see also quality of learning and teachers; schools; teachers and teaching

effectiveness 63, 64–72, 73–80
Eisner, Elliot 96
Eliot, T. S. 65
employment: education and 12, 87–8, 104,
    108
enacting activity 142–4
European Commission 88, 187, 190
European Organisation of School Students
    (OBESSU) 62, 191
European schools self-evaluation project
    10–11, 25–6, 96; benefits of 184–90;
    conditions for success 185–6; critical
    friend in 42, 47, 53, 54–5, 58, 158,
    187–8; declaration from Vienna
    conference 189–90; evaluation tools 35,
    99–101; experts and 62–72, 73–81;
    headteacher's view of 41, 47–8, 53, 60;
    Luxembourg conference 57–9, 177;
    parents' view of 22–3, 26; policy
    making context 85–7, 89–93; pupil's
    view of 11–15; research 62–72, 73–81;
    school case studies 165–83; school
    effectiveness and 63, 64–72, 73–80;
    school self-evaluation group 13–15, 23,
    26, 35, 43, 55; self-evaluation form
    51–2; self-evaluation profile 11–13, 43,
    44, 98–9, 110–14, 173, 188; teachers'
    view of 34, 35, 42, 60; whole staff
    meeting 59–61
European Union of Students 57
evaluation *see* European schools self-
    evaluation project; self-evaluation
exams 66; academic achievement 12, 13,
    47–8, 103–4, 174
expectations 64–6
external evaluation 91
extortion 82–3

Finland 89, 131
Flow 45
focus groups 49, 50, 141–2
focused observation 130
force field analysis 38, 49, 50, 128–9
Frank, Anne: *The Diary of Anne Frank* 3
free observation 130
French 47
further education 104, 108

gender 18; effective schools and 69–70;
    history teaching and 36–7
geography 8, 15–16, 19, 30; visualisation in
    1–2
Germany 186–7
globalisation 86

government: expenditure on teaching 28,
    see also policy making context
Gray, John 191–2
Greece 132, 143
Grisay, A. 192, 193

Hampden-Turner, C. 56–7, 191
Haq, K. 86
headteachers 41–2, 45–8, 53, 60
higher education 104, 108
history 3, 19, 50; creation of 13; gender of
    pupils and attention paid in 36–7; not
    linked 10–11; parents' views of 21–2,
    30–4; understanding of 30; visualisation
    8; what-if 9, 29–30, 37
holidays 27
Holly, M. L. 153
home-school relationships 15, 35, 43–4,
    60, 107, 171–2
homework 5, 6, 9, 24; listening to music
    and 2–3; study of 26; telling parents
    about 19
Hook, C. 129
House, Ernest 95

imaging activity 151–3, 176–83
indicators 145–7; value-added 145, 146,
    148–50
individualism 88
information society 86–7
insanity 47–8
intelligence 24–5, 45, 92
intensity factor 102
interviews 116–18
intimidation 82–3
Ireland 185
Italy 89

jargon 23
Joyce, Bruce 37, 55, 94

Killick, B. 158
Kirdar, M. 86
knowledge society 86–7

language 23
learning 45; academic achievement 12, 13,
    47–8, 103–4, 174; co-operative group
    learning 28; information society and
    86–7; learning organisations 77–8;
    lifelong 87, 89; metacognitive 17;
    methods 8–9; personal and social
    development 13–14, 104; quality of *see*
    quality of learning and teachers; school

as place for 106; time as resource for learning 14–16, 35, 44, 59–60, 104–5, 169; types of 7–8, 43
learning difficulties: support for 105–6, 169–70
life: education for 87, 89
literature 3–7, 30; book reviewing 3–4; idealism about 27
local context 83–5
logs 127–8
Luxembourg conference 57–9, 177

MacBeath, J. 132, 191
management 28, 42, 46
Managing Schools Today (journal) 54
maths 3
Mayring, P. 116
meaning: making of 29
measuring activity 145–50; indicators 145–7; school performance measures 148–50
metacognitive learning 17
Mingat, A. 192
monocular knowledge 56
multiple choice questions 120

national curriculum 73–4
nested layers 68
Netherlands 89, 91

Oakes, J. 145
objectivity 56–7
observation 48, 49, 129–33; peer observation 35–6, 37–40, 49, 131; pupil observation 131–2; shadowing 49–50, 132–3
open interviews 117
open observation 130
open questions 119
oral interviews 116–18

paired (peer) observation 35–6, 37–40, 49, 131
Paltrow, Gwyneth 30
parents 18–19, 33; home-school relationships 15, 35, 43–4, 60, 171–2; parents' view of European schools self-evaluation project 22–3, 26; single parents 83, 84; telling parents about homework 19; views of history 21–2, 30–4
Paris 1
peer observation 35–6, 37–40, 49, 131
peer review 139–41

people-with intelligence 92
Perkins, David 38, 92, 93
personal and social development 13–14, 104
PHOG index 71, 192
photo evaluation 151–3, 176–83
physical education 35–6
picture and photo evaluation 151–3, 176–83
policy making context 85–7, 89–93; achievement of objectives of education and 89–93; decentralisation 89–90; external evaluation 91; knowledge society argument 86–7; quality evaluation 91–3; resource argument 85–6; self-evaluation 91–3; social inclusion argument 86
polyocular knowledge 56, 57
portfolios 138–9
Portugal 125, 187
positive attractors 46
pre-school education 89
prior attainment 66
prioritising 133–6
professional place: schools as 107
profiling activity 155–7
pupil destinations 12, 87–8, 104, 108, 168
pupil observation 131–2

Q sort 133–6
qualitative interviews 117
quality evaluation 91–3
quality of learning and teachers 25–6, 43, 44, 99–100, 105; parents' view of 20; policy making context 85–7; pupils' view of 12, 14, 56; teachers' view of 35, 60
quantitative interviews 117
questionnaires 56, 118–25; on parents' views of history 21–2, 30–4

racism 83–4
rating scales 120–2
reading 24–5, 174–5
Reich, Robert 86
resources 85–6
Roberts, Rocky 83
role play 142–3
Rousseau, Jean-Jacques 15
Roy, Arundhati: *The God of Small Things* 30

Sanger, Jack 129, 130
Sarason, S. B. 102, 158–9

Sartre, Jean-Paul 64
schools 94; case studies 165–83; community and 107–8; decentralisation of authority to 89–90; effectiveness 63, 64–72, 73–80; home-school relationships 15, 35, 43–4, 60, 107, 171–2; improvement 77–80; inspections 20; as learning organisations 77–8; as learning place 106; performance measures 148–50; as professional place 107; school level processes in self-evaluation profile 106–7; self-evaluation for see European schools self-evaluation project; self-evaluation; as social place 106, 170–1
Schratz, M. 95, 129, 176
Scotland: school case study 172–6
self-evaluation 91–3, 94–102; asking 115–29; balance between comprehensiveness and selectivity 95–6; collecting 137–9; diarying 153–5; discussing 139–42; enacting 142–4; imaging 151–3, 176–83; measuring 145–50; methods 115–57; observation 35–6, 37–40, 48, 49, 129–33; profiling 155–7; role of critical friend 101–2, 158–64; school self-evaluation group 13–15, 23, 26, 35, 43, 55, 110; self-evaluation profile see self-evaluation profile; sorting and prioritising 133–6; tools 35, 99–101, see also European schools self-evaluation project
self-evaluation profile 96–9, 103–14; classroom level processes 104–6; in European schools self-evaluation project 11–13, 43, 44, 98–9, 110–14, 173, 188; how to use it 108–10; lessons learned 110–11; outcomes 103–4; relations with environment 107–8; school level processes 106–7
shadowing 49–50, 132–3
single parents 83, 84
Sizer, Theodore 102
Sliding Doors 29–30, 37
social background 65–6, 69–70
social development 13–14, 104
social inclusion 86
social place: school as 106, 170–1
Socrates project see European schools self-evaluation project

sorting and prioritising 133–6
Spain 127, 185
special needs 105–6, 169–70
Steiner-L'ffler, U. 176
Stiggins, Richard 139
story telling 144
structured interviews 117
Stubbs, M. 129
subjectivity 56
surveys 125–7
'Swamp' 54, 55
Sweden 89; school case study 182–3
synergy 16–17

teachers and teaching 18, 27–9; effective 66, 67–8; gender and 36–7; head-teachers 41–2, 45–8, 53, 60; peer observation 35–6, 37–40, 49, 131; peer review 139–41; public undervaluing of 28; pupil observation 131–2; quality of see quality of learning and teachers; teachers' view of European schools self-evaluation project 34, 35, 42, 60
television programmes 4–5
tests 66
thermal imaging 75
Thomas, S. 192
time as resource for learning 14–16, 35, 44, 59–60, 104–5, 169
timetables 15
toilets 18
triangle: interview 117–18
triangulation 26
Trompenaars, L. 56–7, 191

United States of America 144
unstructured interviews 117
unstructured observation 130
urgency 50, 54

value-added 145, 146, 148–50
video evaluation 151–3
Vienna 1; declaration from Vienna conference 189–90
visualisation 1–2, 8

Walker, R. 129, 176
wellbeing 66–7
Wheatley, Margaret 29, 37, 191
Witziers, B. 192